The Rhode Island Gunners

The Rhode Island Gunners

Four Accounts by Union Army Artillerymen from the 1st Rhode Island Light Artillery During the American Civil War

Battery D, First Rhode Island Light Artillery
G. C. Sumner

Three Personal Narratives of the Rhode Island Soldiers and Sailors Historical Society
J. A. Monroe, G. C. Sumner & E. K. Parker

LEONAUR

The Rhode Island Gunners
Four Accounts by Union Army Artillerymen from the 1st Rhode Island Light Artillery
During the American Civil War
Battery D, First Rhode Island Light Artillery
by G. C. Sumner
Three Personal Narratives of the Rhode Island Soldiers and Sailors Historical Society
by J. A. Monroe, G. C. Sumner & E. K. Parker

FIRST EDITION

First published under the titles
Battery D, First Rhode Island Light Artillery
Personal Narratives of the Rhode Island Soldiers and Sailors Historical Societ

Leonaur is an imprint of Oakpast Ltd
Copyright in this form © 2015 Oakpast Ltd

ISBN: 978-1-78282-473-2 (hardcover)
ISBN: 978-1-78282-474-9 (softcover)

http://www.leonaur.com

Publisher's Notes

Contents

Battery D, First Rhode Island Light Artillery

Contents

MEMBERS OF BATTERY D, FIRST RHODE ISLAND LIGHT ARTILLERY, VETERAN ASSOCIATION

At Roger Williams Park, June 1891

Preface

At a meeting of Battery D Association, held at Roger Williams Park, June 6th, 1891, the following resolution was unanimously adopted:

> Resolved, That George C. Sumner is hereby appointed Historian of the Association, and earnestly requested to write and publish a History of Battery D, First Rhode Island Light Artillery.

Comrade Sumner accepted the position, and at once commenced to look up material for the work. He soon found that he had quite a task to perform. At the Battle of Cedar Creek, late in the war, all the books and papers of the battery were captured by the enemy, it thus became rather a tedious undertaking to hunt up facts and dates. Artificer Clark Walker and Corporal Knight had diaries of some parts of their service, which was about all the material on hand to start with.

The Adjutant General's Office furnished considerable information. The roster of the battery was taken entirely from that office. The *War Records* was another source from which facts and dates were collected.

Comrade Sumner took a great deal of interest in this history and had a large part of it written when he was "called away to join his comrades who had gone before." The death of our comrade made it necessary for someone to take up the work. It was impossible to fill his place, and when the writer agreed to take up the history and complete it, it was with a great deal of hesitation, knowing his inability to carry on the work, and not having time to devote to the proper carrying out of Comrade Sumner's ideas.

Comrade Sumner had a great many marginal notes attached to his manuscript which he was familiar with, but to another person they were not very plain. Without doubt he intended to add considerable to his manuscript, but on taking up the work I found it almost impossible to follow out what he had evidently intended to do, and came to the conclusion that it was best to publish it as he left it. I hope the comrades of the battery and whoever else that reads this work, will remember that the author was called away before he had time to even revise his original manuscript.

Very respectfully,

Your obedient servant,

A Comrade of the Battery.

CHAPTER 1

Organisation

At the commencement of the Civil War, in April, 1861, there was in the city of Providence, among other excellent military organisations, one of light artillery, known as the Providence Marine Corps of Artillery, which for years had been interesting and instructing the young men of the city and vicinity in the manoeuvres of this branch of military service. A natural sequence of the presence of this company was to draw attention to this arm, and led Gov. Sprague to offer the government a fully equipped light battery, in addition to the First Regiment of Infantry. The offer being accepted, a battery was speedily organised for three months service, and on the 18th of April, six days after the firing upon Fort Sumter, it left Providence, fully equipped, for Washington.

When it became evident that more troops and a longer term of service would be needed, Gov. Sprague at once began the organisation of a regiment of light artillery. The second battery (or A, in regimental orders) was mustered into service June 6th, 1861, for three years or the war, and left home for Washington June 19th. After which, at intervals of less than a month, a battery left Providence for the seat of war, until eight had been sent, which completed the First Regiment Rhode Island Light Artillery.

Battery D was the fifth in number, but fourth in the regimental formation, that was recruited, its organisation commencing immediately upon the mustering of Battery C (Aug. 25th). Its quota was filled perhaps the most rapidly of any of the batteries, for by the 2nd of Sept. it had its complement of men, and was sent to Camp Ames, on the Warwick road, just beyond Pawtuxet, where, on the 4th of Sept., it was mustered into the service of the United States.

On Sept. 10th, the battery moved to Camp Greene, near the Stonington Railroad. While in this camp the men were uniformed, divided into gun detachments, and drilled in the manual of the piece, marching, etc.

On the 13th the battery left Camp Greene on the steamboat train for Stonington, under command of First Lieut. Geo. C. Harkness, the other officers being First Lieut. Henry R. Gladding, Second Lieuts. Stephen W. Fisk, and Ezra K. Parker. From Stonington it proceeded by boat to Elizabeth City, N. J., from which place it continued on by cars to Washington *via* Harrisburg, reaching its destination shortly after noon on the 15th, and marched immediately to Camp Sprague, where Capt. J. Albert Monroe, who had just been promoted from First Lieutenant to Captain, and transferred from Battery A to Battery D, took command.

The personnel of the company was particularly well adapted for the especially active work appertaining to the successful manoeuvring of light artillery. Its members were young; scarcely one in ten had reached his majority: most of them had left good homes, where they had received the advantages of a fair education, and except in rare instances their physiques were such that camp life and the exercise of the drill speedily developed endurance and suppleness. To no one was the possibilities of this command more apparent than to Captain Monroe. His experience in the home company, and three months of practical service with Battery A, convinced him that here was material from which, by persistent hard work, and by a proper and judicially administered discipline, there could be evolved a battery of light artillery which would honour itself and the State from which it came: and he immediately proceeded to work for the accomplishment of that idea.

Requisitions were speedily obtained for horses and guns, and the battery was soon fully equipped, the battery consisting of four ten pound Parrotts and two twelve pound howitzers. Drilling was commenced immediately, both field and the manual of the piece, and continued without cessation from the 18th of Sept. to Oct. 11th, and such was the progress made by the company that at a review held on the 9th of Oct., on the grounds back of the Capitol, of all the artillery in the vicinity, at which Gen. Scott was reviewing officer, the battery was complimented for the excellence of its movements.

Oct. 12th Capt. Monroe received orders to report with his battery to Gen. Fitz John Porter, near Hall's Hill, Va., and as soon as possible the company commenced its first march, passing through Washington *via* Pennsylvania avenue, thence through Georgetown to the Potomac River, crossing at Aqueduct Bridge. Hall's Hill was reached about 7p.m., and the battery went into camp. Having no tents, the men were obliged to spread their blankets on the ground, and had their first taste of a field camp in Virginia.

Oct. 14th orders were received to report to Gen. McDowell, and the battery moved about three miles, to Upton's Hill. While here they were given their first impressions of war. It was intimated that the enemy was in the immediate vicinity, and were liable to make an attack at any time. Each night one section of the battery was sent out on picket. At no time in their service did they feel the responsibility of their situation more keenly than on these occasions, and not a rebel soldier within twenty miles. The two sections which were to remain in camp were obliged to work upon the earthworks with picks and shovels, an occupation they did not relish.

Oct. 29th camp was moved just over Munson's Hill, on the north slope, and a camp laid out. under the direction of Capt. John Gibbon, who had assumed command of the artillery in our division. His own, Battery B, Fourth U. S., was placed upon the left (instead of the right, as it should have been according to strict military etiquette, presumably because the ground was higher and drier). Our battery came next, then the First New Hampshire, Capt. Gerrish, and the Pennsylvania battery, Capt. Durrell, on the right. Tents of the Sibley pattern were now issued in place of the small A tents. These were circular in form, and large enough to accommodate ten or twelve men comfortably. When the weather became cold enough to require them, stoves were issued, and when the tents were properly ditched, the bunks built and filled a foot deep with straw, they became very comfortable homes, even in the coldest of weather. We soon had orders to prepare this camp for a winter's sojourn. Details were made each morning to work upon the stables for the horses, and in the course of a few days the finest camp in the history of Battery D was completed, and named Camp Dupont.

The battery was parked in regular style, pieces in front, caissons in the rear; on the right and left of them the stables were built. The tents for the men were pitched in the rear of the stables. The officers' tents were in the rear of the battery, the captain's being in a line with the centre of the guns, and two others, one on each side of the captain's, a little in advance, for the four lieutenants. The cook-house was at the upper end of the right tents, and the guardhouse was placed quite a distance in front of the battery.

In this camp the battery remained from Oct. 29th, 1861, to March 10th, 1862, occupying its time in drill, inspections, sham fights, target practice, etc. Everything calculated to increase its efficiency was indulged in. Days were spent in perfecting the men in horsemanship. Heroic measures were used: no saddles or bridles were allowed; men were expected to learn to manage their horses successfully bareback, and with only the halter, and they did it, but there were many laughable and some serious incidents occurred before they thoroughly mastered the art.

The sham-fights were particularly exhilarating and entertaining to us, the whole corps, numbering fifteen or twenty thousand, participating in them, and blank cartridges were used without stint. A change of front would sometimes necessitate a long run for the battery, and if over open ground, was participated in with a relish; but if as it sometimes happened, the route lay through what had been woods, but had been freshly cut off by the soldiers, leaving stumps of irregular height, it sometimes became very annoying to the cannoneers, as the carriages struck first one stump and then another, throwing them about, making it very difficult to retain their places on the boxes.

CHAPTER 2

Campaign to Centreville

For some time rumours had prevailed of a forward movement, but nothing of a definite nature occurred until March 9th, when orders were issued that four days rations be cooked, and the battery prepared to march at an early hour the next morning; the limbers of the pieces and the caissons were supplied with ammunition, and everything put in order for a campaign against the enemy.

At an early hour on the 10th of March, "boots and saddles" was blown, the battery was speedily hitched up, and in a short time Capt. Monroe gave the order, "Right piece, forward," and we moved out of park, from Camp Dupont, where we had spent four months, for the last time. The line of march was toward the Centreville Pike, and when we reached Baily's Cross Roads, a halt was made near the road until our turn should come to join the column. The entire Army of the Potomac was on the march for Centreville, where the enemy was reported to be in force. It was several hours before our turn came, but at last we were ordered to move into the road, and commenced our march in earnest. It was a most disagreeable day, very cold, and a heavy mist prevailed, which soon wet our clothing; the freezing temperature soon converted this moisture into a coating of ice, making it exceedingly uncomfortable for the men, particularly the drivers, who were obliged to sit their horses without any opportunity to warm themselves by exercise.

Our progress was slow and tedious. Six o'clock found us in the vicinity of Fairfax Court House, where we made camp. Early next morning we hitched up and had barely time to prepare coffee for ourselves, when we were ordered to join the column, and proceeded on our way towards Centreville, but after marching about a mile we were ordered to make camp.

It had been discovered by our advance that the enemy had retired upon our approach, and there was to be no opportunity to display our valour. We remained in this camp until the 15th.

On the morning of the 15th, the army started on its return towards Washington. Soon after starting it began to rain, and by noon the water was coming down in torrents, soon wetting the men to their skins. The column marched much more rapidly than they did when going out, they evidently hoping to find shelter at their old camps.

About 7 o'clock p. m., Battery D turned into the dooryard of Mr. Cloud, at Cloud's Mill. Both officers and men were in a miserable condition, and they immediately set about improving it to the best of their ability. The fence in front of the house was soon demolished, and a fire started, around which all hovered until morning. During the forenoon of the 16th we marched back to Camp Dupont, after an absence of just one week. This seemed like home to us, and we all felt that we would like to stay here for a while at least; but that was not to be, for next morning we were ordered to proceed at once to Fairfax Seminary, where we remained until April 4th. While in this camp, on March 29th, our first batch of recruits, nine in number, were received from Rhode Island.

At daylight on April 4th, the battery, with the First Division of the army, under Gen. McDowell, the rest of the Army of the Potomac having gone by transports to Fortress Monroe, marched to Fairfax, and bivouacked for the night, early the next morning continued on to Manassas, remained overnight, and at daylight next morning started on to Bristow Station.

The weather on this trip up to this time had been pleasant and fairly comfortable; but on the night of the 8th there came a change; it grew rapidly cold, and about 10 p. m. began to snow. Those of the men who were not frozen out and obliged to hover around the camp-fires, found themselves covered by a blanket of snow about four inches deep in the morning.

We remained at Bristow until the 16th, and then continued on the march to Catlett's Station, remaining one day, and on the 18th marched to within three miles of Fredericksburg, camping near the village of Falmouth. Some of our men started into the village and attempted to make small purchases, but the people of the place were very loyal to the South, and at this early period of the war had great confidence in the Confederate money, and but very little in Uncle Sam's crisp greenbacks, and refused to take them in exchange for their goods.

Now it so happened that an enterprising firm in Philadelphia had just issued a facsimile of the rebel money, of various denominations, and the men had purchased several thousand dollars worth, as curios. These were offered the rebellious tradesmen, and accepted with great glee, as an indication of the final success of their side, that the Yankees were already being obliged to use their money. They soon discovered that the bills were not genuine, someone having pointed out to them the printer's name and location in the margin, and they refused to take any more, notwithstanding the Yankee customers assured them that the bills were worth just as much as the genuine. A complaint was made to head-quarters, but the general, after hearing both sides, decided that they were entitled to no redress.

On the 19th the battery marched to a position directly opposite Fredericksburg, on the north branch of the Rappahannock River. The guns were placed in position, pointing directly at the city, but the next day the pieces were limbered and a regular camp laid out, tents were pitched, and preparations made which indicated that we were to tarry here for some time. Drill received our undivided attention; from four to six hours a day being given to that work, excepting on Sundays, which were given up to inspections of the men and material of the battery. Cleanliness was important, and was carefully looked after.

On the 10th of May the battery was ordered to move down to the bank of the river, near the railroad bridge, for the purpose of protecting it from an expected attack of the enemy; but they did not come, and things soon quieted down and assumed their normal condition, and the battery resumed its usual occupation of drilling.

The effect of such long-continued and constant work in this direction began to show itself in the accuracy with which the movements were executed. The efficiency of the battery began to attract attention, and almost every day when we reached the ground where we were to have our field-drill there would be quite an audience awaiting us. Senators and Representatives from Washington, visiting officers, and distinguished people from all over the country, would be taken out to see the show.

As an illustration of how it impressed one individual from our own State, I quote from an article which he sent to the *Providence Journal*:

> The proficiency attained by the sturdy fellows of Battery D, is really surprising, and would do credit to a company of cadets fresh from the rapid practice of West Point. I saw them yes-

19

terday, under command of Captain Monroe, performing the evolutions of field-drill with such accuracy as to command the admiration of old army officers who were present.

On the 26th of May the battery crossed the Rappahannock River into Fredericksburg, and made camp on a common in the centre of the town, remaining until the 29th.

Union soldiers were not welcome guests in that city at that time, and the citizens took no pains to disguise the fact. Their manner towards us and treatment of us left no doubt in our minds that they wished we were anywhere but in their presence. We did not mind it, however, and made ourselves just as much at home as though we were welcome.

Early in the morning of the 29th the battery recrossed the river, and joining our division, commenced our journey for Thoroughfare Gap, for the purpose of aiding Gen. Banks, who was being badly pressed by the rebel Gen. Jackson, in the Shenandoah Valley. We made only a short distance the first day, but did better next day, making nearly twenty-five miles, and reached Catlett's Station.

On the 31st we marched only four miles, but pushed on the next, and reached Haymarket, near the Gap.

June 1st was a day of rest for us, but on June 2nd the troops were early in motion, and after marching through the Gap were halted for an hour, then countermarched, passing through the Gap, and encamped on almost the same spot that they had left in the morning.

This was a movement which at the time was very confusing to us, but time developed the fact that the emergency which demanded our presence in the Shenandoah Valley had passed, Jackson having accomplished what he desired, and his troops being wanted at Richmond by Gen. Lee, he had left the valley, and at the moment of our arrival at the Gap, was well on his way. Our stay at Haymarket continued for three days.

On the 6th we had orders to move. Our destination was Warrenton, where we arrived after an easy march, late in the afternoon. Here we remained until the 8th, moving on that date to Warrenton Junction, bivouacking for the night, continuing on the next day towards Catlett's Station, which we reached on the 10th, and made a stay of four days. This trip was very pleasant to us; the weather was good, the roads were fair, our marches were not long, and the whole more of a pleasure trip through a rather interesting country.

June 15th we marched to Cannon Creek, and after remaining for five days we continued our journey to Spotted Tavern, and, after a stay of forty-eight hours, returned to Fredericksburg on the 23rd, after nearly a month of marching, and made camp within a short distance of the old one, in which we remained until Aug. 5th, our time being occupied with the usual duties of camp life, drills, inspections, etc.

July 2nd we turned in our battery of Parrotts and howitzers and drew one of light twelves or Napoleons. These guns were of brass, smooth bore, and had fixed ammunition. They were of short range, which would necessitate our coming in close contact with the enemy; but the fixed ammunition would enable them to be fired much more rapidly; and as they had the reputation of being very destructive when used at short range, the exchange was on the whole very acceptable to the men.

July 4th was celebrated by a salute in the morning, and repeating it in the afternoon.

Aug. 5th the battery, with a portion of our division, started on a reconnaissance towards the Rapidan River. Towards noon on the second day out, a portion of our troops had a slight skirmish with the enemy, but it was of short duration.

Early on the morning of the third day of the reconnaissance our column countermarched, and marched rapidly towards Fredericksburg. Our cavalry were constantly skirmishing with the enemy. When within fifteen miles of the town a regiment of infantry and our battery went into position, but after firing a few shots the enemy fell back, and we rejoined the column. Continuing our march we reached our old camp on the Rappahannock Aug. 8, where we remained until Aug. 22nd.

CHAPTER 3

Rappahannock Station

August 22nd King's division to which Battery D belonged, left camp opposite Fredericksburg, it having been ordered to report with all possible haste at Rappahannock Station. The battery pulled out of park at daylight, and after a hard day's march, made camp within eight miles of the station, some time after dark. Very early next morning as we were aroused, the battery hitched up, and everything made ready to proceed, we heard heavy and continuous firing, which indicated to us that someone was having a hot time of it.

At 9 a.m. we were ordered to continue on to the station, which we reached about noon, remaining until dark. All the afternoon troops were continually recrossing the river and moving to the rear, and just before we left, the buildings around the station were fired. The light from this fire illuminated our way for some distance. At the station, and for a mile or so beyond it, as we passed along the road, men were engaged in tearing up the railroad, heating the rails and twisting them beyond any possibility of their being used again.

Everything indicated that we had commenced a retrograde movement, and the constant picket firing, which would occasionally increase in volume, as though a regiment or brigade had become engaged, with the added noise of cannon, told us plainly that the enemy were pressing our rear vigorously.

In order that our situation may be fully understood, it may be well to give a brief description of the general military events of a few weeks previous to our arrival at the station.

On the 27th of June Maj. Gen. John Pope assumed command of the Army of Virginia, composed of Fremont's, Banks's and McDowell's Corps, in all about 38,000 men. The first two of these commands were at Middletown, in the Shenandoah Valley. Of the latter command, one division, under Gen. Ricketts, was at or near Manassas Junction, and King's (to which Battery D belonged) at Fredericksburg. It was the first intention of Gen. Pope to unite these widely separated troops, and in concert with Gen. McClellan, who was occupying an advanced position on the peninsula, attempt the capture of Richmond; but in the interim between the assumption of this command by Gen. Pope and the uniting of his forces, Gen. McClellan had decided to retire from his advanced position, to the James River, at Harrison's Landing, which was accomplished after seven days of continuous and severe fighting.

The rebel commander. Gen. Lee, being relieved from any anxiety for the safety of Richmond, determined upon a demonstration towards Washington, and sent Gen. Jackson with a large force to oppose Gen. Pope. The two armies met at Cedar Mountain, on the 9th of August. A severe battle was fought, resulting in the defeat of our army, which was driven from its position at dark.

It was soon discovered by Gen. Pope that Gen. Lee was moving nearly his whole force from Richmond, for the purpose of crushing his (Pope's) army, and it was now determined by the authorities at Washington to transfer Gen. McClellan's forces from the peninsula to the Potomac, as a reinforcement for Gen. Pope.

On the 23rd of August, the day the battery arrived at Rappahannock Station, Gen. Longstreet had reached our front, and made an attack upon our troops at Beverly Ford. It was the firing from this engagement which had been sounding in our ears all day.

We continued our march well into the night. Just after midnight the battery pulled into a lot and halted without unharnessing. The men were told to lay down near their pieces and get what rest they could. About daylight we were aroused and started on again, reaching Warrenton about dark on the 24th. Early next morning the battery was on the road, and after a slow, tedious march of five or six hours bivouacked at Sulphur Springs for the night, without unhitching.

The evening of the 26th found us in the neighbourhood of Waterloo Bridge. Twenty-four hours later we were on the Warrenton Pike, about halfway between Warrenton and Groveton, wet through from a drenching rain which had prevailed for several hours.

After a very uncomfortable night we took the road again on the morning of the 28th, headed towards Groveton. About 5 p. m. the battery moved off the road into a field upon the right, came into park, and, without unhitching, the men commenced to prepare supper.

Just as Capt. Monroe and the other officers, with Gen. King as their guest, had seated themselves at the camp-table, a few picket shots were heard on our left, followed almost immediately by a considerable volley. Gen. King immediately mounted his horse and started in the direction of the firing. Capt. Monroe ordered the drivers to mount, put the battery in motion down the pike, then galloped on ahead; soon he returned, gave the order "Trot, march," and, after going a short distance, turned the head of the cohimn towards a hill upon the left of the road.

We had almost reached the base of the hill when a staff officer was seen coming over the top towards us, waving his sword in the wildest manner and calling upon us to go back as quick as possible. He hurriedly made the captain understand, but before our direction could be changed, we saw the lead horses of a rebel battery appearing over the brow of the hill—we were both after the same position and they had beaten us. Our direction was soon changed and we made every possible effort to get under cover before they could do us much damage, but they succeeded in getting in a few shots, which, however, did us no damage. Soon we reached a sunken place in the road which afforded us protection, and we were halted while Capt. Monroe searched for a new position.

After a stay of five minutes we were again ordered forward. About one hundred yards of our way was fully exposed to the fire of the rebel battery. They took every advantage of it, and threw their shells thick and fast at us. It did not seem possible that we could pass this exposed part of our journey without being seriously damaged; but notwithstanding the shots flew around us, only one took effect, hitting the stock of one of our caissons, breaking it and disabling the carriage and necessitating its being blown up. Lieut. Parker was ordered to accomplish this, and although he was exposed to great personal danger, both from the enemy's fire and the explosion, he successfully accomplished it.

The battery soon turned from the road into the fields on the left, and with all possible speed made for the top of a hill not far distant; on reaching the top of which it came into battery and immediately commenced firing at the rebel battery which had taken the first position from us.

I quote from Capt. Monroe's account of this battle:

It was evident that we were in for it, and I hastened back to the battery, which started at a quick trot for a knoll that I had observed, and which appeared to be a good position. As the leading carriage reached the foot of the knoll an officer rode rapidly towards me from its top saying, 'For God's sake, Captain, get out of this; they are putting a battery right on this hill.' I lost no time, for I could see the horses of the rebel artillery above me, and we turned back to the road. We took cover in the road where timbers skirted both sides of it for a short distance. We were very uncomfortable here, for the battery that had stolen the hill from us knew our position, and at less than six hundred yards range, sent its shot and shell crashing through the trees and over them, exploding their shells directly above us.

We were where we could do nothing, and I determined to run the gauntlet of fire that swept over the open road beyond the timber we were in, to another copse that would afford more shelter, and at the same time probably an opportunity to get our guns into action; therefore the necessary order was given, and the battery passed over the space intervening at a rapid gallop. This movement resulted in few if any casualties to the men, but a shot struck the stock of a caisson, disabling it. To prevent its capture by the enemy it was blown up by Lieut. Parker.

It had now grown quite dark, and the opposing lines were easily traced by the sheets of flame and flashes of powder pouring from each, while the positions were plainly discernible. The ground the battery had secured appeared in the darkness to be unfavourable for the use of all the guns; therefore two were posted in the road, where they had a flank fire upon both the infantry and artillery of the enemy. A captain of one of the rebel batteries engaged here told me several years afterwards that the guns away off to his left, which he had understood were those of a Rhode Island battery, inflicted terrible punishment upon him, and that he lost more heavily in men, horses and material, than in any one action of the war. Considering that we had but two guns in this position, this was a high compliment to the efficiency of Battery D.

Before or about nine o'clock the action was over. Its close was terrific: fire leaped in waves from the musket's mouth, and men saw in the darkness the angry flames; bullets filled the air, or struck with heavy thud a living mark, and men heard the cruel sound; but neither fire, scream nor blow, nor the presence of almost certain death, appalled the Federal lines.

Soon after nine o'clock the heavy firing ceased, and in a half hour everything was quiet, save occasional shots from the pickets. By ten o'clock the men were sleeping quietly, the drivers near their horses, and the cannoneers in their positions about the guns.

About midnight a staff officer entered the battery, found the captain and ordered him to awaken his men, have the guns limbered, and move the command into the road with the least possible noise. Sergeants were awakened and sent around among the men, who were awakened with great care, and cautioned not to speak save in a whisper. Everything about the harnesses and carriages which would rattle or make a noise of any kind was muffled. When everything was ready the battery started out of its position, and gaining the Warrenton Pike, took up its line of march back towards Gainesville.

The explanation of this movement was, that our division commander had become very much exercised in his mind as to the wisdom of his remaining in this position, as it seemed to him untenable; and as Gen. McDowell, our corps commander, was inaccessible, he decided not to remain.

After-knowledge has made it plain that it would have been much better for our side if our position had been firmly held, for our army had the rebel Gen. Jackson at such disadvantage and his supporting force, under Gen. Longstreet, was so far away, that in all probability had he (Gen. Jackson) been assaulted by our combined forces at daylight, he would have been so disabled as to have been of no service to his side in the fighting of the two following days.

Upon reaching the intersection of the Warrenton and Manassas Pikes, just beyond the village of Gainesville, the direction of our march turned towards Manassas Junction, to which place we now marched, reaching there just as the day began to dawn. The battery was parked without unharnessing, and the men allowed to prepare their breakfast.

About the middle of the forenoon we left the Junction, taking the Sudley road towards the old Bull Run battlefield. Our progress was slow and tedious, the road being filled with troops and wagon trains. As we neared our destination we could hear the sound of battle, which grew louder and seemingly more extended with every mile we travelled. Our halting and hitching-along progress became very annoying to the men of Battery D, for it seemed to them that with such delay it was extremely doubtful about their reaching the battlefield in time to be of any service.

About 3 p. m. we left the road and entered the fields at a smart trot, and soon reached the "Henry House" plateau, with the full expectation of immediately entering the fight: instead of which the captain indulged in a field-drill, for the purpose, as he has since said, of satisfying himself as to whether his men would remain "steady" with the immediate prospect of coming under fire. The result was entirely satisfactory to him, and he has been pleased to say since, "that after that experiment he would not have hesitated to have marched through the whole Confederacy with those men."

Towards night we were ordered into a position on low ground between the Stone House and Dugen's, north of the Warrenton turnpike, but after a few moments found that the position was untenable, because of our own batteries, who, from a position on a hill in our rear, persisted in cutting their fuses so short that most of their shells exploded in close proximity to us.

From here we marched back and took position on very high ground, overlooking quite an extent of territory towards an unfinished railroad, where Jackson had been fighting our troops since morning. We were not near enough to take part, but could see the struggle quite plainly, and frequently the shot and shell from the enemy would strike or burst in close proximity to us.

We now began to get our first impressions of what war really was, and soon became thoroughly convinced that it was very serious business. We had hardly settled down in our new position before wounded men began to pass through our intervals; those with light wounds on foot, and the more seriously wounded were brought upon stretchers.

This night we spread our blankets, and lay down in our positions, the cannoneers about the guns, and the drivers at their horses' heads, and were soon fast asleep.

At daylight on the 30th we were awakened by picket firing upon our right, which in an hour or so increased into a constant roar of musketry and artillery, which, until about noon, seemed to be confined principally to our right, but soon after noon we began to see great clouds of dust on our left, and column after column of our troops could be seen hurrying in that direction, which indicated to us that trouble was brewing there. Batteries were taken from positions near us, and hurried along with the troops, but we were allowed to remain in ours until nearly three o'clock, when we were ordered to move down to the Warrenton Pike, upon reaching which we moved along for perhaps a half mile in the direction of Groveton, then moved into a field upon the left of the turnpike and halted. We remained here for nearly an hour.

It was in the neighbourhood of four o'clock that a staff officer from Gen. McDowell rode up to Capt. Monroe, upon the full gallop, and, after a few hurried words had passed between them, the order "Forward, trot, march" was given. The battery was countermarched, and back we went, bearing off to the south of the pike, and making for a hill perhaps eight hundred yards distant. Upon reaching this hill (by name Bald Hill), we moved down about two-thirds of the way to the bottom, and there being a piece of level ground, we went into position. The ground in our front descended quite abruptly for a hundred yards or so. At the foot of the hill a brook ran, in which at this time the water was very low, and when we reached our position the farther bank was occupied by a single battle line of our troops, consisting of two brigades of infantry. Gen. Milroy's independent brigade formed in line of battle in our rear.

A great cloud of dust which we had been watching for some time coming from the direction of Gainesville, has finally reached our front, and we earnestly watch for the first appearance of the enemy. Soon we notice a cloud of dust and considerable commotion upon a hill perhaps a mile away. The dust has hardly settled when we see a puff of smoke, and in a few seconds a case-shot explodes in our midst, we receive orders to open fire, and our struggle has commenced.

Our guns are short range, and we find it impossible to reach the rebel battery; but it became certain that rebel infantry are moving through the woods in our front, and we begin to throw shell and solid shot in their direction. Soon the line of battle in our front opens upon the rebel line coming through the woods, and a sharp and vigorous fire is kept up for a while, when the rebels charge our thin lines, which break and run up the hill towards us, passing through our intervals to the rear.

Battery D is now face to face with the enemy, who have halted in the depression of the brook for the purpose of perfecting their alignment. Soon they make a rush for the battery, probably without the least doubt but that we will prove an easy prey; but Capt. Monroe had drilled the men of that battery for nine months, and it had prepared them for just such an emergency as this. Every man was perfectly familiar with his duty, and determined to do it. Guns were never served faster than were these; round after round of canister is thrown into this mass of approaching rebels; and it is thrown in such a manner that it is most effective, and more than the enemy can stand, and they fall back to the brook.

While Battery D had been thus engaged, battery after battery had been placed in position by the enemy, and these were now filling the air with bursting shell and case-shot; but our position being so far down the hill about all of their shots went over us.

Soon the enemy appear again, but this time their lines extending way beyond both our flanks, the right and left pieces change the direction of their fire so as to protect our flanks. We became anxious about our support, who ought now to be ready to assist us, but a hurried investigation gives us the information that they have left us to our fate—not an infantryman is in sight save their commanding general and three or four of his staff officers.

Gen. Milroy is standing on his dead horse cheering us on, and his staff officers are trying to help us work our guns. We appreciate their motives, but not being versed in light artillery duties, they are rather a detriment to us. In justice to his brigade which has retreated, it may be well to take into consideration that they were in position some thirty yards in our rear, which brought them well up the hill, and they were exposed to the artillery fire which was passing over us.

To add to our trouble word is brought from the limbers that our canister has been exhausted, and only a few rounds of solid shot remain. We cannot do much execution with this kind of ammunition, but we keep it going at a lively pace. The enemy in our front soon discover that we are not using canister, and taking advantage of it are fast approaching us. Will Capt. Monroe delay too long, and shall we be obliged to leave our guns as we have seen two batteries do just a few moments before? No; he has his eyes upon them, and we soon hear the welcome order, "Limbers to the rear." The limbers are whirled across the trail, the pieces are limbered and hurried away almost from the possession of the enemy!

Lieut. Pardon S. Jastram, of Battery E, of our regiment, saw the latter part of Battery D's engagement, and its withdrawal from its position, and has described it in the following story:

The heat of the battle was over on the right of our line, at the second Bull Run, and we were watching the movements of the troops away up on the plains at the top of Bald Hill. Kearney

29

was there with us, as well as a large number of officers and men of the line, all watching with breathless interest the operations of the contending lines clearly exposed to our view, save where a clump of timber hid a portion of the rebel line, and concealed what was going on. There was a line of our batteries, supported by infantry, all heavily engaged in an effort to repel a determined attack that the enemy's artillery and infantry were making.

It was evident Lee had concentrated his efforts upon this point, and that he proposed to carry it by hurling all his available force against it. It was so plain from our standpoint that he would be successful that Kearney remarked, "You will see a second stampede from this field before night."

Slowly the rebel line advanced, and rapidly the rebel artillery poured shot, shell and shrapnel into the Union lines, which stood steady and unbroken, but all aglow from the rapidity of the fire streaming from it, which had a sulphurous hue as seen through the enveloping smoke which rose in the air and floated away in great clouds. Guns were served as it seemed they never were before. It appeared as if the heavens would be rent in twain by the thunder of the artillery and the discharges of the small arms on both sides combined.

The rebel line never faltered, but continued to move on, notwithstanding the deadly havoc in its ranks. Finally came the charge, and, with yells that rang out clearly over the space between them and us, they impetuously dashed upon the apparently firm, immovable line before them. The quickened fire of the artillery told that they were throwing canister with all their might and main, and if human power, so far as those men were concerned, could stem the approaching crest of glittering steel, they would do it. It looked as if it was an impossibility for any living force, however determined, to advance through that storm of iron and lead; but the rebel line wavered for a moment only, then it gathered its strength again almost in the very second that it appeared to lose it, and with renewed ardour swept on.

Our advanced line of infantry, occupying a sunken road in front of the artillery, broke and rushed pell-mell through the intervals between the guns and limbers; and the second line just behind the limbers of the batteries, joined them in their mad race to the rear, and down the hill. Double canister went from the well served guns, and great gaps appeared in the hotly charging line; but it was only for a few seconds, for in that brief space of time they were in among the guns and gunners, the latter seeking safety in precipitate retreat; there was nothing else to do except to remain and become prisoners. The guns were silent; they could hardly be seen on account of the great number of the enemy in among them. The drivers hastily mounted the horses of the limbers, and making a short "left about," hurried away with the fleeing cannoneers.

Not so, however, the limbers of one battery: like lightning they dashed forward towards their pieces, and almost in the twinkling of an eye, they emerged from the confusion in an unbroken line with a light twelve pounder attached to every one of them, the captain of the company proudly riding before, wildly waving his sword!

It was a bold movement, and evidently one the enemy had not anticipated, and so quickly had it been executed, he did not have time to realise it until the guns were beyond his reach. Except the men with these guns, not a Union soldier nor Union commander of any kind save in hasty retreat, could be seen on that, the south side of the Warrenton Pike, while the rebel lines continued to increase in extent, and to advance as rapidly as formations could be made.

Our interest was centred in the battery, now all alone, entirely without support, and all expected to see it gallop to the rear and join the general stampede. To our infinite surprise, after advancing two hundred or three hundred yards to the rear, the captain again went into battery, as if, single handed, to defy the whole centre of the rebel army. The assurance of the battery commander, his effrontery and impudence, were as much of a surprise to the rebels apparently, as to us, and they seemed to be staggered for a few moments, as if in doubt whether or no our lines had reformed and were about to advance again. Their doubts were soon dispersed, and they charged with such a dashing impetuous rush that apparently the battery could by no possibility escape.

Again the horses and limbers plunged wildly forward, and it seemed as if the pintle-hooks of the limbers actually shot into the lunettes of the trails of the gun carriages. Before the charging line reached the ground that the guns stood upon and fired from, the battery was moving away at a smart trot:

It looked as though the battery captain was now playing and trifling with the enemy, for when he reached the crest of the hill leading down into the valley, he went into battery again, to pay a parting compliment to the Johnnies, but he failed to surprise them for a third time, and they resumed their formation for a charge. The captain saw his danger and without firing a shot he limbered to the rear and coolly moved down the hill, where he was lost to our sight.

Several of us were light artillery officers, and we knew from our own experience on the drill ground and under fire, what skill must have been exercised by a battery commander in training his men and horses to enable him to handle his battery like a plaything in the face of overwhelming numbers of the enemy, and to take what would have been enormous and unpardonable risks with a command not almost absolutely perfect in drill and discipline.

Such was the manner Battery D retreated from its position at the second Bull Run.

After limbering the pieces as narrated in the preceding pages, the battery moved down the hill, and, following the edge of the woods, soon reached the Warrenton Pike, near the Stone Bridge. We found the road to be filled with wagons, parts of batteries, infantry, cavalry, etc. We halted at the bridge and Capt. Monroe tried to get some ammunition for the battery, but it was impossible to do so. The battery was now ordered forward onto the bridge, but the bridge at this time was blocked tip with wagons, etc., which we had to remove, and by the time we crossed it was quite dark. We moved tip the pike about half a mile and entered a field on the left, and remained there until about nine o'clock. We took advantage of this halt to have supper.

While we were halted at the bridge we supplied the battery with coffee, sugar, and hardtack from an abandoned baggage wagon. Just before we reached the bridge there was a large number of camp-kettles that were filled with corned beef. The fires were about out under them owing to the bullet holes that had let out the water from most of them; but we found a number that were all right and took them along. We had a good square meal, which put us in first class condition.

At about nine o'clock we were again put in motion, and reached

Centreville Heights about midnight, parked the battery, unhitched the horses, without unharnessing, and the men lay down in a drizzling rain for a very much needed rest, and slept soundly until morning.

Our stay on these heights was extended through the whole of Sunday, the 31st, and until nearly two o'clock p.m. of Sept. 1st. We were then put in motion, and proceeded along the Centreville Pike towards Washington. We moved along very leisurely, and it was in the vicinity of four o'clock that we reached a point about half way between Centreville and Fairfax Court House, when our ears were again filled with the roar of volley after volley of musketry, seemingly not a great distance away. Our column was halted immediately, and for an hour or more we stood in expectation of being momentarily called upon. To add to the impressiveness of the occasion, a very severe thunder storm commenced about the same time with the engagement, and the noise of the thunder added to that of the battle, made it seem terrific. The rain fell in torrents, wetting us through in a few minutes, and increasing our discomfort.

This engagement was the Battle of Chantilly, and was brought about by the rebel Gen. Jackson's endeavour to intercept and cut our retreating column, moving along the Warrenton Pike, by marching *via* Little River Pike, a road which leaves the Bull Run battlefield from a point near his position upon that field, crossing the Warrenton Pike near Fairfax Court House; but the watchfulness of our cavalry had discovered the movement, and it was promptly frustrated. Soon after dark the firing ceased, and the battery was moved into a field upon the right of the road, parked, and notwithstanding that the ground was thoroughly soaked, and the men wet to the skin, they rolled up in their blankets and were soon asleep.

Tuesday, Sept. 2nd, we continued our march towards Washington, reaching the vicinity of Bailey's Cross-roads about dark. Since the 22nd of August, the battery had been upon the march day and night, not once had the horses been unharnessed, and they had been short of forage for most of the time, and it may be imagined were in a very exhausted condition. The men were thoroughly used up; what with the excessive duty, lack of rations, and the discouraging termination of the campaign, they were very much disheartened.

On our arrival in the vicinity of our old camp, at sometime in the early evening, considerable cheering was heard down the road leading to Alexandria, which increased in volume as it approached. Our interest in the singular and unexpected demonstration drew us out into the road, and we could soon see in the growing darkness the approach of a large cavalcade, and by a close inspection we were able to distinguish the form of Gen. McClellan. We immediately added our cheers to the others, and when a few moments later it was said that he had been reappointed to the command of our armies, our enthusiasm was unrestrained.

From Sept. 2nd until Sept. 6th, we remained in camp near our old camping grounds at Upton's Hill and Dupont. Each night a section of the battery was sent out on picket, but nothing of importance disturbed us.

CHAPTER 4

South Mountain and Antietam

About nine o'clock on the evening of Sept. 6th, the section on picket was called in, and as speedily as possible the battery packed up and started towards Washington, passing through the city towards midnight, and early on the morning of the 7th made camp about twelve miles from the city, on the Maryland side of the Potomac River, where we remained until the 10th, when we marched to Lisbon. On the 12th we reached New Market, continuing on to Frederick City the next day. Here the head of our column began to encounter the rebels, and on the 14th our troops fought a severe battle with them at South Mountain, and after persistent and hard fighting, succeeded in driving them over the mountain.

Battery D was not engaged in this battle, but from its position, which was upon very high ground, the men had an excellent view of the engagement.

Let us pause a moment, for the purpose of narrating the movements of the Confederate Army, which had caused this sudden departure of ours into Maryland. After the check given to Gen. Jackson at Chantilly, Gen. Lee decided to invade Maryland. He hoped by this action to have his army largely recruited from the great number of Southern sympathizers in that State, whom it had been said were only waiting for just such an opportunity as this would give them, to join the Confederate Army. Gen. Jackson was ordered to march for the Potomac, and between the 4th and 5th of Sept. the whole Confederate Army had crossed into Maryland, and was encamped near Frederick, on the Monocacy River.

Gen. Lee issued an address to the people of Maryland, inviting those who were in sympathy with the Southern cause, to join the army; but it fell flat, and he lost more by desertions than he gained by recruits from the Marylanders. On the 9th of Sept. Gen. Lee issued Special Order No. 119, in which he ordered Gen. Jackson to proceed to Harper's Ferry, and oblige its surrender. Gen. Longstreet and the rest of the army were ordered to proceed to Boonsboro,—thus his army was divided. Happily this order fell into the hands of Gen. Mc-Clellan, who acted upon its information immediately by following the main part of the Confederate Army, attacking it and driving it over South Mountain down to Antietam, and it was late in the afternoon of the 17th before Lee's army was fully united.

The morning of the 15th saw Battery D upon the road again, and by noon we had reached the summit of South Mountain. As we passed along we saw numerous evidences of the severe struggle. Many of the dead, both of our own and the rebel forces, lay by the roadside and in the fields, burial parties being then at work digging graves.

During the afternoon we continued our winding way down the mountain, following the pike road which led through the village of Boonsboro, and went into camp just beyond the village. On the morning of the 16th we were hitched up and ready to move, but did not get the order to move until about noon; when, passing through Keedysville, we followed the pike until near McClellan's headquarters, the vicinity of which we reached just before dark, and turning to the right crossed Antietam Creek, and after marching for sometime in a somewhat circuitous route went into park about nine o'clock, with a number of other batteries. Our position was on cleared ground and on the summit of a commanding ridge, as we discovered next morning.

As our infantry advanced to establish a picket line, they were met with a heavy fire, which convinced us that the enemy were in our near presence, and in large force. Their artillery shelled us continually, and the flight of the shells with their burning fuses, together with the flash of the small arms, made a very pretty display, but we were all glad when the exhibition came to a close, just before ten o'clock.

The teams were not unhitched, but the bridles were dropped, giving the horses an opportunity to feed. It was late before the horses were fed and the men had eaten their suppers, but finally all had disposed themselves for sleep, either upon the ground, or on the chests of the caissons, and were soon utterly indifferent to their surroundings and the prospects of trouble on the morrow.

Just at daylight the next morning we were awakened by shell that went screeching over the battery, and in a minute or two it was followed by quite a lively lot of them, but their elevation was just a little too high, and they passed over us, only one doing any damage.

Cannoniers rushed to their posts, drivers to their horses: bridles were hastily slipped on, and in less time than it takes to tell it, were executing the movement "Action front," in answer to an order from the captain. As the men succeeded in rubbing their eyes open, and recovered from their astonishment, they looked about for an explanation of this disturbance. It was in the gray of dawn, and the few first rays of the rising sun had made it possible for us to see the surrounding hills. From one of these a battery or two of rebels had discovered our position, and gotten in the first blow; but they had no idea what a hornets' nest they were stirring up, for it so happened that upon that ridge there lay four batteries: upon our left lay Battery B, Fourth United States, upon our rear Battery L, First New York, and the First New Hampshire, and as quickly as possible every gun, twenty-four in number, was firing in reply to the enemy.

Capt. Monroe says of this part of the action:

I have always thought that but one battery opened upon us, though others believe there were two or three opposed to us. Whatever number there was, they must have found their position a warm one, for the gunners of three of these (our batteries) could not be excelled for marksmanship, estimation of distances, and all the good qualities which go to make a skilful gunner. The previous winter they had been exercised by Capt. Gibbon in firing at target, sighting, etc., and they had acquired great proficiency in these points. The fuses of the shell and case were accurately timed, and the projectiles burst where it was intended they should, among the guns and limbers of the enemy, who had stirred up a hornets' nest, and the hornets proved too many for him.

After the rebel battery had retired, and the firing ceased, the men of Battery D had an opportunity to look about them, take in the lay of the land, etc. In our front the ground sloped gradually for several hundred yards, at which distance it was crossed at nearly right angles with our position by a sunken road, in which the rebel line of battle was posted.

Immediately upon our left was a thin belt of woods, and beyond that an extensive cornfield, in which was done as stubborn fighting as was ever seen. During the whole day its possession was hotly contested; first one side and then the other would occupy it, and so vigorous was the assault, so brave the defence, that by noon it was possible to trace where the various stands had been made, by the continuous lines of dead and wounded, extending from one side of the cornfield to the other.

After the cessation of the artillery fire, the men of Battery D were kept busy replenishing the limber chests with ammunition, and various other duties, until about nine o'clock, and for an hour afterwards had a comparatively easy time. Two batteries in our line, Campbell's and Reynolds's, were moved from their position near us to a new one just beyond the woods in the edge of the cornfield, where they received very warm treatment.

About ten a.m. one of Gen. Hooker's staff came to Capt. Monroe and ordered him to report to Gen. Hooker. After ordering the drivers to mount, and putting the column in motion, left in front, under Lieut. Fisk, Capt. Monroe sought Gen. Hooker, whom he found at the front of our line of battle, mounted upon a white horse, altogether the most conspicuous object in that vicinity, and less than five hundred yards from the rebel line. As coolly as though in a drawing room, he pointed out to the captain the position he desired him to occupy, and the work he wanted him to do. The position was upon the top of a slight elevation fully a hundred yards in front of our line of battle, and the work was the silencing of a rebel battery which had secured a position from which they had an enfilade fire upon our line of battle, which was very destructive.

Upon receiving this order, Capt. Monroe returned to the battery, joining us just as we had passed through the woods and were entering the cornfield. Our passage through this field was necessarily slow, because of the impossibility of moving in a direct line in consequence of the great number of dead and wounded; frequent stops had to be made for the purpose of moving them out of the way.

Just after crossing the Smoketown road Capt. Monroe halted the caissons and advanced the pieces a short distance and gave the order "Form line advancing, trot, march," and soon gave the order "In battery, action front," "Commence firing." This manoeuvre brought us upon level ground nearly in front of the Dunker Church, and about one hundred and twenty-five yards from the Hagerstown Pike.

The battery that we were to silence was south of the church on the east of the pike. They did not seem to pay any attention to us until we were fairly in battery, and had opened on them, then it was give and take for a few minutes. They had been firing at quite long range, and did not get their guns depressed so as to do us any damage, all of their shots going over us. Our gunners were putting case shot in among them at a rapid rate, and soon their fire slackened and in a little while ceased altogether. After the smoke had cleared away we found that they had retired, leaving one limber and several dead men and horses on the ground they had occupied.

We stopped firing and watched a brigade of our infantry which was going into position on our right and rear. They moved to the right until they were on a line with our right piece, and then faced to the front and charged into the woods just to the north of the Dunker Church. In the meantime we began to get a few minie balls from the south of the church, and sent back a few shells; but we soon had orders to cease firing, as there was some doubt about whether the brigade that had just passed into the woods had not moved to that side of the church. It was not over six or eight minutes before volley after volley was fired in the woods just behind the church, and the brigade which had charged into the woods but a few minutes before in such dashing style now came pouring out in a confused mass. They had run into a large force of the rebels and could not hold their ground.

We expected now to get the order to limber up and move to the rear; but instead, we were ordered to "Commence firing." Up to this time we had lost but two men and two or three horses. We directed our fire into the woods in our front, and in a few minutes we saw a hne of rebels coming through the woods just to the right of the church. Knowing that if that line was not stopped that Battery D was in a bad place, as they would flank us on the right, and the ground to our left was such that we could not get out that way, we sent round after round of canister at them in quick succession, and had the satisfaction of seeing the line waver and then break and return to the woods.

We were now feeling that we had things our own way again, but the minie bullets were beginning to come again, not so thick as before, but with a great deal of accuracy, and we soon found, that although we had driven the main line back, in the meantime quite a number of sharpshooters had dropped into the depression on the east side of the pike, and also behind a pile of rails on our right not over seventy-five yards away, and were making it very uncomfortable for us. The right piece of the centre section had three number ones shot down before they could load their piece, and had lost every man but Corp. Gray and Private Mills. The piece was finally loaded, and a shell was sent into the pile of rails, which must have done some damage. The right piece had lost every horse on its limber, and the other pieces were suffering losses in men and horses.

It was now apparent that it was time for us to fall back if we wanted to save our battery. Capt. Monroe soon gave the order, and we fell back to Mumma's house, just under the hill to our rear. We had to leave one piece, but Lieut. Fisk soon returned with some men and the piece was taken to the rear with the prolonge, leaving the limber, which was recovered next day.

The battery soon moved back to the position we occupied in the morning, and replenished our ammunition. Lieut. Parker went on a hunt for horses to replace those that were killed and wounded. He succeeded in getting horses enough so that we were in shape to move at a moment's notice.

In this battle our battery last four killed, sixteen wounded, and two missing (six of the slightly wounded staid with the battery). We lost thirty-eight horses. Capt. Monroe's horse was shot six times.

Capt. Campbell, of Battery B, Fourth Ignited States, having been severely wounded, Capt. Monroe succeeded him as Chief of Artillery, and the command of Battery D passed to Lieut. Fisk.

The afternoon was well advanced when an order was received that we take position "In battery" along the ridge occupied by us in the early morning, and with us went four other batteries, making twenty-nine guns. Every officer was ordered to keep a sharp lookout, and at the first indication of an attempt by the enemy to place artillery in position, all the guns in that line were to commence firing, concentrating their fire upon that spot.

About five o'clock a horseman was seen to ride over the hill from which the rebel battery had shelled us in the morning, followed almost immediately by the teams of a battery, and rapidly making the left about, drop their pieces into battery, but before they had fired a shot, twenty-nine projectiles of various kinds and sizes were flying towards that unfortunate battery, creating, a few seconds later, the greatest consternation, as they exploded among the pieces and limbers; round after round followed in quick succession, and that battery beat a hasty retreat. Other batteries tried to maintain the position, but it was of no use; our fire was too frequent and well directed for anything to live upon that hill for any length of time. Gradually it became more and more quiet, so that by nine o'clock all firing had ceased, save an occasional picket shot.

Battery D remained in position. Through the night rumour had it that we had practically destroyed Lee's army, and that it only remained for us to up and at him in the morning, to drive him into the Potomac. But the next morning we were very much surprised at the entire absence of noise; instead of the roar of battle, we could not hear even the noise of a single picket gun. Our curiosity kept us hunting for a reason, until it was ascertained that we were under a flag of truce.

All day long we lay in our position, expecting that the truce would end, and we should resume the fight. During the forenoon we took advantage of the inaction to recover the limber left on the field, visit our wounded in the hospitals, refitting our disabled pieces, caissons, etc., and at last night closed in without our having fired a shot. This was not entirely satisfactory to us, for although we were not actually starving for a fight, still the impression of all, even the privates, was that we had our enemy at great disadvantage, which we were by this delay losing.

On the morning of the 19th of Sept., the battery was early prepared for an advance movement, but it was nearly noon before we moved out of park. Since early morning we had seen troops moving forward along the Hagerstown Pike, and were momentarily expecting to hear the roar of battle, but not a sound reached our ears until near the middle forenoon, when distant artillery could be heard. What has happened? Soon mounted messengers returned at full speed to Mc-Clellan's headquarters, and the mortifying intelligence is given that there is no enemy in our front. Gen. Lee having taken advantage of the darkness of the night and moved his entire command across the Potomac at Shepherdstown Ford.

It is well that it was not possible for Gen. McClellan to hear all that was said of him by the soldiers of his army when this was fully understood by them; the feeling that here was one more illustration of the superior generalship of the enemy was very depressing.

About 12 o'clock our battery pulled out of park, moved across the fields to the Hagerstown Pike, and started towards Sharpsburg. Our route carried us along that part of the road over which there had been such a fearful struggle on the 17th; nothing had been disturbed (except that the wounded had been removed), but lay just as it had been left on the evening of that day. As we reached that part where the cornfield was upon our left and the Dunker Church upon our right, the sight became sickening, even to men who had become inured to such scenes, for there lay within the reach of our vision hundreds, yea, thousands of dead, just as they had fallen, swelling into most horrible shapes, twice their natural size, and mortification, which had been hastened by a light rain on the night of the 18th, and a very hot sun on the morning of the 19th, had turned the exposed parts of the bodies black. We were glad when we had passed beyond the battlefield.

It was our impression that we had started in pursuit of the enemy, but that was soon corrected, for before we reached Sharpsburg we were ordered into camp, upon ground which had evidently been occupied very recently by the rebels, as was made plain to us by the debris which lay around, and emphasized by large numbers of a certain kind of live stock, which for some reason (probably an over-crowded condition) had left them, and now proceeded to fasten themselves upon us, much to our discomfort.

On the 20th our camp was moved to a more acceptable place, and we remained in it just one month.

Oct. 1st President Lincoln visited the army, and remained four days. During his stay a grand review was held of the Army of the Potomac, which had been increased to nearly 150,000, and was in superb condition, while Lee was at Winchester, Va., with his army, reported to be in a wretched condition; still McClellan did not show any disposition to move upon him, notwithstanding he was urged time after time by the President to do so.

All through October the weather was of the finest, just such as was needed for a campaign, but all through the month Gen. McClellan was inactive, and it was not until Nov. 1st that he was ready; then he moved, but it was too late, for on the 7th there was a heavy snowstorm—winter had commenced, and now movement would be necessarily slow and tedious. His opportunity had been thrown away.

Oct. 20th Battery D left camp near Sharpsburg and marched to Bakersville, going into camp with our division artillery, where it was said we were to quarter for the winter; but at two o'clock in the afternoon of the 26th, orders were received to pack up, and we were soon on the march again, which was continued until nine o'clock, through a drenching rainstorm, and finally made camp in a ploughed field, which was very inconvenient for men and horses, as the mud was ankle deep.

On the 28th, our march was confined three or four miles, and we made camp near Crompton's Pass. The next day we continued on, went through the gap, and camped near Knoxville, Md. We remained here over the 29th.

A new disease had broken out among our horses, three-quarters of them having swollen tongues, and so badly affected that their tongues would protrude from their mouths, rendering it impossible for the poor animals to eat their grain or hay; and added to this, a hoof disease, caused by their being so constantly in the mud, had become so bad that in many cases the hoof nearly rotted off, necessitating the shooting of a considerable number of them.

Oct. 30th we crossed the Potomac into Virginia, at Berlin, and next day commenced our pursuit of the rebel army, with a four gun battery, being obliged to leave two of our guns because of lack of horses.

From the 31st of October to the 6th of November, we continued our march, reaching Warrenton on the afternoon of the 6th, where we remained until the 11th.

On the 7th the battery was ordered into position, expecting an attack. A furious snow storm prevailed all day, making us very uncomfortable, and as we were without tents, we were obliged to depend entirely upon our blankets for protection.

On the 10th it was officially announced that Gen. McClellan had been relieved from command of the army, and Gen. Burnside appointed to succeed him. Their addresses, one of farewell and the other assuming command, were read to us upon parade that night.

Towards the last of October Capt. J. Albert Monroe left us, having been promoted to Major of our regiment, and assigned to duty at Washington. He was a strict disciplinarian and a thorough and efficient drillmaster. Early in November Major Monroe was assigned to the duty of organising and commanding the Artillery Camp of Instruction at Washington, in which duty he made a national reputation as an artillerist of the first order.

Lieut. Fisk, being the senior officer present, had command of the battery from a short time after Antietam until our arrival at Bakersville, when Lieut. Harkness, having returned from his sick leave, assumed command.

CHAPTER 5

Fredericksburg

On the 11th of November the battery marched to Waterloo, remaining until the 17th, and then continued on to Morristown. Here it was again rumoured that we were to go into winter quarters, and a removal on the 19th into a fine grove rather strengthened our belief that there was some foundation for the rumour; but orders which were received late on the 21st that we were to be ready to move early the next morning, settled effectually the winter camp question at this place.

Next morning the battery made an early start, and at night reached Brook Station, on the Fredericksburg & Aquia Creek Railroad. The weather was perfectly horrible, a cold drizzling rain prevailing all day long, made the march very disagreeable.

Our stay here was extended until the 7th of Dec. Twice during that time we received marching orders, but heavy snowstorms necessitated their being countermanded; but on the 7th we started, but after marching four or five miles we reached a hill so steep and icy that the horses were unable to pull the carriages to the top, and we made camp upon the hill with our pieces and caissons strung along from the top to the bottom. The next day we managed to get over the hill, and continued on to Fredericksburg. On the 9th we moved to a position opposite the city, and made camp.

Gen. Burnside, upon assuming command of the army, with the consent of Gen. Halleck, abandoned Gen. McClellan's plan, which was, by a rapid march upon Gordonsville, to interpose between Gen. Lee's divided forces (he having sent Gen. Longstreet over the Blue Ridge to resist the Union advance upon the Confederate capital), and beat them in detail, and adopted a new plan of operations. The capture of Richmond, rather than the destruction of Gen. Lee's army, was to be his objective.

The Union Army at this time was 120,000 strong. Some precious time was wasted in its reorganisation. Instead of the old corps formation, it was now organised into three Grand Divisions, each consisting of two corps. Gen. Sumner was placed in command of the right. Gen. Franklin of the left, and Gen. Hooker of the centre, and a large reserve commanded by Gen. Sigel.

The plan as stated by Gen. Burnside was to concentrate the army at Warrenton, make a feint of crossing the Rappahannock, leading the enemy to believe that an attack was about to be made upon Gordonsville, and then move the whole army to Fredericksburg, and thence march rapidly upon Richmond; but here again some one blundered. To cross the Rappahannock, it would be necessary to construct pontoon bridges. Gen. Burnside supposed that the matter had been fully attended to, and that the pontoons would be on hand at the time of his arrival, Nov. 15th; instead of which it was the 25th of the month before they arrived, and the 10th of December before things were ready for throwing the bridges across the river.

In the meantime the enemy had discovered the plan, and on the 22nd Gen. Burnside and his division commanders had the mortification of seeing the opposite heights covered with the enemy's batteries, and filled with his infantry. Gen. Lee's army, some 80,000 strong, had all been brought up, and it lay in a semicircle around Fredericksburg, each wing resting on the river—its right at Port Royal below the city, and its left a short distance above it.

On the 10th of December, everything being ready. Gen. Burnside gave orders that the bridges should be thrown across at an early hour the next morning; three were to be constructed immediately in front of Fredericksburg, and two a couple of miles below. The morning of the 11th was cold and raw, a dense fog prevailed, amid which the work commenced.

The heights upon the Falmouth side were close to the margin of the river, which at this point is about three hundred yards wide. Upon these heights there were placed in position one hundred and forty-seven guns. The bridges below the city were laid without much opposition; but in front of the city a galling fire, from behind stone walls and from windows, was opened upon the bridge builders, driving them back, and effectually preventing further work upon them.

About six o'clock another attempt was made, with the same result. Then Gen. Burnside ordered the guns mounted upon Safford Heights to open fire upon the city, and batter it down if necessary. More than a hundred guns responded immediately to the order, and a roar commenced which could be heard miles away, and that fairly shook the earth, lasting nearly three hours.

In the midst of this firing another attempt was made to lay the bridges; but, strange to say, there still were sharpshooters to oppose them, and they were obliged to fall back; then volunteers were called for to cross the river and drive the enemy out of their hiding places. Three regiments responded to the call, were quickly conveyed across, and in a brief space of time the sharpshooters were driven away, nearly a hundred of them being made prisoners, and the bridges laid.

Before dark Sumner's and a few of Hooker's Division had crossed to the south side of the river. Considerable skirmishing occurred as the troops forced their way through the city and out upon the plains beyond.

Early on the morning of the 12th, the rest of the army crossed. and Battery D went with it. Our progress up the streets from the river was extremely dangerous, from the fact that the enemy had a perfect range, and succeeded in ricocheting shot after shot down the very centre of the street, obliging us to use the sidewalks. Occasionally they would explode a shell uncomfortably close; but we succeeded in reaching the upper part of the town without any serious casualty. Here we sought protection behind a large stone warehouse, where we remained all day, and until before light next morning, when we were moved up nearer the enemy.

All day of the 13th we lay under fire, protected by buildings. The enemy shelled Fredericksburg all the morning, and about noon the order was given for our infantry to advance upon Marye's Heights. The mist had cleared, and every movement of our troops could be distinctly seen by the rebels upon the heights. Then commenced a most furious cannonading, followed in a few moments, as our troops reached the stone wall at the foot of Marye's Hill, by volley after volley of musketry. So terrific was the fire from Marye's Hill that our artillery could not be advanced, and the infantry had to fall back.

The men of Battery D were soon convinced of the terrible work that was going on in front, from the great numbers of wounded which passed them, going to the rear. In fifteen minutes, of the 5600 led into battle by Gen. Hancock, 2000 were disabled. All day and until nearly dark on the 14th our battery remained in the place we had moved into in the morning.

Just before dark we were ordered to move forward across the plain to the left of the city and shell the works on Marye's Heights. We came into position on the edge of an embankment which was at least five or six feet high. We placed our pieces in position and then took our limbers and caissons back under the embankment, and when all was ready, we opened with a will. We thought we had quite a snap on our enemy, but in about three minutes they convinced us that we had "*barked up the wrong tree*," for they just sent in a shower of shells and minies that made us seek cover. We laid close to the embankment until they let up, and then loaded all our pieces and gave them a broadside. We fired two or three rounds, and then they had their turn again; this was repeated three or four times; but at last we were denied the privilege of even getting in a round or two, as their fire was kept up for a long time, and they were putting their shells just in the right place. We afterwards found out that they had platted the ground in their front, and knew to a nicety every position, and could drop a shell into any of them; and then it became apparent to all of us that we were not wanted there anyway, so we limbered up and retired to the lower part of the city.

Here we remained until two o'clock in the morning of the 15th, when we recrossed the river, and returned to our old camp. By daylight all our army had recrossed the river to the Falmouth side, and the Battle of Fredericksburg was over.

Battery D, although under fire all the time, did not become engaged, save in this single instance, and was but little injured—First Sergeant R. Henry Lee's wounded hand, and a broken stock of a caisson being our only casualties.

Capt. W. W. Buckley, who had been promoted from First Lieutenant to Captain on Oct. 30th, and assigned to Battery D, reached our camp on Dec. 10th, just in time to participate in this fight.

Dec. 17th the battery was moved about a mile and a half back from the river into a grove, and began to build winter quarters. A cellar about a foot deep, six feet long and four feet wide, was first dug; this was fixed around with pine slabs, dirt was then tamped around the outside of the slabs, a ridgepole was raised in the crotch of two upright poles and covered with our shelter tents, and a mud chimney was built on the outside, the tent being tacked tightly around the fireplace. We had a bunk on either side, raised from the ground and filled with boughs. When these houses were completed and we had built good rousing fires in the fire-places, we were just as comfortable and happy as it was possible for soldiers to be.

From this time to Feb. 6th, 1863, our time was occupied in performing the ordinary duties of the soldier, such as drills, having inspections, etc., varying the operations between Jan. 10th and 21st, by being under marching orders for the purpose of crossing the Rappahannock River on an expedition against the rebels.

Gen. Burnside desired to redeem, if possible, the disaster which had befallen the Union army, and he originated a new plan, the purpose of which was an immediate advance upon Richmond. His plan was to make a feint above Fredericksburg, and to cross with the main body six miles below. A large force of cavalry with four guns was to cross at Kelly's Ford, push towards the Rapidan, destroy the railroad and bridges in the rear of Gen. Lee, traverse Virginia, and join the Union garrison at Suffolk.

This movement was stopped by order of the President, representations from dissatisfied officers had had their effect, and Gen. Burnside was ordered not to make the movement.

By Jan. 10th the plan had been changed. It was now proposed to cross the Rappahannock above Fredericksburg, flank the enemy and force a battle. The President gave his permission, and the troops were placed under marching orders. The pontoons were brought up to the vicinity of Banks' Ford, and everything made ready to throw the bridge across the swollen river. Most of the army had been brought up to the vicinity of the ford, and it was contemplated to make the movement on the morning of the 21st of Jan., but on the evening of the 20th a fearful storm of wind, sleet and rain came on, such as is seldom seen in that region, which continued all night, and when morning came the entire country had been converted into a vast bed of mud, and for hours the troops were hopelessly mired—it was impossible to move in either direction—every attempt to move only sank the wheels of the artillery and of the wagons deeper into the soft sticky mud. Orders were finally issued to the troops to return to winter quarters, and what is known as the "Mud March" was ended.

Battery D was fortunate enough not to have left its camp on this occasion; for ten days we were hitched up ready to move at a moment's notice, but happily were not called upon, and thus escaped a most disagreeable episode.

Stormy and cold weather prevailed during the last week of January, but as we were comfortably housed, rations plenty, and duty light, we managed to get through it without much discomfort.

February came in like a lion—the 2nd was very cold, the 3rd still colder, and on the 4th the men could do little else than sit by their fires, the cold was so intense.

On the 6th orders were received to pack up as soon as possible, and be ready to march in an hour. About eight o'clock the battery moved out of our winter camp and took up its line of march in a cold drenching rain, towards Bell's Landing on the Potomac River, distant about twelve miles. The roads were exceedingly muddy, so that our progress was necessarily very slow; the very best we could do was about six miles on the first day; the pieces and caissons would become fast in the mud, and we would have to double our teams to pull them out. Our condition may be imagined—tired out, wet through, and no way of protecting ourselves from the cold storm, which continued through the night.

We succeeded after great difficulty in pulling our pieces and caissons through to the landing on the next day; but the battery wagon and forge not having arrived, six teams of horses were sent back after them, and they were found about five miles back, the forge being bottom side up in a creek, having run off the bridge the night before. We finally got it on the road and hauled it and the battery wagon to camp.

About two o'clock in the morning of the 9th, the men were aroused, and commenced loading the battery on canal boats. At nine o'clock the loading of the battery was completed. The boats were shoved out into the stream and anchored until four o'clock in the afternoon, when a steamer took our tow-line and towed us down the river a few miles, where we again anchored, and remained until the nth, when we continued our journey; but about noon it commenced storming, and we put into St. Mary's Bay for a harbour. All day of the 12th the storm continued, and we remained in the harbour.

Within a hundred yards of where our boats lay, were some immense rocks, and at low tide large numbers of oysters could be seen clinging to their sides. Permission was given that the men could use the small boats to gather them, and soon large quantities were secured, and, as it may be imagined, to men whose diet had been principally "salt junk" and pork, this change in their diet was very acceptable.

The 13th opening clear and pleasant, an early start was made, and we moved on down to the mouth of the river, but the bay was found to be so rough that it was not considered safe to attempt crossing it, and we made harbour until three o'clock in the afternoon, when the wind having gone down, we started again towards Fortress Monroe. We reached Hampton at daylight, and immediately disembarked. The next day we went into camp near Hampton.

Hampton at this time was in ruins. When the rebel Gen. Magruder evacuated the place, he burned it, hardly leaving a house standing. It must have been a beautiful place before the war, but at the time of our arrival it had been given over to the negroes, who had built huts out of the ruins, and were taking life very easily.

One enterprising darkey had established an oyster house, and as soon as we were in camp he solicited our trade, but as we had not been paid in some time, about everybody was "broke;" we did have some "Kalamazoo" greenbacks, but they had lost their value. We felt that our constitutions needed a change of diet, and oysters were about the proper thing to tone us up, so we sent one of our number over to the oyster house and he bought a gallon of oysters and offered in payment a two dollar "Kalamazoo." The darkey had some doubts about the bill, but was assured it was genuine, and that he could go up to the captain and convince himself that it was all right; but before the darkey had time to go, the captain walked in; the bill was produced, and the captain gave him two dollars and eighty cents in good Government greenbacks, remarking that it was worth three dollars to him. This move established the worth of Kalamazoo greenbacks, and we had a fair supply of oysters. (Capt. Buckley was at this time on a sick furlough, but *his dress coat* was in camp.)

From the 15th of February until the 11th of March, we remained in camp at Hampton, the time being occupied with the regular round of camp duties. Snow and rain alternated with pleasant weather. Duties were light, and, with plenty to eat, a good comfortable place to sleep in, and the privilege of passes to visit the numerous places of interest in the vicinity, made us feel very well contented with our situation.

On the 27th of February Capt. Buckley returned from a sick furlough. Lieut. Parker, taking his turn at a furlough, left the battery on March 2nd, for Rhode Island.

At two o'clock in the morning of the 6th, John T. Green died of measles, and was buried at three o'clock in the afternoon of the 7th, with military honours.

First Lieut. G. C. Harkness, at his request, was mustered out of service, and left for home on the 7th.

March 11th the battery moved to Newport News, where it remained until the 16th, on which day the camp was changed about a mile back towards Hampton.

Just at night on the 18th, orders were received to prepare five days rations and be ready to march at an early hour next morning. At six o'clock in the morning of the 19th, we started for Fortress Monroe. It began to snow soon after leaving camp; the storm rapidly increased, and by afternoon became a blizzard. It was found impossible for us to reach our destination, and we were obliged to camp. We passed a most disagreeable night; wood was very scarce, and it was with great difficulty that we gathered enough to keep us from freezing. Snow fell to the depth of eight or ten inches, adding much to our discomfort.

Next morning we continued on to Fortress Monroe, and from the wharf at that place loaded our battery upon the steamer *John Brooks*, and the horses upon two schooners, and started early on the morning of the 22nd, in tow of the steamer, for Baltimore, Md. Our passage across Chesapeake Bay was rather tempestuous, indeed so rough was it at one time that the steamer was obliged to cut the tow-line and cast us adrift. She lay then she picked us up again, and we proceeded on our journey without further interruption, reaching Baltimore at sunrise on the morning of the 24th.

The battery was transferred as rapidly as possible from the boats to the cars, and at three o'clock in the afternoon left Baltimore over the Baltimore & Ohio Railroad for Parkersburg, on the Ohio River. Our train consisted of flat cars upon which the pieces and caissons were loaded, and freight cars in which the men and horses were accommodated, the only difference between those occupied by the men and those in which the horses were, being the placing of a few pine planks across the car for the men to sit upon. Two nights and one day were occupied in making this journey, arriving at Parkersburg on the 27th. Frequently long stops were made which enabled the men to make little foraging trips, and, as they were almost always very successful, there was a sudden increase both in the quantity and variety of their diet, which was very acceptable to them, and this, together with the constant change of scene, made the trip very enjoyable.

Most of the 27th was occupied in transferring the battery from the cars to a river steamboat, and in the evening commenced our trip down the Ohio River, which was continued all night, and until eight o'clock in the evening of the 28th, when the bow of our steamer was run up against the bank of the river some six or eight miles above Cincinnati. Early next morning we continued on down the river to

Covington, where our mode of conveyance was again changed from boat to cars. We reached Lexington, Ky., about eight o'clock on the morning of the 30th, and unloaded our battery and went into camp about six miles from that city.

After the failure of Gen. Burnside's last movement with the Army of the Potomac, which resulted in the "mud march," he was relieved at his own request from that command, and went immediately to Washington, and formally tendered his resignation as Major General of Volunteers to the President, but Mr. Lincoln refused to receive it, remarking that he had "*other fish for him to fry.*"

After a short furlough, during which he visited Providence, where he received an enthusiastic ovation from his townsmen, Gen. Burnside returned to Washington, hoping to have command of his old Ninth Corps, but the President, after several consultations with him, on the 26th of March placed him in command of the Department of the Ohio. Upon accepting this command Gen. Burnside requested that he might be allowed to take the Ninth Corps with him. His request was granted, and as Battery D had been transferred to that corps, we were thus enabled to follow the fortunes of our much loved Burnside.

The battery remained in camp at Lexington just a week. On the evening of April 7th marching orders were received, and early on the 8th we packed and hitched up, but were delayed until nearly noon, while the men were paid. As soon as this was accomplished we commenced our march, but after making eight or ten miles, bivouacked until morning, when we continued our march, reaching Camp Dick Robinson before dark, after a pleasant journey of about twenty miles over one of the best of roads.

Battery D's camp was upon one side of the road and directly opposite the Seventh Rhode Island was encamped. As there were many acquaintances in the two organisations, this proximity made it very pleasant for the men of both commands.

On our way from Lexington to Camp Dick Robinson some of our men had stopped by the way to inspect the country in general and the whiskey distilleries in particular. An irresistible desire had seized them to learn just how that beverage—which, for a small outlaw would so soon make a millionaire of a pauper, or a brigadier of a private soldier—was made; so great was their interest that they took no heed of time, and their inspection lasted two days. The men of the battery began to think they would never see their comrades again; all of them were popular fellows and their return was anxiously awaited.

At last, one afternoon a great cloud of dust was seen rolling down the pike towards our camp, and occasionally as the curtain of dust was blown aside, a family carriage, with a coloured driver mounted upon the box, a soldier by his side, with the horses upon the dead run, could be seen. As it drew nearer the soldier was recognised as one of the absentees, and when the carriage whirled from the pike through our camp, drew up before the captain's tent with a great flourish, while from inside our missing comrades one after another crawled out, formed a line, and as the captain appeared, saluted him and reported for duty, it was so ludicrous and audacious that it brought a shout of laughter from the men, and made it impossible for the captain to say anything more than "Go to your quarters," while he maintained a straight face.

Frequent trips were made by the men to distant villages in the vicinity; the weather for the most part being very pleasant and warm, made these trips through this beautiful country very enjoyable.

On the 26th we started early in the morning for Stamford, about eighteen miles distant. We reached our destination about three o'clock in the afternoon, and made camp, in which we remained until the 30th, when an order was received to pack up as soon as possible and proceed to Columbia, about twenty-five miles distant. We were soon on the road, and after marching about twenty miles, went into camp at Carpenter's Creek.

The next day, May 1st, was spent in bivouac, momentarily expecting orders to march, but nothing was received until evening, when we were ordered to prepare to march at five o'clock in the morning. At daylight the order was countermanded.

May 2nd we were allowed to pitch our A tents, which led us to think our stay at this place was to be prolonged. Fortunate it was for us that we pitched our tents, for a heavy thunderstorm prevailed all day of the 3rd, and nearly all day on the 4th, and without the tents we should have been in a sorry condition.

Late on the 4th orders were received to cook two days rations, and be ready to march at midnight, and shortly after that time "Boots and saddles" was blown, and we commenced a march of about fifteen miles, over a very rough road and through an all day rain, which, with the rain of the two previous days, transformed the red clay into several inches of a sticky paste, which made our progress very slow and tedious. Early on the morning of the 6th we continued our march, reaching the town of Bumpus about noon. Stopping only long enough to feed our horses and eat dinner, we then pushed on and made camp a few miles from Somerset.

On the 7th we moved our camp to Somerset, where we remained until June 4th, our time being occupied with general camp duties, drills, etc. Hay was very scarce, and every other day the horses were taken out and allowed to graze. These trips proved very pleasant for the men, as it brought them in contact with the farmers, and gave them opportunities to buy butter, eggs, and other desirable eatables.

On the 22nd orders were received to turn in A tents and all our surplus baggage, and rumour had it that we were soon to start for East Tennessee; but day after day passed and nothing further was heard of such a movement.

On the 25th, the drivers being some three or four miles from camp grazing their horses, an orderly rode furiously into camp with an order to have the battery hitched up as soon as possible, and bringing the startling information that our pickets had been driven in by the enemy, who were fast approaching Somerset.

A messenger was immediately dispatched for the horses, and upon his reaching them there commenced as grand a hurdle race as one would care to witness—every one upon his own responsibility starting for camp—across fields, over fences and through ditches they went, making for the men in camp a most interesting and amusing finish. Upon their arrival the battery was hitched up, and remained in that condition, ready to move at a moment's notice until dark, when everything quieted down and assumed its usual condition.

It was while in this camp that the men of the battery had a rather startling illustration of the cavernous condition of this part of Kentucky. Our camp lay upon the ridge of quite a sizable basin, in the bottom of which there was a pond of perhaps five or six hundred feet in circumference. It had been there ever since we came to the place, and we had no reason to think that it was not a permanent fixture to the landscape; but one night about midnight the men were aroused by strange and unusual noises, evidently proceeding from the pond. Investigations were made, but nothing was ascertained beyond the fact that the water in the pond was falling very fast. Daylight was patiently waited for, when it was discovered that our pond had disappeared, and in the very centre of the depression was a hole as large as a hogshead, evidently leading into one of the numerous caverns with which the country thereabout is filled.

Gen. Burnside left Cincinnati on the 30th of May for Hickman's

Bridge, Ky., for the purpose of leading the Ninth and Twenty-Third Corps over the Cumberland Mountains into East Tennessee, but when he reached Lexington he was met by an order from the War Department directing him to reinforce Gen. Grant, at Vicksburg. Gen. Burnside had at this time the Twenty-Third Corps, formed from small bodies of troops which had been scattered about in Kentucky, Ohio and Indiana, whose organisation he did not consider thoroughly perfected, and his old staunch and true Ninth Corps. With his usual unselfish noble-heartedness Gen. Burnside put behind him all his plans and desires and immediately put two divisions of the Ninth Corps in motion for Vicksburg, and telegraphed the Secretary of War for permission to accompany them, but the secretary would not permit it, and Gen. Parks assumed command.

The order for this journey of the Ninth Corps reached Battery D at its camp in Somerset just before one o'clock on the morning of June 4th, and at sunrise the battery pulled out of park and started on its march for Lexington.

On the evening of the 5th we reached Stamford, and the men were kept up until after midnight signing the payroll and receiving their pay. The night of the 6th we occupied our old quarters at Camp Dick Robinson.

At ten o'clock in the forenoon the battery arrived at the depot in Lexington, and the men immediately commenced to load the battery upon the cars for the purpose of commencing our proposed journey, but after having nearly completed this work, the order was countermanded; the battery was unloaded and moved about three miles from Lexington and encamped.

During the night word was brought to us that Louis La Font, a member of the battery, had fallen or been thrown downstairs at the guardhouse in Lexington, and his neck broken. La Font was a genial, good-natured man, much liked by his comrades, and his death cast a gloom over the whole company.

The next day the battery received orders temporarily transferring it to the Twenty-Third Corps, together with marching orders for the 11th, and on that day it moved to Camp Nelson, about five miles distant, where the battery remained until July 12th. Our situation here was very pleasant, in the very centre as it was, of that beautiful blue grass country, surrounded by the most luxuriant fields of corn, wheat and rye, and such fields of clover. Our horses enjoyed it, and it made the drivers feel glad to see them growing so fat and sleek upon this excellent fodder.

As the 4th of July drew near we began to make great preparations for its celebration. Clark Walker, our carpenter, went to Nicholsvale and built a platform for dancing; arrangements were made with the citizens to provide a banquet for a fair consideration; in fact everything that could be thought of that would add to the success of the day was arranged. By daylight on the morning of the 4th the men were astir, cutting grass to be used as wadding (for at sunrise we were to fire a national salute), and piled it up near each gun.

Just as the sun appeared above the horizon, every cannonier was at his position—the guns having been previously loaded, filled almost to the muzzle with the wet grass—number four stood with his lanyard held taut in the position of ready, when out broke upon the morning air the order "By battery, fire." At that instant there came a report from the six guns of the battery that was heard for twenty miles, followed as rapidly as possible by other reports until one volley had been fired in honour of every State then in the Union.

After stable call had been attended to, the men were allowed to go to the village and carry out the programme previously arranged. The violinist of the battery, Dan Elliott, provided the music for the dancing, fairly eclipsing all of his former efforts. It was a very enjoyable occasion, the men returning to camp about six o'clock, well satisfied with the entire success of the celebration. At sunset the salute of the morning was repeated, thus making everyone feel that the day had been properly observed.

July 5th rumours of the approach of Gen. John Morgan, at the head of about 3000 mounted men and six guns, began to excite the citizens. Farmers made all possible haste to drive their cattle, horses, etc., within our lines; the battery placed its guns in position commanding the roads, while the infantry dug rifle pits and made every provision to give these raiders a very warm reception should they have the temerity to come our way.

The excitement continued for the next five days, but on the 11th it was learned that Morgan had avoided us, having passed many miles to the west of our position, and on the 8th had crossed the Ohio River into Indiana, where he was committing all sorts of depredations.

July 12th orders were received for the battery to march at nine o'clock in the forenoon for Lexington, load upon the cars and proceed at once to Cincinnati. At eight o'clock on the morning of the 13th Covington was reached, and as quick as the battery could be unloaded, we crossed the river into Cincinnati. That city was in a state of great excitement—Morgan was expected to ride into their streets at any moment, and with the greatly exaggerated reports of the enormity and cruelty of his depredations constantly ringing in their ears, it was not surprising that they should welcome with open arms anything which promised them protection from such a monster. All the militia was under arms, but the advent of a battery of light artillery, particularly a veteran organisation that they knew had seen service, and lots of it, like Battery D, was very reassuring to them. Their pleasure was evidenced by the welcome they gave us; indeed so royal was the welcome I am afraid had John Morgan appeared to us that night he would have met very little resistance from us, a circumstance which happened but once in the nearly four years service of Battery D.

No sooner had we landed on the levee than we began to receive an ovation which increased with every block, and when we crossed the Rhine—a canal which ran through the centre of the city—the demonstration reached its climax. This part of the town was largely occupied by Germans. There was a lager beer saloon upon each corner, and sometimes one or two between. As we passed, the saloon-keepers came out to us with each finger of both hands holding a glass of beer. Capt. Buckley had mounted the cannoneers and given strict orders that none should dismount without permission; but this precaution was wholly unnecessary, for the men had no desire to dismount with all this beer surrounding them. A few indulged once, more twice or thrice, and a much larger number so frequently that when we arrived in camp on the outskirts of the city, it was found that quite a number of the men were ready to turn in at once, and the temperance men would have the privilege of doing all the work of unharnessing, watering and feeding the horses, as a reward for their good behaviour.

Early next morning the three sections of the battery were sent out upon three principal roads approaching the city from the north, and selecting positions which commanded these different roads for a considerable distance, went into battery. Our support was the militia from the city and the surrounding country, who felt, and we agreed with them, that should Morgan attempt to enter Cincinnati he would meet with a very warm reception. But Morgan did not attempt to enter the city, but passed some miles from our front, and was finally captured by Gen. Shackleford on the 26th, near New Lisbon.

July 16th the battery was withdrawn from picket duty, and encamped upon Vine Street Hill.

July 17th Gen. Burnside ordered Capt. Buckley to move the battery to Ninth Street, within a short distance of his headquarters, place the carriages in a wagon yard, the horses in a stable, and furnish the men with quarters in a hall nearby. To say that the men were very much pleased with this arrangement but mildly expresses their feelings. It was a matter of much speculation among them as to just why this good luck had fallen to them. At first the men were inclined to think that it was because Gen. Burnside was kindly disposed towards us, and having an opportunity to give us a "soft snap," had improved it; but with the light of future events, they were inclined to think that, added to this reason, was a desire to keep the battery in the city near him, that he might use it as an intimidator against the draft rioters, whose grumbling and growling were growing louder and louder, and their nightly meetings in the different market places more numerously attended, as the draft proceeded.

The first intimation that the officers of the battery received that such duty would be required of us came a few evenings after the commencement of our new arrangement, when an orderly from headquarters came to the hall and inquired for Capt. Buckley, who could not be found; in fact it unfortunately happened that the highest officer that could be found was a duty sergeant, which fact the orderly was obliged to report to the general, who ordered him to return to the battery, find an officer, and order him to report at head-quarters immediately. Lieut. Parker had returned by this time, and he immediately reported to Gen. Burnside, whom he found very wroth, and who proceeded to lecture him upon the great lack of attention to duty by the officers of Battery D, and ordered him to inform Capt. Buckley that he desired him to have his battery prepared to hitch up at a moment's notice, at any hour of the day or night. This gave us the knowledge that we were not in these comfortable quarters just for our own pleasure, but that there was a probable duty connected with our situation. After this only a few men were allowed to leave at a time, all others were expected to be within hailing distance of the hall.

As often as every other day the battery was called out for parade, and was taken through the different portions of the city. On Sunday we were marched down to the levee, where we went through an inspection, and afterwards were drilled for an hour or two, just to remind the evil-disposed citizens that there was a six-gun battery still in their city, that would make short work with any mob who attempted any violence.

About half-past eight one evening the battery was ordered to hitch up as soon as possible, and as soon as ready it started for a market-place situated nearly in the centre of the city, where a crowd was reported to be gathering. As we neared the place the captain gave the order "Trot, march," and the battery swept around the corner into the market-place in a column of sections, dividing as it reached the market-house, the right pieces passing it on the right, the left pieces upon the left, uniting as they passed the house and continuing on to the end of the square, then countermarched and came back. By the time we had reached the end of the market-place there was hardly a person to be seen, everybody seemingly having become satisfied that Gen. Burnside was determined that there should be no hostile gathering in Cincinnati.

This was the only occasion when it was necessary to make such a demonstration as this. Everything quieted down, and from this time until the end of our stay, Aug. 10th. Battery D was not called upon to do any more intimidating.

At nine o'clock on the morning of Aug. 10th we crossed the Ohio River, loaded the battery on the cars, and at two o'clock in the afternoon left Covington *en route* for Lexington. Arriving just after midnight, the men were immediately put to work unloading the battery, and as soon as this was accomplished, and they had prepared and eaten their breakfast, "Boots and saddles" was blown, and the battery started for Camp Nelson, where we remained until the 15th, the time being occupied in general repairing and refitting, and every care was taken to get our battery in the best possible condition. New harnesses were drawn, the battery wagon was thoroughly overhauled and replenished, and clothing was issued to the men. Those of them who drew a liberal supply had reason to be thankful that they had done so; these who did not, regretted it before the coming campaign was over.

CHAPTER 6

The Campaign in East Tennessee

On the 11th of August Gen. Burnside arrived at Hickman's Bridge, Ky., and began making the final arrangements for his movement into East Tennessee. He received information that the Ninth Corps had been relieved by Gen. Grant, and was then on its way north, the advance regiments having already reached Cairo, and could be expected to arrive in Cincinnati not later than the 15th.

The Twenty-third Corps, under Gen. Hartzuff, had rendezvoused in three columns, at different points; one, under Gen. White, at Columbia; another, under Gen. Hascall, at Somerset; and the third, under Gen. Carter, at Crab Orchard. With this last column Gen. Burnside was to go.

On the 20th the general issued orders for a forward movement to take place on the 21st, and *at last* this long delayed, much wished for, and most fervently prayed for expedition was to start.

What significance those two words—*At Last*—had for thousands, yea, tens of thousands at this time. It signified to President Lincoln that at last one load which had been upon his heart for a year and a half—namely, his sympathy for the loyal people of East Tennessee—was about to be removed; it signified to those three great leaders of the Union men of that section—Andrew Johnson, Edward Maynard, and Parson Brownlow, that at last all their labour, efforts and prayers were about to bear fruit in the accomplishment of their most cherished desire.

It signified to Gen. Burnside that at last he could push forward an expedition which had had full possession of his heart—primarily, for the relief of a long-suffering, intensely loyal people—and secondly, to seize and hold as much as possible of the East Tennessee and Georgia Railroad.

It signified to Gen. Rosecrans that at last he need give himself no uneasiness about the rapid transfer of any portion of the Army of Virginia to Chattanooga, *via* the East Tennessee and Georgia Railroad, and after being used successfully against him, to be as rapidly returned back again.

But what an infinitely greater significance did these words have for the thousands of women and children in East Tennessee. In imagination I can see those mothers, wives and sisters (as they receive the news carried by some fleet-footed messenger over the Cumberland Mountains, by secluded paths, gather on their mountains, in their valleys, in towns and cities, and turning their eyes towards the mountains at the north, cry out in all the ecstasy of lightened hearts, "At last, thank God, dear fathers, husbands and brothers, you are coming back to us!" And in answer I can hear, coming from the throats of those fathers, husbands and brothers, who had come over the mountains into Kentucky in such numbers that they had organised eight full regiments of infantry and three of cavalry, "Yes! dear ones, at last we surely are coming, to protect you and our homes."

Our battery having been thoroughly refitted and prepared for the expedition, was ordered upon the 15th to report to Gen. Hascall, at Danville. Here it remained until the morning of the 17th, when it continued its journey to Stamford, laid over one day, and at two o'clock on the morning of the 19th was aroused by "Boots and saddles," marching as soon as ready, for Crab Orchard.

This place had in ante-bellum days been noted as a watering-place, or perhaps more properly speaking, sanatorium, it being possessed of numerous medicinal springs. If my memory serves me, it was more fortunate than most fakes of this sort, in that these springs were supposed to contain waters of different therapeutical effect. There was the alterative, tonic, and aperient water, a liberal and intelligently administered course of which would rejuvenate the most thoroughly used-up system in the world. No wonder that it was the Mecca toward which all the chronics of the South journeyed.

Any veteran will remember how apt an old soldier was who had been living upon salt junk, salt pork and hardtack for a considerable time, to allow his imagination full scope whenever his surroundings reminded him of a full course dinner or banquet. Thus it was with Battery D on the evening that we spent at Crab Orchard.

A lot of us gathered on the *piazza* of the vacant hotel and gave orders for dinners that would have taxed the ability of a Delmonico or a Tillinghast to have filled; and the fearful drop that came when the men who had been personating waiters to help along the joke and had dashed away for the kitchen on receiving our orders to have them filled, and returned with a raw pork sandwich for each, profuse with their apologies from the proprietors, that they were unable to fill our orders because of the great rush of business, which had entirely destroyed their assortment of eatables.

We ate the sandwiches, using all the imagination that we possessed, then went to the springs and tried a course of the waters. One of the springs, which I suppose must have been the alterative, was loud in its smell and loud in its taste, and we vowed we would have no more of it.

Crab Orchard is situated at the beginning of the foot-hills of the Cumberland Mountains, and from here the difficulties of the way will increase with every mile we travel. From this on for some eighty miles we are to march through a wilderness, from which we cannot expect to gather anything in the way of forage, consequently we must secure all the grain and hay that can be found, to take with us. All day of the 20th we spent in this work, scouring the country for ten miles around with indifferent success.

On the 21st we marched to Cub Creek, a small stream emptying into the Cumberland River. Next day we moved to Cumberland River and camped on its bank, near Smith's Ford. On this day our battery made twenty miles, which was considered astonishing by our corps commander. In a report to Gen. Burnside he said that the roads were the worst he ever saw, particularly the last five or six miles before we reached the river, but thought they would be better when we had crossed to the other side.

I think that my comrades of Battery D will smile at this prophecy when they remember what we really did find in the line of roads after we crossed the river. The approach to and exit from Smith's Ford were two of the steepest hills I ever remember to have seen, and the next morning when we began to cross I contemplated the work with fear and trembling; for I considered my position of wheel-driver on the sixth caisson a dangerous one. But as I stood upon the top of the hill and watched piece after piece and caisson after caisson go down safely, and feeling that I was perhaps as expert a driver as any of the others, and had a pair of horses—of which I propose to have something more to say later on—as reliable as any in the battery, I began to have more confidence, and when my turn came made the descent successfully.

On the other side it required the united efforts of six pairs of horses and all the cannoneers that could get a hand on the carriages, to make the ascent.

We spent the 24th in foraging for grain, and succeeded in finding enough for three or four feedings, which was very unsatisfactory. We had hardly enough to feed the horses, on small rations, for more than three days, and as on the morrow we were to commence our climb to the top of the Cumberland Mountains, should our horses give out we would be in a sorry plight.

On the 25th we continued our march, and to our surprise found the roads in much better condition than we expected, and were able to make about eighteen miles. We began to feel that perhaps our way was not to be so difficult after all; but the next morning before we had been on the road an hour we found that the good road was a delusion and a snare—a sort of "will-o'-the-wisp" to lure us on, and then suddenly throw before us difficulties which were almost insurmountable.

The road began to narrow rapidly, until it became simply a bridle-path, over which I do not believe a carriage had ever passed before. The ascent became steeper and steeper, many places being encountered over which the carriages had to be lifted by the men. The horses could hardly be driven over these precipitous places, much less be made to pull.

The infantry which had been ordered to accompany the battery to assist in getting us over the rough places, became tired very early, and the men of the battery becoming disgusted with their continual grumbling, and the awkward manner in which they rendered their assistance, drove them away, preferring to do it alone. Both men and horses performed herculean labour that day.

During the afternoon we had been encouraged by the report that there was very little more of this terribly hard labour to be performed. If we could only hold out just a little while we should reach the top of the mountain, and after we passed the "Pine Knot Tavern," the road would be level, and in much better condition.

I do not know whether it was the hope of getting through with the labour, or the anxiety to reach the tavern—many of them picturing to themselves an establishment something after the style of the good old New England tavern, filled with plenty to eat and drink— that stimulated the men to greater exertions or not, but for an hour or two our progress was much more rapid. It was after dark when we reached a spot large enough to park the battery at very close intervals, and bivouacked for the night.

Early on the morning of the 27th, after giving our horses all the corn left, we started on. Very soon we passed "Pine Knot Tavern," which consisted of a cellar half filled with the debris of what had been a small log cabin, the supports of which had rotted off and allowed the cabin to fall into the cellar.

Several natives, who had come from their homes, located in the ravines on either side of the mountain, to see us pass, and sell a few chickens (their stock had been exhausted long before we passed), were the first people we had seen since we entered the wilderness.

All day we marched at this high elevation. Occasionally a cloud would sweep across our path, enveloping us in fog for a while; then there would be places where we would pass out of the woods and a most magnificent landscape would unfold to our view. Sometimes it would be Kentucky, at others East Tennessee upon which we were looking. Taken all together it was the most enjoyable panoramic sort of a march that the battery ever made.

It was left, however, for the morning of the 29th to unfold the most magnificent sight that most of us had ever looked upon. As we gazed about, we found that our location gave us a view on both sides of the mountain. To the north we could see back into Kentucky, almost to our starting point, and trace the route which we had just come over, dotted here and there with the towns and villages through which we had passed. Many of us had wondered why that section of the State had been called the "Blue Grass Region;" the reason was plainly evident to us now, for there it lay before us, as blue as though it had been dyed.

Then we turned our eyes towards the south, and looked upon that land into which we were about to enter; beautiful it was to look upon, divided into valleys by spurs of the Cumberland Mountains, the ever-changing colour of the landscape as the sun rose higher and higher, enabling us to see farther, until our eyes could discover the Smoky Mountains, the tops of which were covered with a smoke-like cloud, located beyond Knoxville.

As our eyes became tired of looking such a distance we fastened them upon the scenery near at hand, and found it as grand and romantic as any we had ever looked upon. Taken all together it was a most magnificent sight, and did not fail to arouse the most unenthusiastic nature in the battery.

While we are contemplating the scene before us, and before we commence our descent into these valleys, it will be well for us to consider what manner of people these are whom we are going to succour. That they are a peculiar people is perfectly evident from the fact that, living as they do in the almost geographical centre of the Slave States, they are by a large majority opposed to the institution of slavery. This is evidenced by the fact that the first abolition paper ever published in the United States emanated from a press in Jonesboro, Tennessee. Among the first abolition societies ever organised in this country were those of Eastern Tennessee, and in the year 1816 the Manumission Society, of Tennessee, held a meeting at Greenville, and issued an address advocating the abolition of slavery. Whence came this abhorrence of slavery, and this love of liberty? Certainly the origin of this people must have been different, totally different, from those who surrounded them on all sides.

I am indebted to my friend William Rule, Esq., of Knoxville, for the following account of the first settlement of East Tennessee:

On the first day of May, 1769, a young farmer started out from the banks of the Yadkin River, in the State of North Carolina, accompanied by five stalwart hunters. It was about the time that the descendants of the Pilgrim Fathers in Massachusetts were denying themselves the luxury of tea rather than pay tribute to a tyrant king. About the same time the House of Burgesses was dissolved by the Colonial Governor of Virginia, for having dared to pass resolutions condemning the Stamp Act, and Governor Tryon, of North Carolina, was serving his royal master by oppressing the patriots of that colony.

The name of the young farmer was James Robertson, the founder of the first colony in Tennessee; and one of the hunters who accompanied him was Daniel Boone, whose daring exploits are familiar to everyone. They went, as did the messengers of old sent by Moses, to spy out beyond the Alleghanies a land where they and those who sent them might live free from the restraints and oppression of English rulers.

One year afterwards a colony was established beside the swift-running waters of the beautiful Watango River. It was composed of men and women of heroic mould, filled with inspirations of patriotism, resolved that their abiding place in the wilderness, surrounded by savages, should be "Freedom's home or Glory's grave." It was the descendants of these patriots who became the first Abolitionists. It was these same people that, in February, 1861, when voting upon a proposition proposed by the Legislature as to whether a convention should or should not be called for the purpose of passing an ordinance of secession, declared by a majority of more than twenty-three thousand out of a total vote of forty-three thousand, against holding the convention.

It was these same people who furnished to the Union Army during the Rebellion thirty-five thousand troops—two thousand more than our own State.

It should be borne in mind that these men could not go quietly and peacefully to enlisting places, situated in their own towns and cities, place their names upon the rolls in the presence of friends who encouraged and praised them for so doing, nor could they leave their families with the assurance that they would be looked after and taken care of by a kind and sympathetic State.

On the contrary they were obliged to travel on foot by night over mountains, swimming swift-running rivers, avoiding all roads, taking only unfrequented paths, because the Confederates, who realised that these men were bound to serve the Union cause, and were willing to endure any hardship or privation necessary to accomplish that object, were patrolling all the roads leading into Kentucky, for the purpose of capturing these patriots and carrying them off to rebel prisons. Journeys varying from two to three hundred miles were made by tens of thousands of these men, for the purpose of fighting for their country, leaving their families to the tender mercies of an enraged enemy.

Show me a people possessed of greater heroism, patriotism and love of country, than the men and women—of whom I propose to say more—of East Tennessee!

It had been the custom of Capt. Buckley after we entered the wilderness, to ride on before the battery after he had seen it under way, taking with him as orderly, William Fisk, and hunt for forage. On this morning they started as usual, and were nearly the first to pass the tavern. They were successful in securing two of the chickens beforementioned, but could get no information as to any grain in that vicinity. Continuing on, it was well into the afternoon before they came across any other citizens. Turning a bend in the road they suddenly came in sight of a log cabin just off the trail we were following. No one was in sight, but a few vigorous hulloas from the captain brought into view two men and three women, evidently father, mother, son and two daughters.

Capt. Buckley, in his most suave manner, asked if they had grain or any knowledge of any in that vicinity. They very promptly answered that they had none, neither did they know of any, and the captain was about to continue his journey, when the younger daughter said, "John Cooper has some."

"Who is John Cooper, and where does he live?" asked the captain.

"A right smart piece down that road, on Pond's Creek," she replied, pointing to a path which opened from the main road directly opposite where they were standing.

Mounting their horses the captain said to Fisk, "We will go and see John Cooper," and started down the path.

After riding a little more than two miles, they reached a log cabin, and noticing what appeared to be a grist-mill a little further on, the captain thought he would investigate before going to the house. The result of this investigation was between twenty-five and thirty bushels of corn, wheat and oats, upon which the captain's seal was immediately placed.

They went to the house and were pleasantly greeted by Susan Cooper, wife of John Cooper, as the lady informed them. In reply to the captain's question as to whom the grain belonged, she informed him that some of it was John's and the balance belonged to neighbours. No objection was made by her when informed by the captain that he should be obliged to take the grain, but he would leave a receipt for it, which would be paid if her husband was a Union man.

At the captain's suggestion Mrs. Cooper expressed a willingness to provide dinner for her guests, the number of which had been enlarged by the arrival of an artillery-captain and two buglers, who had come down into the ravine in quest of grain, and had been invited by Capt. Buckley to partake of the meal then being prepared by Mrs. Cooper, which consisted of fried chicken and bacon, with a liberal supply of corn bread. The lady was considerably embarrassed by her inability to supply dishes for so large a company, and apologised for her impoverished condition in this direction by saying that "It was a long time since John had been where dishes could be put off."

Three things in connection with these people are thoroughly impressed upon my mind:—First, the very small environment within which they lived; secondly, their entire lack of interest in anything not entering upon their own lives; and, thirdly, the exceeding simplicity of their lives, and the little that was required to make them apparently contented and happy. Mrs. Cooper, for instance, living at the bottom of that ravine, the only entrance to which was down a narrow mountain pathway, in a log cabin having but one room, with about two acres of cleared land, surrounded upon all sides, save at the entrance, by a solid wall of rock towering seventy-five feet in height, passing months at a time without seeing anyone save the members of her own family, certainly had as monotonous an existence as could be imagined.

The grain secured by the captain did not reach our bivouac at Chitwood until late at night, but so badly was it needed by the horses—they having been without any grain for one day at least—that the drivers were aroused and their horses fed immediately.

The time had now arrived when we must commence our descent from the mountain top. It is less laborious for the cannoneers, but much more so for the wheel-drivers, of which I, unfortunately, happened to be one. It has always been a matter of surprise to me that we brought the battery safely to the foot of that mountain. I consider that the agility displayed by me in dodging that pole as it flew about in every direction—sometimes over one horse, then the other, at one time pointing to the earth, and then to heaven, caused by the dashing (sliding would perhaps be a better word, as the wheels were locked) of the caisson over the rocks, sometimes making necessary a jump of four or five feet, and be able to shout to my comrades as we reached the bottom, "It never touched me," was one of the best things I ever did.

I claim no special merit for the successful manner in which I guided the caisson down that awful road, because there were thirteen other wheel-drivers who were just as successful, but all the same, I believe it was my thorough knowledge of the peculiarities of my horses that enabled me to do it. I was intimately acquainted with both of them, as I had driven them for twenty months. Both were powerful animals, but with entirely different notions as to how their strength was to be used. Hercules, the nigh horse, which I rode, was always willing to do his full share of the pulling, and if upon occasions it became necessary for him to make an extra effort, he would, at my bidding, take the whole load of the caisson upon his shoulders.

The off horse, with almost as much strength, did not believe in pulling, and would not unless he thought I was watching him, when he would put in apparently for all there was in him; but when asked to hold back, he entered into the performance of that act with all the enthusiasm of a horse's nature. I have frequently stopped the whole team by signifying that I wanted him to do his best at holding back.

I have always regretted that I obliged that horse to go down to his grave with a name which entirely misrepresented him. He had the most vicious expression I ever saw upon a horse. His ears were always lopped (I never saw them erect), and he had a habit of parting his lips, showing his teeth in such a manner that it gave one the impression that he only awaited an opportunity to attack. His appearance led me, when the sergeant presented him, saying, "George, here is a horse just suited to go with Hercules," to exclaim, "He looks like Old Satan himself!" and from that moment he was known through the battery as "Old Satan."

It was wrong thus to name him, and I desire on this occasion to do him justice by declaring, after two years constant association, during which I learned to think a great deal of him as a horse, that I never saw any evidence of his possessing a single attribute said to be possessed by his namesake. Kind and gentle, he never gave me any trouble. He seemed to have acquired a perfect understanding of how that caisson should be managed upon the march, and I soon learned to trust him with its management. Upon long marches at night, when I found it almost impossible to keep my eyes open, many were the restful naps I enjoyed sitting on Hercules' back with my head pillowed upon the valise in "Old Satan's" saddle.

Speaking about horses, I wonder if my comrades of Battery D have forgotten what an amount of affection was lavished upon the horses by their drivers. Certainly no one of the sixth detachment will ever forget "Old Curley," driven so long as the nigh leader upon their piece, by Anson Mathewson, possessed of an intelligence which enabled him to reason more successfully than some animals of the human species.

We all remember the affectionate regard held by St. John, Billy Mills, William Stalker and many others for their teams. Any of them would tramp miles after dark to some haystack which they had seen during the day, make as large a bundle of the hay as they could carry, bring it to camp, spread it before their horses, and then sit up half the night watching until the horses had consumed it, from fear that some one would steal it and feed it to his own team.

At last we are over the mountains, and the great difficulties of our journey passed. This march of the Army of the Ohio over the Cumberland Mountains has been likened to the crossing of the Alps by Bonaparte, and it seems to me the simile is well taken. Certainly it is hard to imagine difficulties greater than those encountered by our army. The rebel Gen. Buckner, who is said to have had an army of 20,000 men to oppose our entry into East Tennessee, while Gen. Burnside had but about 15,000, was so thoroughly satisfied of the absolute impossibility of the passage of an army from Kentucky to Tennessee at this point, believing that they must come by way of Cumberland Gap, that he made no attempt to oppose us; consequently when we appeared before him his astonishment was so great, and his retreat so precipitous, he failed to notify a detachment of his army, numbering 2,000 men, who were guarding Cumberland Gap, and who soon were obliged to surrender to Gen. Burnside.

Our march of the 28th and 29th had been through a wilderness of rocks; that of the 30th and 31st was through a wilderness of woods. The troops in advance of the battery had worked the road-bed into an almost impassable condition. Our horses having had but little forage since the 21st, and had been forced to work beyond the limits of their strength, now began to give out, many falling from sheer exhaustion. It began to look as though if grain could not be secured for them our chances for getting through would be rather slim. Quartermaster Remington was scouring the country in search of it; but on his return gave the discouraging information that no forage could be secured until we should reach a point about twenty miles further on. There was no other way out of our present difficulty: that point must be reached, and the cannoneers must help the horses pull the carriages.

Our progress was necessarily very slow, but patience, perseverance and lots of hard work, finally accomplished the task, and late in the afternoon of the 31st, as we drove into park, we had the pleasure of seeing Quartermaster Remington ride into camp, followed by two wagons loaded with corn. It gave the drivers much satisfaction to see their teams enjoying the first good feeding which they had had for ten days.

We had now gotten out of the wilderness, and were just about to enter one of those fertile valleys which we had seen from the mountain top. The men who had accompanied the wagons upon the forage trips after the corn, gave us our first impression as to the kind and friendly treatment which we might expect from the people whose country we were just entering, in their description of the reception they had received from those at whose places they had secured the corn.

On the morning of September 1st, after another good feeding, the horses seemed to be in much better condition. About ten o'clock in the forenoon the battery pulled out into the road and joined the division, which had been ordered to make "Big Emery," about twenty miles distant, before dark. We accomplished the task easily, and formed a junction with the column under Gen. Carter, with whom Gen. Burnside had crossed the mountains.

Foraging was now reduced to a perfect system. Gen. Burnside issued an order calling attention to the fact that as it would now be necessary for the army to depend upon the country largely for its subsistence, he desired to remind us that we were among a loyal people, who were our friends, and he was unwilling that they should be robbed or despoiled of their property except in a legal manner, and by the proper authorities. Officers were to be held strictly responsible for any depredations committed by the men under their command; division, brigade and regimental quartermasters were ordered to receipt for everything taken by them for their commands, which would be paid upon presentation to the proper authority, provided that the loyalty of the person could be proven. Officers and men must pay for anything taken by them for their personal use. The quartermaster sergeants of batteries were allowed to give receipts for forage, but they must be countersigned by the commanding officers to secure payment.

Details were made each day to do the work, and the privilege of going upon these trips began to be much sought after. The kind manner in which we were received by the citizens, made such excursions very pleasant for the men.

September 2nd we remained in camp near Big Emery River, resting and grazing the horses until two o'clock in the afternoon, but the time lost in the morning was made up by continuing the march well into the night, it being eleven o'clock before we pulled off the road and parked the battery for the night.

Very early the next morning we started for Clinch River, crossing some five miles above Kingston, and continued on towards Knoxville, camping that night about twenty miles from that place.

Next day, September 4th, our battery countermarched some six or eight miles, and taking a road leading to Loudon, where the rebels were reported to be in strong force, in a fortified position, marched rapidly to that place.

Early in the afternoon artillery firing in our front convinced us that at last we had come up with the enemy. Two hours afterwards, as

71

we came out upon the bluffs of the Tennessee River opposite Loudon, we saw our cavalry crossing the river, under the protection of our artillery, and driving the enemy beyond the town. Before the arrival of our troops the enemy had fired the bridge over the river, and it was soon totally destroyed.

Next day our infantry crossed the river and took possession of the town, occupying as many of the fortifications as they could use, and destroying the rest. The battery remained in camp opposite Loudon until the 15th of September, enjoying a much needed rest. Both men and horses had become thoroughly used up by this long and difficult journey, which had just been completed, and the opportunity to recuperate was thoroughly enjoyed and appreciated.

The rebels in their hurried flight had left us a few horses, mules, and beef cattle, which were appropriated by our troops with thanks. A large amount of wheat and corn were found in possession of the farmers, which was immediately seized by our quartermaster. A steam flourmill in Loudon was found to be in perfect condition, and was soon at work converting the wheat into flour, which was issued to the army for the first time on the fifth. Corn meal was soon added to our rations; flapjacks and corn-dodgers became plenty; chickens and fresh pork could be obtained without much trouble; and we were soon able to get up a dinner the quality and quantity of which was very satisfactory to us.

September 14th orders were received late at night for the battery to be prepared to march at an early hour next morning. The men were aroused by "Boots and saddles," the battery hitched up, and marched to the railroad, where all the knapsacks, together with the chests of the caissons, were removed and placed upon flat cars. In this light marching order the battery left Loudon at two o'clock in the morning of the 15th. Our first camp was made near Knoxville, second at Strawberry Plains, and the third at New Market, where we arrived early in the afternoon of the 17th. It began raining on the evening of our arrival, and continued throughout the night and the next day. Happily we were not ordered to march and could spend the time fixing up our tents for protection. The cooks were ordered to prepare rations for a march on the following day.

September 19th we left New Market for Loudon, arriving on the 21st, having been absent about one week, during which we had covered ninety-eight miles.

The emergency which had occasioned this long march seems to

have been of double origin. Our movement to New Market had been occasioned by a reported raid of the rebels of Southwestern Virginia upon Gen. Scannon, with the view of driving him out of West Virginia, and our movement had been made with the intention of leading the rebel commander to believe that we were about to move upon him from the rear.

The occasion of our quick return was a dispatch from Gen. Halleck to Gen. Burnside, notifying him that three divisions of Lee's army had been sent to reinforce Bragg, and he desired him to go to Gen. Rosecrans' assistance as soon as possible.

September 23rd the battery was ordered to cross the river at Loudon. Our crossing upon this occasion was a long, tedious work, occasioned by the fact that it had to be accomplished by the use of one flat-boat, just large enough to accommodate one carriage and the team at a time, and the first streaks of day were appearing before it was fully accomplished.

As soon as everything was across, the battery started for Sweet Water, a station sixteen miles south of Loudon, on the East Tennessee and Georgia Railroad. We had just arrived at that place, when we were ordered to counter-march and return as rapidly as possible to Loudon. We were all night upon the road, arriving at our destination at daylight, when the troops were ordered into position upon the south side of the river. Our battery was placed in a fort commanding the approach by the road.

The 20th was a day of excitement among the citizens, who flocked to us in great numbers for protection. It was reported that the rebel Gen. Forrest was coming up the railroad from Athens *via* Cleveland, with a large body of men, and it was also rumoured that a large force of rebels had crossed the Little Tennessee at Meyerton, a village about fifteen miles to the left of Loudon, which it was supposed would unite with the main column at or near this place. Skirmishing in our front was continued all day; desultory firing to the left of our position, but at considerable distance, was heard, convincing us that the rumours which had been circulated had considerable merit of truth in them.

Early in the morning of the 27th we hitched up, expecting an attack. A pontoon bridge had been completed during the night, and at daylight troops began crossing the river from the north bank and moved to the front, but it soon quieted down, and the day passed without further incident.

Next morning cannonading could be heard from a distance, and our troops fell back, forming three lines, making elaborate preparations for a battle; but, as on the previous day, the cannonading soon ceased, and everything became quiet.

On the 29th it was reported that the rebels had fallen back. Our cavalry moved to the front, while our battery remained in position upon Loudon Heights, with the three lines of infantry in front.

All excitement had subsided by the 30th, and although cannonading could be heard occasionally, it was at such a great distance that it had no terrors for the citizens, and they began slowly to return home. Several regiments of cavalry and mounted infantry passed our position on their way to the front.

It will be of service for a fuller understanding of our situation if we spend a few moments in explanation. It was expected by Gen. Burnside when he entered East Tennessee with the Twenty-Third Corps, that the Ninth would soon follow; but the surgeons' reports convinced him that this would be impossible, fifty *per cent.*, perhaps more, of the men of that command were down with malarial fever. The commander, Gen. Parks, was very sick, and could not be expected to do duty for a month at least; Gen. Welch, the second in command—a man much admired by the members of the Ninth—had died from the disease, at Cairo. Regiments had been reduced until many of them could not muster more than a hundred men for duty; while the batteries could hardly find men enough to take care of the horses. Truly, the swamps around Vicksburg had proved to be a more destructive enemy than the rebels.

Becoming convinced that the corps must be allowed to recuperate before attempting a march so full of difficulties as the crossing of the Cumberland Mountains, he ordered that they should rendezvous at Crab Orchard, and give the corps a much needed rest, but they had not had time to fully recuperate when Gen. Burnside's pressing need of more troops compelled him to order the corps to join him in East Tennessee as soon as possible.

On Sunday, Sept. 20th, the advance of the Ninth Corps passed through Cumberland Gap and bivouacked in Tennessee, and by long, difficult and continuous marches, reached Knoxville on the afternoon of the 26th.

It was the timely arrival of the Ninth which enabled Gen. Burnside to send the Twenty-Third Corps to Loudon and below, making a demonstration of such strength that the rebel Gen. Forrest concluded not to hazard an attack, but fell back towards Chattanooga.

From Oct. 1st to the 5th our battery remained in the forts at Loudon. Each day details were made to accompany the three wagons upon forage trips, and many are the pleasant episodes recollected of those occasions. Seldom did those teams return to camp without the carcass of a slaughtered hog or a fine sheep underneath its load of corn on the ear. The citizens had kindly planted a liberal supply of that improvement upon the sweet potato—those golden yams—and any foraging trip which did not produce a large stock of them upon its return, was pronounced a failure.

Most of the boys will remember trips of this sort, when the distance from camp made it necessary that they should remain out over night. How gladly they accepted an invitation to spend the night with the people at whose house they happened to be—if they received such invitations—and how persistently they demanded such hospitality from those who did not extend the invitation.

It is well remembered by some of us how much we were embarrassed upon the occasion of our first experience in spending the night with those people. Most of their homes were log cabins, containing but one room, and as it most always happened that the family consisted of mother and from one to seven daughters, it became a vexed question with us as to how the act of retiring would be accomplished; and as the time for retiring approached, we became anxious. It was all unnecessary, however, for when the time came, the women arose, threw a straw bed upon the floor, with blankets, produced a curtain, which they hung across the centre of the room, bade us goodnight, and retired to their side, leaving us to go to bed at our leisure.

Oct. 5th our troops fell back from Athens, and crossed to the north side of the Tennessee River upon the pontoon bridge at London.

Oct. 6th our battery received orders to report to our old division (First) Ninth Corps, at Blue Springs, distant about ninety-seven miles. It was reported that the enemy were advancing from Virginia, threatening our communications with Cumberland Gap, and on the 3rd Gen. Burnside had ordered the Ninth Corps to oppose them. All the infantry were carried on the cars, and in order that the battery should reach the objective point as soon after the infantry as possible, they were hurried along at the rate of thirty miles a day.

Fortunately our horses were in a much better condition than they had been for some time. Since our long march to New Market and back, Sept. 15th to 21st, they had had but little work to do, and with liberal feeding on grain and much opportunity to graze, they had gotten into very good condition.

We left Loudon at noon on the 6th, and reached Bull's Gap about dark on the 9th. We found the roads in very good condition, the streams were low, lessening the difficulties of fording, in fact everything seemed to work favourably for the accomplishment of this long march.

Oct. 10th we passed through the Gap towards Blue Springs, but very soon came up with our division, posted in line-of-battle along Lick Creek. Capt. Buckley reported his arrival, and was told to hold himself in readiness to move against the enemy.

Soon Gen. Burnside appeared and ordered the line to advance. Our cavalry encountered the enemy a mile or two south of Blue Springs, and a rattle of musketry ensued for a few minutes, when the enemy retired to their reserve line and maintained a fire upon our skirmishers.

It was Gen. Burnside's desire to capture as many as possible of the enemy, and for that purpose he sent Col. Foster's brigade of cavalry around to seize and hold the roads in the Confederates' rear. When sufficient time had been allowed for the colonel to reach his position, our troops in front attacked the rebels, and a sharp, hotly-contested battle upon both sides was continued until dark.

Our men had succeeded in driving the enemy from their position, and after forming in a new position were ordered to lay upon their arms during the night, prepared to assault the enemy at daylight. Next morning our line advanced at day light, only to find that the enemy had abandoned his position—Col. Foster not having reached their rear in time to intercept their retreat.

Our battery had been in position all day, but did not open fire until nearly dark, when we threw a few shots at a rebel battery.

Our troops pursued the enemy nearly twenty miles, Battery D accompanying them. Cannonading was heard in the vicinity of Greenville soon after we started, showing that the enemy were some distance in advance of us. It was nearly noon when we passed Greenville, and four o'clock as we reached Rheatown, about nineteen miles from our bivouac of the previous night. Continuing for a mile further, we halted for the night.

On the 12th our cavalry reported the enemy so scattered that further pursuit would be useless. Early in the afternoon the battery moved back through Rheatown and encamped on the other side of the valley, in proximity to the troops of our division.

Next morning, Oct. 13th, the army started on its way back to Knoxville. Although there was no special haste in our return movements, it seemed to me that very good time was made by the battery. Our first bivouac was made at Blue Springs, near the battlefield, a distance of twenty miles; that of the 14th at Morristown, a distance of twenty-five miles; that of the 15th at New Market, a distance of twenty-three miles; that of the 16th at Armstrong's Ford, on the Holston River, a distance of twenty miles; and that of the 17th at Temperance Hill, Knoxville, a distance of eight miles, making ninety-six miles, which added to one hundred and seventeen, the distance from Loudon to Rheatown, gave a total of two hundred and twenty-six miles travelled by the battery between the 6th and 17th of October—an average of a little more than twenty-two miles for each of the eleven days. Oct. 18th and 19th, the battery lay in camp in Knoxville.

Late in the afternoon of the 19th orders were received to have the battery prepared to move at an early hour next morning. Requisition had been made for more horses, and the division quartermaster had promised Capt. Buckley that he should have them promptly; but as yet they had not materialised.

Next morning, the horses not having arrived, the battery left Knoxville with only four pieces, one section being left behind because of lack of motive power. During the march cannonading was heard in the direction of Kingston. We were getting rather used to that sort of thing, and would not have been much surprised had the sound of cannonading reached our ears from all points of the compass at one and the same time. We bivouacked that night near Campbell's Station, about seventeen miles from Knoxville.

Oct. 21st our battery was in motion at daylight, towards Loudon. After passing Lanoir's Station we continued on towards Loudon for about two miles, where we halted for about an hour, after which we countermarched back to the station and made camp. Lanoir's Station at this time was a large—perhaps the largest—plantation in East Tennessee, belonging to a Dr. Lanoir. Its land was very extensive and beautifully situated. The station consisted of the doctor's mansion, farm buildings, yarn factory, houses for his overseers, and a hundred or more negro huts, making a very sizeable settlement. Lanoir was a large owner of slaves, and, as may be imagined, a very pronounced secessionist.

A good many of us felt inclined to forgive the doctor for all the hard things he said of and to us Yankees, because of his wisdom—from

77

our standpoint—in planting such an extensive cornfield, many of us being willing to make oath that it extended for four miles along the road towards Campbell's Station—for our use. It certainly was for our men, and the doctor's part in it was simply that of an instrument in the hands of a higher power.

Oct. 22nd we were ordered to Loudon. We moved out of park about one o'clock in the afternoon, crossed the river on the pontoon bridge, and camped at sunset. On the next day it looked a little as though we should have a brush with the enemy.

On the 24th the battery wagons, forge, and all surplus baggage was sent to the north side of the river. The right section of the battery, left at Knoxville for want of horses, returned to us on this evening.

Oct. 25th, 26th and 27th were days of perfect quiet. Towards evening on the 27th we received orders to be ready to move in the morning.

On the morning of the 28th all our troops on the south side of the Holston River were withdrawn, the pontoon bridge taken up, and the Ninth Corps fell back to Lanoir's.

On the 29th our camp was changed a short distance, just on the edge of a fine grove of pine trees. When the battery was parked, the men were ordered to the front, and Capt. Buckley addressed them, saying: "This spot will probably be our winter camp, and I desire that each detachment build for itself log cabins, from the materials in sight."

As soon as the line was dismissed, the men commenced staking out their locations, and felling the trees preparatory to the building of their houses. The material was of the very best, straight as an arrow, and of about uniform size; they were just what was needed for this purpose, and could be laid one upon the other so closely that it was unnecessary to do but very little "chinking."

Day after day the men worked at this hut-building, and as they progressed became more and more interested in them. An immense amount of labour was expended upon these huts, the desire of each detachment to equal if not excel the others, resulting in the production of some very excellent cabins.

Chimney-building was by far the most difficult and intricate part of the work. These were built of wood and clay, the base being built of quite large logs, growing smaller as the chimney rose in height, until as it neared completion the sticks were the size of ordinary kindling-wood. As the woodwork was laid it was thickly plastered with clay both inside and out, which soon became as hard as a brick after fires had been kindled in the fireplaces.

By the 5th of November many of the huts had been roofed in and were occupied by the men. Improvements, however, were being constantly added, such as securing boards for flooring, and building of bunks one above the other. The making of mattresses, by carefully picking over pine boughs, removing the larger sticks, then with an old blanket covering the boughs and carefully tacking it all around, resulting when finished in a most delightful bed.

The officers' quarters were of course finished before those of the detachments, because they had at their command the whole mechanical ability and muscular strength of the battery, and were occupying their finished huts by the 6th of November.

With perhaps a single exception, the detachments did not occupy theirs, fully completed, until the 13th. Certainly no member of Battery D will fail to recollect that night; seated around those fire-places in which were roaring fires, they gave perfect freedom to their imagination and built castle after castle of great magnificence, in which the certainty of a winter of ease, comfort and happiness predominated. Luxuries were promised, a rumour prevailing that some of our enterprising scientific comrades of the centre section had secured a still, and within a week or two would be prepared to furnish us good Bourbon whiskey, at a moderate advance over the cost of production. We went to bed that night feeling that we had all the comforts of home that a soldier could possibly' expect, and were soon lulled to sleep by the contentment of our surroundings, and the delightful aroma of our pine beds.

At daylight on the morning of the 14th we were awakened from a most refreshing sleep by first call, and almost immediately were astonished to hear heavy artillery firing in the direction of Loudon. Each man sat up in bed and looked at his comrade. "What does that mean?" they asked each other.

Just at that moment a member of the detachment who had been on guard entered, and was eagerly plied with questions as to what was up. He could only tell us that there seemed to be considerable commotion among the infantry around us, and that two regiments of cavalry had just passed our camp in the direction of Loudon. Five minutes of such cannonading as we had been listening to convinced us that this was not an ordinary cavalry raid such as we had been engaged in following for the past three months, and our hearts sank within us. Evidently there was trouble ahead.

We were soon dressed, and hurried into line to answer to the assembly call. After rollcall had been completed and the line broken, the buglers were ordered to sound "Boots and saddles," which thoroughly convinced us that we were in for it. Breakfast was hurriedly prepared by the men, and by the time it had been partaken of, the troops in our vicinity were in motion, going in the direction of Loudon. A cold rain which had set in sometime during the night, added much to our depression.

From a despatch-bearer we learned that Gen. Longstreet had been detached from Gen. Bragg 's army at Chattanooga and sent north to capture or delay the Army of the Ohio, and was now attempting to cross the Holston River, at Huff Ferry, just below Loudon; in which effort he was being opposed by Gens. Potter and White and part of the Ninth and Twenty-Third Corps, with success.

From our information of today we know that these generals, together with many others in our army, and also the members of Gen. Burnside's personal staff, believed that it was possible for us to prevent Gen. Longstreet from crossing the river, or even defeat him in battle, and so expressed themselves to Gen. Burnside, who had astonished them by declaring his intention to retreat to Knoxville.

Understanding the plan of Gen. Grant (who had succeeded Gen. Rosecrans in command of the Army of the Cumberland) as he did, he realised that he could do Gen. Grant a greater service by drawing Gen. Longstreet to Knoxville, thus taking him away from Gen. Bragg, and making that general's defeat by Gen. Grant more certain.

Our battery remained all day of the 14th in park, with the teams hitched up and attached to the carriages, expecting every moment to be ordered to the front. One battery of our division, Capt. Roemer's, moved out of park, and started toward Loudon about eleven o'clock in the forenoon, and again we looked for the expected order.

Sharp skirmishing, with an occasional artillery duel, continued all day. Just at night our troops advanced upon the enemy and drove them back to their bridge-head, where they held them during the night.

On the morning of the 15th Gen. Burnside ordered a retreat upon Lanoir's Station, and by daylight the whole command was upon the road, followed by the enemy, they pushing their skirmishers forward with considerable caution. At dark that night our army bivouacked at Lanoir's, and with the exception of a rather vigorous attack upon our lines at ten o'clock in the evening, which was easily repulsed, we were not further molested.

After dark on the 14th the men of the battery not on guard improved their last opportunity to enjoy one more night in their huts. It was noticed that there was none of that happiness and hilarity which had prevailed to such an extent the night before. The faces of the men expressed an amount of seriousness which had not been present then.

The morning of the 15th still found the battery waiting for orders to move. Early in the morning troops of the Twenty-Third Corps began to pass our camp, and as it seemed to us, in some confusion, but Gen. Burnside soon appeared and restored order, after which everything moved with clock-like precision.

Just before five o'clock in the afternoon the battery moved out of park to the road, and commenced its march towards Campbell Station. Not more than three miles had been accomplished before we began to have trouble. The rain which had commenced the night before still continued, and had softened the clayey soil of the road into a clinging substance which made it almost impossible to move the battery. There was a series of hills to climb, and our only way was to take the horses from the caissons and put them on the pieces, and haul them to the top of the hill, and then go back and haul up the caissons; this was repeated several times before we had reached the railroad crossing. It was now three o'clock in the morning, and the officer commanding the rear guard informed us that we must get ahead at once, as he should be unable to hold his position after daylight, as Gen. Longstreet's advance was close at hand. Capt. Buckley had in the meantime sent word to Gen. Burnside of our situation, and he had ordered some mule teams to our relief. The teams soon made their appearance, and the mules were quickly hitched on, and we were on the move again. The wagons that had been left in order to send us (and also the other batteries) the mule teams, were burning as we passed them, as it was impossible to move them.

By this time it had grown quite light, and the rapidly increasing fire in our rear and on the left convinced us that we were being pushed by the enemy. As an incentive to increase our efforts and hurry us along during the night, we had been frequently told that unless we reached the junction of the Kingston and Loudon roads before daylight, we should be cut off and become prisoners of war to Gen. James Longstreet. It was now long past daylight, and we were several miles from the junction. Fortunately for us our pursuers had been unable to reach that point.

Gen. Longstreet had detached a column under Gen. McLaw and ordered him to proceed by the Kingston road to this point. Having secured a guide perfectly familiar with the road, but who, unfortunately for Gen. Longstreet's plans, happened to be a staunch Union man, who became so strangely mixed in his bearings that when daylight appeared Gen. McLaw found himself several miles from his objective point.

In the meantime Gen. Burnside had sent Gen. White with his division out upon the Kingston road, with orders to extend his line to the left until it joined the right of the Ninth Corps, and hold the enemy until the artillery had passed.

It was shortly after ten o'clock in the forenoon when Battery D passed the Kingston road, and continued on towards the village of Campbell Station, noted as the birth-place of Admiral Farragut. Passing through this village we were ordered into position upon the right of the road, about half way up a long, steep hill, above the village.

Just before we went into position our hearts were rejoiced by the discovery of one of our pieces and its caisson which we had about given up as lost, fearing that it must in some manner have missed its way and been overtaken by the enemy. Sergeant Gray explained his early arrival by saying that, becoming convinced that being obliged to render assistance to less fortunate teams was rapidly exhausting his own teams, he determined to push on as fast as possible, and wait for the battery at the station.

At this time Benjamin's battery of twenty-pound Parrotts was in position upon the right of the road, Some distance below our battery. Gettings was on his right, while Von Sehlen was in position in line with us, on our left.

When at twelve o'clock the enemy opened upon us, it was found that Benjamin's and Gettings' positions were not favourable for their heavy rifled guns, and they were moved to the left of the road, upon higher ground a little in our rear.

Our infantry was posted across the Kingston road, beyond the creek which ran through the village at the foot of the hill upon which we were. The centre was held by White's division. Twenty-Third Corps, while the Ninth, which had retired from the front and formed in the rear of these troops, took position upon the right and left of this division.

Benjamin, Roemer and Gettings opened upon the enemy a most

terrific fire from their rifled guns. Our battery was unable to throw its shells far enough to reach the enemy, and was obliged to content itself with an occasional shot at their skirmishers.

We soon saw a heavy line of skirmishers advancing out of the woods in our front, and with perfect nonchalance approach a ravine only a short distance from one of our batteries, carrying their guns at a trail. The coolness of the act made it somewhat doubtful as to whether they were friend or foe.

Sergeant Gray, who was some distance in front of the battery on the pike, took in the situation at once, and tried a shot at them with his carbine, and was severely reprimanded by an officer standing near, for firing at our men. A moment settled the question, however, for no sooner had they reached the ravine than they dropped out of sight, and instantly there came the *pop, pop, pop* of their rifles, and the officer who had objected to their being treated as foes, had lost a horse.

The rebels who had so boldly sought this position had failed to notice one of our regiments, which lay under cover of a building to their right, which position gave then an enfilading fire the entire length of that ravine, and in a few seconds the rebels found themselves in a place hotter than they had ever been in before, and one which they were glad to vacate as soon as possible.

Soon after the failure of the enemy to drive our centre, they made a vigorous assault upon the right of Christ's brigade. Ninth Corps. Our battery was ordered to change its position and direction of its fire, to co-operate with this brigade, and we shelled the woods upon the right with such good effect as to check the progress of the enemy in that direction. It was while executing this movement that the men of our battery became thoroughly convinced of the utter impossibility of successfully manoeuvring light artillery with mules as a motive power.

No sooner was the attempt made to limber the pieces than each individual mule commenced a performance of his own, entirely at variance with that of his mate, which soon resulted in a tangle that was exceedingly discouraging to the men. In some of the teams half the mules seemed determined to run away, frightened by the bursting of the shells, while its effect upon the rest of the team was to create a determination not to move a step. Some of them were seized with an irresistible desire to climb over each other, in many instances elevating themselves to such a degree as to lose their balance and go over backwards, in one or two instances falling upon the men who were trying to control them.

An instance of the perverseness of these animals came very near depriving the battery of one of its most valued members, Sergeant Spencer, of the first piece, who found himself at the beginning of the execution of this order to change positions, with his gun limbered, to which was attached a team of mules, but without a driver, who had mysteriously disappeared. There were none of his companions present who felt competent to drive this team, nor did the sergeant himself have the utmost confidence in his ability to successfully manage them; but something must be done, and that quickly.

Riding up to the nigh wheel mule he seized the jerky-line—the use of which he knew to consist of a rapid succession of jerks when it was desired that the leaders should turn to the right, while a steady pull would cause them to turn to the left—and started the team. It was his desire that the gun should move in the middle of the road, but the mules preferred the side close to the fence, and as they were masters of the situation, that was where the gun moved.

It was very uncomfortable for our comrade, the uneven character of this part of the road constantly throwing the wheel mules against his horse and obliging him to lean for support upon the rail fence at his side. Very little progress had been made, and the sergeant had but just rested his hand upon the fence when a rebel shell carried away the uprights of the fence within a foot of his hand. It was a natural impulse which caused him to remove his hand instantly from its resting place. This convinced Sergeant Spencer that it was time to assert his authority over those mules. Dropping the jerky-line, he rushed to the leaders, forced them into the road, and soon had the gun up with the rest of the battery.

This last position held by our battery, was upon very high ground, overlooking the entire field occupied by both Union and Confederates, and save an occasional disappearance behind a ravine or into scattered clusters of woods, the manoeuvring of the Ninth and Twenty-Third Corps was in plain view. It was a grand panoramic martial picture which was unfolded to our vision that afternoon.

The rebel host, commanded by Gen. Longstreet, upwards of twenty thousand strong, composed of such well-known fighting troops as McLaw's and Hood's divisions, of Alabama, South Carolina, Georgia and Mississippi regiments, to which had been added for this occasion Buckner's division, commanded by Gen. B. R. Johnson, had started from Chickamauga, flushed with their recent victory over Gen. Rosecrans, upon a pleasure trip up the Tennessee Valley as far as Knoxville. Pardonably proud were the first two divisions of that army at the record of their prowess and success gained upon many of the hardest fought battlefields of the war; and when camp rumours placed the foe opposed to them to consist of a single corps of inexperienced troops, it was not surprising that they should have entered upon this campaign with a feeling that there would hardly be excitement enough in the journey to make it interesting. This feeling was strengthened somewhat when, upon arriving at Huff Ferry, on the Tennessee River, they found us so willing to leave their front and retreat.

It is entirely probable that our foes entered upon this, their first battle with us, having very little respect for our fighting abilities, and a somewhat exaggerated opinion of their own, forgetting that "*pride goeth before a fall*," and that it is always well to respect your enemy's ability until you have proved his weakness.

The independent, indifferent way in which the rebel skirmish line advanced, has already been described. The advance of his main force in three columns, soon followed the repulse of his skirmishers, and then began to occur surprises of which our enemy had little dreamed.

The eight or ten batteries of the Ninth and Twenty-Third Corps opened upon their lines as soon as they became uncovered, with such an accuracy of range and correct judgment of distances as to keep the air in front and about them well filled with bursting shells and case shot, which must have convinced them that if these were new and inexperienced troops which were opposing them—which they had been told we were—then we must have made wonderfully good use of our time.

It will be easy, they think, to brush asunder this line of blue which they see just in advance; but this line of blue rises up and delivers volley after volley into the rebel ranks, absolutely refusing to be brushed aside, and in a moment our over-confident foe is falling back in a confused, uncertain way, as though they were not quite sure what had happened. Indeed, it required one trial more before they were willing to believe that our troops would not throw down their arms and retreat at their approach.

A second repulse convinced our enemy that a direct attack would not be a brilliant success; he then opened his artillery, and began a series of flank movements, which were promptly and successfully met and frustrated by Gen. Burnside.

About half-past five o'clock in the afternoon our battery was ordered to pull out of our position, section at a time, and commence our march towards Knoxville. The right section went first, then the centre, and last the left. During this time a long-range battery of the rebels was making it very uncomfortable for us. The twenty-pound shells were falling and exploding unpleasantly near, creating a great disturbance among our mules; indeed it required the united efforts of our own men, together with a large detail of infantry, to control them sufficiently to limber our pieces. At last it was accomplished, and considerably after dark we reached the road, and made as rapid progress as possible towards Knoxville.

This was our second night out, and it found every man thoroughly exhausted. For thirty hours the men had not slept or partaken of food, excepting a little corn bread, and were covered with mud from head to foot, which the freezing weather had stiffened, making it difficult to walk, adding to our uncomfortable condition. Many would have lain down by the roadside for rest if they had been allowed to do so, but infantry carefully patrolled the road and for a considerable distance on either side. Anyone found inclined to take a nap was aroused and started on his way.

The battery reached Knoxville at about three o'clock in the morning, and went into camp near an earthwork, afterwards called Fort Sanders. The troops began to arrive about daylight on the 17th, and were assigned to positions in the defence line of Knoxville, by Capt. O. M. Poe, Chief Engineer, Army of the Ohio.

CHAPTER 7

The Siege of Knoxville, Tennessee

The site occupied by the City of Knoxville, which we were to defend, was in front of a plateau of about half a mile in width, running parallel to and near the Holston River. This plateau was intersected by three creeks, First, Second and Third, giving the position the appearance of separate hills. First Creek separated Knoxville from East Knoxville, or Temperance Hill; Second Creek separated the town from College Hill; and Third Creek ran into the river beyond our lines.

To the north and west of the town the plateau descended gradually to a valley or basin of about three-quarters of a mile in width, beyond which was a small plateau similar to the one just described, and of about the same height. On this ridge the enemy's forces were stationed, with their batteries at prominent points.

The line of defence established commenced at a point on the river and ran at nearly right angles with the river to a fort which the enemy had commenced on a hill north of the Kingston road and about a thousand yards in front and to the right of the College. From this point it ran along and nearly parallel to the river, across Second and First Creeks, over Temperance Hill to Mabey's Hill near to Bell's house, thence to the Holston River.

Our forces at this time in Knoxville numbered about twelve thousand effective men, exclusive of the new recruits of loyal Tennesseans. The enemy was estimated at from twenty to twenty-three thousand, including cavalry.

In the line of our defence occurred the following strategic points: College, Loudon, Summit, Temperance, and Mabey's Hills, all of them of considerable height, and upon these hills were built forts of varying strength, those upon Loudon, Summit, and Temperance Hills being bastioned earthworks, protected by ditches of considerable depth and

87

width, while those upon the other hills were merely earthworks without ditches. The parapets of all these forts were protected by cotton bales, covered with raw hides.

Upon Loudon Hill was constructed by far the most important work of the entire system. As has before been intimated, this fort was commenced by the enemy before Knoxville was occupied by the Army of the Ohio. From its strategic situation, coupled with the fact that the single assault made by the enemy upon our lines during the siege of Knoxville was upon this fort, when a force of less than three hundred men successfully repelled and disastrously defeated nearly four thousand picked men from Gen. Longstreet's army, it would seem to require a somewhat detailed account of its principal features.

There have been several different ideas expounded in relation to the build of Fort Sanders (called by the enemy Fort Loudon); the atlas accompanying the War Records has been taken as the most accurate one, but that differs very materially from what was built as Fort Sanders. Capt. Poe, Chief Engineer of the Army of the Ohio, laid out the works in quite an elaborate style, but on our arrival at Knoxville we went to work on the old fort that the Confederates had started, on Loudon Hill. The bastion on the extreme northwest corner was where the members of our battery put in hard labour with pick and shovel, and when it was completed we had a good defensible work. Perhaps it was not quite up to the engineer's idea; every fort is expected to have a berme, ours did not; the western face of the bastion was as near a straight line as possible; the line from the bastion running to the Kingston road took a slight curve outward (or towards the west).

The following are the dimensions as we knew them at that time, and by actual measurements:

Starting at the northwest corner of the bastion it ran about south four hundred feet, then east one hundred and thirty-five feet, then south to the Kingston road, six hundred and seventy feet; from the northwest corner of the bastion running east one hundred and fifteen feet, then southeast eighty feet, then in an easterly direction until it reached the creek at the foot of the hill.

When we arrived at the fort it was simply a rifle-pit, but in two or three days it was in good shape. The irregularity of the site was such that the parapets of the bastion varied in height, the one on the north being thirteen feet, while the western front was twelve feet. The ditch on the west was twelve feet wide and eight feet deep; on the north it was eight feet deep at the corner of the bastion, and ran back to almost nothing at the northeast angle; on the south side of the bastion the ditch ran from eight feet deep to about a level where it joined the line running south. There was one embrasure on the west and one on the north side of the bastion. On the northwest angle the ground was built up so that a gun could be fired in barbette.

The line running south was quite heavy, where it joined the bastion, and had four embrasures, which were occupied by Benjamin's regular battery. As the line ran down the hill it was lighter, being about four feet with no ditch, or only a slight one where dirt had been thrown up from the outside, except in two places where the ground inside the breastworks had been dug lower to allow a piece of artillery to be placed and an embrasure cut in.

In front of the northwest angle of the bastion Capt. Poe had some telegraph wire stretched from stump to stump. Sometime after the siege was over a fort was built south of the bastion, so as to command the ditch on the west, but during the siege there was no line of fire that could enfilade the ditch on the west side of the bastion.

During the siege the Seventy-Ninth New York had a plank laid over the ditch from the embrasure on the west, which they used in going to and from the picket line, and when the enemy was looking for a good place to assault the works, they saw some men of the Seventy-Ninth crossing on this plank, and came to the conclusion that there was no ditch in front of the bastion. Gens. Longstreet and McLaw both speak about this in their report of the siege and assault.

All of the large forts, such as Sanders, on Loudon Hill, Comstock, on Summit Hill, Huntington Smith, on Temperance Hill, were connected by a line of rifle-pits; on and near this line were built batteries for from one to six guns, which could command both a direct and enfilading fire for a considerable distance in their vicinity. Battery Noble, located to the left of the Kingston road, below College Hill; Battery Zoelner, to the right of Fort Sanders, commanded the railroad for a considerable distance on the left of Second Creek; Battery Galpin, on the right of Second Creek, overlooked the railroad for a considerable distance; Batteries Wiltsie and Billingsley were located between Gay street and First street, covering the ground near the depot and beyond; Battery Clifton Lee, east of Fort Huntington Smith, together with Battery Fearns, on Flint Hill, were in the second line of defence; Battery Stearman was located in the gorge between Temperance and Mabey's Hills; Fort Hill, the extreme northeastern limit of our line, was situated upon Mabey's Hill.

It must be remembered that upon the morning of the army's arrival at Knoxville, Nov. 17th, almost none of the immense work contemplated in the line of defence which we have been considering, was begun. As fast as troops arrived and were assigned to their positions, they were ordered to select either a shovel or pick and dig for all there was in them.

Early in the morning Gen. Burnside, in order to relieve his exhausted troops, and also hurry along the work as rapidly as possible, had started patrols through different parts of the town with orders to arrest every able-bodied citizen, white or black. Union or Confederate, and put them at work on the fortifications. Relief gangs were organised, and the work continued night and day.

By the 20th our line was in such a condition as to inspire the entire command with confidence that we could hold the town against any rebel force that might be brought against us. First and Second Creeks had been dammed, the back water creating quite large ponds, the overflow from which made most formidable wet ditches in front of a considerable portion of the line.

The pieces of Battery D remained in Fort Sanders from their arrival until the 20th, when the right piece, right section, under Lieut. W. B. Rhodes, was moved into what afterwards became Battery Noble. The lieutenant felt that he would like to take both pieces of his section, and asked permission of Gen. Ferrero to do so, but the general refused, giving as his reason that "he thought one piece quite enough to be sacrificed." This remark, overheard as it was by the men, created in their minds the impression that in the general's opinion he was placing them in an extra-hazardous position, and they were constantly on the alert expecting an assault down the Kingston road.

On Wednesday, the 18th, the men of our battery, together with those from Benjamin's, and a large detail of citizens, commenced active labour upon the ditch and bastion of the fort. During the afternoon we were joined by the Seventy-Ninth New York Highlanders. Lieut. Benjamin, who was appointed to the command of Fort Sanders, had requested that this regiment be assigned to duty as defenders of the fort, and it had been so ordered. While all of the regiments of the Ninth Corps had the thorough confidence of their comrades of the artillery service, the old Seventy-Ninth was held in especial esteem because of its long service, and it was very gratifying to have them with us in the fort.

The work upon the fort was pushed forward with the greatest

rapidity. The men were arranged in details and required to work a certain number of hours, then allowed a certain number for rest. In this way there was no cessation in the work.

The morning of Tuesday, the 19th, opened dull and cloudy. A heavy fog obscured the valley below the fort, and occasional picket shots made us very anxious that the mist should clear, that we might locate our enemy. The previous afternoon he had made his appearance upon the heights in the vicinity of the Armstrong house, where he had been held at bay for several hours by a force of mounted infantry and cavalry, under command of Gen. Sanders, of the Twenty-Third Corps.

Gen. Longstreet had ordered Gen. McLaw to force his way into the town, and sent reinforcements to enable him to do so. Our troops were finally forced down into the ravine below the Armstrong house, and the enemy getting within easy range of our guns at the fort, both batteries improved the opportunity to shell them.

Gen. Burnside was in the fort at the time, and watched the battle over the parapet. He went from point to point along the west front, speaking encouragingly to the men, advising them to "keep cool, fire low, and be sure and hit something every time."

Towards evening the enemy ceased his efforts to push us further, seemingly contenting himself with occupying the heights in front of the Armstrongs'. When the fog cleared we found that during the night the enemy had occupied a range of hills running from a point on the river south of the Armstrong house, thence along our west and north front to a point on Second Creek, while their pickets extended nearly to the Farwell road. A little later they established a battery upon this road and from it threw the first shells into the city. This line of the enemy was from three-fourths to one mile distant from our works, and as it became light enough we could plainly see their men at work throwing up breastworks for almost the entire length of their line.

All day long the pickets kept up a constant exchange of shots, which near the Armstrong house assumed the proportions of a fair-sized battle on several occasions during the day.

In the afternoon we raised a flagstaff in the fort and in a short time a flag was unfurled and heartily greeted by the men with cheers. The enemy desiring to honour the occasion, opened a furious cannonading upon the fort, fortunately doing us no damage. During this, the second day of the siege, bullets began to sing right merrily over the parapets and through the embrasures of the fort, a music which we were obliged to listen to day and night from this on for the seventeen days of the continuance of the siege.

The morning of Friday, the 20th, was cool and misty. The enemy had been very quiet during the night and allowed us to get a full night's rest; but at nine o'clock, when the new pickets made their appearance, they increased the vigour of their fire, causing the relieved men to hustle for all they were worth to get inside the fort.

During the afternoon bales of cotton had been hauled into the fort from the town, and gangs of negroes were employed to roll them onto the parapets for the better protection of the men. The interior crest being only about four feet above the banquette tread, the upper part of the bodies of the infantry were exposed to the enemy's fire. The bales of cotton were covered with raw hides to prevent their being ignited from musket fire. It began raining during the afternoon, and continued well into the night, and, as we were without tents, it made our situation rather uncomfortable.

A brick house on the Kingston road in the ravine below the Armstrong house had become a source of annoyance to our men; the rebel sharpshooters occupying it had from the windows kept up a most disastrous fire upon our pickets and the fort, the distance being about five hundred yards.

Gen. Ferrero determined to destroy this building, that it should furnish no further protection to the enemy, and ordered Col. Humphrey, commanding the brigade in its front to detail a regiment to proceed under cover of darkness of the evening, dislodge the enemy from the house and burn it. The Seventeenth Michigan, under command of Lieut. Col. Comstock, was chosen for this dangerous and difficult work.

The sortie was made at eight o'clock in the evening, so quietly and with such alacrity as to completely surprise the enemy. Many of them were captured, while others had very narrow escapes, such as taking advantage of the opening of a door by one of our men to slip under his arm and escape. This was not an easy thing to do, as many found, quite a number losing their lives in the attempt.

As our men were returning from this successful assault the enemy seemed to suddenly realise what had happened, and opened furiously upon our lines with three or four batteries; but by that time our troops were back within the works, the light from the burning building enabling both infantry and artillery to pour a most destructive fire into the enemy's line, who, by half-past nine, confessed their willingness to call it enough for this day, by discontinuing their firing.

Work upon the rifle-pits and north front of Fort Sanders was continued during Saturday, Nov. 21st, strengthening them in every possible way. We were not molested by the rebels, and nothing worthy of mention occurred during the day.

A rumour reached the battery about noon that the enemy had commenced the construction of a raft at Boyd's Ferry, some distance above Knoxville, on the Holston River, which they proposed setting adrift, hoping that it would carry away our pontoon bridge, and thus break our connection with the south side. At five o'clock in the afternoon Chief Engineer Poe commenced the construction of a boom, made by stretching an iron cable across the river above the bridge. This cable was finished and placed in position by nine o'clock on the next morning.

Sunday, Nov. 22nd, was passed quietly. Up to this time the pickets had been relieved about nine o'clock in the morning, but as many of the men had been badly wounded while performing this duty, the commanding officer decided to change the time for doing this work, to early morning before light, and this Sunday morning was chosen to make this change. The wire entanglement which had just been completed on the northwest in front of Fort Sanders, proved its efficacy upon this occasion, for notwithstanding the men of the relief party were perfectly familiar with its existence, nearly one-half their number were sent to the ground before they were reminded of the entanglement.

On Monday, Nov. 23rd, two pieces of Battery D were moved from their positions on the northern portion of Fort Sanders, and placed in Battery Galpin, a small earthwork upon the eastern side of Second Creek. From this point they covered a considerable extent of territory, reaching from the pond made by the damming of Second Creek, along the railroad to the west and north for several hundred yards.

The section had but just reached this position when the enemy made an assault on Col. Christ's brigade, driving in his skirmish line, who, as they were driven back, set fire to a considerable quantity of combustible material which had been placed in the large round-house for just such an emergency. This fire soon communicated with adjacent buildings, and created an illumination which enabled our troops to see the entire field. This was not satisfactory to the rebels, and they soon retired.

Tuesday, Nov. 24th, it began raining at daylight. During the night the rebels had dug and occupied a rifle-pit which gave them a flank fire along our west front. This proved very troublesome, and it was decided that it must be stopped if possible. As soon as it was light enough to see, the Second Michigan made a charge on the enemy's new line at this point. The brave men of this regiment formed near the ditch of our fort, pushed rapidly forward, reached the objectionable ditch and had nearly destroyed it, when the enemy hurled a very heavy reserve force against them and drove them back. Further to the right a second determined assault was made by the Forty-First Massachusetts and the Forty-Eighth Pennsylvania, our men driving the enemy from the rifle-pits and taking many prisoners.

On Wednesday, Nov. 25, the enemy made a determined effort to push forward their lines on the south side of the Holston River. It was evidently his desire to force us from our position opposite Knoxville. This would have given him the key to our position, and made it untenable for us.

Thursday, Nov. 26th, the work of strengthening our works continued, and all of the entrenching tools were kept busy.

On Friday, Nov. 27th, the enemy still appeared to threaten our troops on the south side of the river, moving their forces from one part of their line to another, but did not attack us.

Saturday, Nov. 28th, opened cold and rainy. The water in and around the fort formed into quite heavy ice during the night, while men woke with a coating of ice on their clothing which occasioned them much inconvenience in moving about. All the afternoon the enemy were moving large bodies of troops towards our right, constantly pushing our pickets nearer our works. In front of the northwest angle of Fort Sanders our picket line was only a few yards from the fort.

That the assault was near at hand, and must come in a few hours, we were all certain. That everyone was on the alert was proven when at about ten o'clock in the evening a general alarm was sounded; our artillery immediately opened from Battery D's section at Battery Galpin, under Lieut. Parker, around Fort Sanders to Battery Noble, occupied by the right piece of Battery D, under Lieut. Rhodes.

Our fire at this time was only continued for a short time, ceasing as soon as we ascertained that the enemy were not coming. One of the greatest difficulties laboured under by us was the absolute necessity of using the closest economy with regard to ammunition.

This ten o'clock attack had been for the purpose of driving in our pickets close under the fort, where they now lay. This enabled the enemy to advance within one hundred yards of our guns, and at that moment they were lying in a depression a short distance from the northwest angle of the bastion of the fort, waiting for the first dawn of day that they might rush on to what?—victory, they thought, but we had quite a different idea, and our idea was nearer right than theirs.

By five o'clock on Sunday morning, Nov. 29th, every man in our line had been aroused, and was occupying his position, either at the parapets or embrasures. The third piece of our battery was located on the north side of the fort some two hundred feet from the bastion; the fifth piece was located on the line running south about one hundred and fifty feet from the Kingston road; while the fourth had been mounted in the northwestern bastion, in barbette. This gun, under command of Sergt. Chas. C. Gray, was by far the most serviceable in the fort on that morning, as will be seen as our story progresses.

All of the guns were loaded with double canister, and at half-past five the cannoneers were at their posts in the position of "Ready," every number four holding his lanyard taut, ready to pull at a second's warning, and send the gun's charge of death into the ranks of the enemy.

It was a minute or two of half-past six when a signal gun was fired from the rebel battery near the Armstrong house, the shell passing over Fort Sanders and exploding in its rear. Instantly all the artillery in the enemy's line opened, and for twenty minutes poured a furious fire of shot and shell into and beyond the fort.

Suddenly the firing ceased, and the cannoneers who were straining their eyes trying to pierce the gloom and mist of the early winter's morning, saw our pickets hurry across the plank which gave them passage over the deep ditch through the embrasure into the fort, and rapidly fall into their places. Then we were certain that there was work before us. At this instant the first gun in the fort to fire—Sergt. Gray's—was discharged.

During the twenty minutes cannonading by the enemy not a gun had been fired from our side, every man having been cautioned to reserve his fare until he could see or hear the enemy. Soon the cannoneers caught the sound as of the rushing of many feet, followed quickly by a confused sound as the rebels encountered the wire entanglement, over which many of them stumbled and fell. Then we saw them coming through the mist, and greeted them with the contents of our double-shotted guns.

Sergt. Gray soon discovered that the position of his gun (in barbette) was a failure, because of the ease with which the rebel infantry could prevent his men from loading the piece—they being obliged to expose a considerable portion of their bodies in the performance of that duty. Ordering the piece taken down from its elevated position, the sergeant had it run into the embrasure upon his right, from which he rapidly poured round after round of canister among the mass of rebels that were charging the bastion on the north side.

Either the rapid and terribly destructive work of this gun, or the desire of the enemy to find some easier way of entering the fort, caused them to swing away from this point around to the western front, and soon our sergeant noticed that there was apparently no enemy in his front. Not being of the kind to throw away ammunition, and having in mind the necessity for observing economy in its use, after taking the precaution to load the piece with double canister, and have the number four affix his friction primer, with the lanyard held taut in his hand, he awaited events.

It was only a moment before the head and shoulders of a rebel officer appeared above the brow of the ditch, who, after a hurried glance around, sprang into the embrasure, rushed up to the muzzle of the gun and placing his sword upon it, ordered its surrender. William Mills, the number four, turned to his sergeant and asked, "Charlie, shall I let him have it?"

"No," replied Gray, "don't waste a double round of canister on one d——d fool."

Not long, however, did the sergeant have to wait for more victims. Before his words were hardly spoken three more brave rebels had followed their leader. Gray gave the order to "Fire!" and when the smoke cleared away not a vestige of the four heroes who had stood before that gun a moment before remained.

This seemed to quiet the enemy on the northern front of the bastion, but a fresh column now commenced a furious assault upon the western front, the noise and confusion of which attracted the attention of Sergt. Gray, who, glancing around to the embrasure in his rear, discovered that the gun from a New York battery, which occupied it, was evidently in trouble. Hurrying across, he ascertained that the horses had run away with the limber, thus depriving the gun of ammunition.

Sergt. Gray had the gun replaced with his own, and during the remainder of the battle, ably and heroically supported by the men of the fourth detachment, did such efficient service that although many desperate attempts were made to drive them from their position, none were successful.

Benjamin's twenty-pound Parrotts had opened fire at the same moment with our own, and were sweeping the opposite side of the glacis with double canister.

The infantry support in Fort Sanders consisted of the Seventy-Ninth New York and two companies of the Twenty-Ninth Massachusetts. These men were posted along the parapets and angles of the fort, every place that would afford opportunity for a shot at our assailants being fully occupied. Full cartridge-boxes, with hundreds of extras, were placed in front of each man, to facilitate the most rapid work. Men who could not find a place in the line were employed to load muskets and pass them to their comrades who were in position.

Soon we were in the midst of the very hottest work, the enemy charging in "Column by division, closed *en masse*," and although the entanglement prostrated many, the weight of the column carried them over it to the edge of the ditch, the formidableness of which caused them to momentarily hesitate. Then it was that the terrific fire from the double-shotted guns of our artillery and closely posted infantry, delivered almost in their faces—not ten yards distant—caused them to melt away as grass before the mower's scythe, and jump into the ditch for safety; but, alas! no sooner had they reached the ditch than Lieut. Benjamin had some of his twenty-pound Parrott ammunition with fifteen second fuses brought into the bastion of the fort, and lighting the fuses with a burning stick they threw them through the embrasures or rolled them down the parapets into the ditch.

Acts of heroism followed each other in rapid succession; the brave rebels were making every effort to scale the twenty feet from the bottom of the ditch to the parapet, under the greatest difficulties; digging with their fingers into the slippery surface they would raise themselves up the embankment for a short distance, only to lose their hold and slide back into the ditch; and if perchance one did reach the top without being shot on the way up, the moment his head showed above the parapet it would be pierced with a bullet, and back he would roll into the ditch. Two or three times the enemy succeeded in reaching the top of the parapet, upon which they placed their flags, but they were instantly killed.

An incident illustrative of the fierceness with which this battle was fought is described in the *History of the Seventy-Ninth New York (Highlanders)*:

Sergeant Dunn, of Company K, owing to the excitement, had forgotten to withdraw his ramrod when he last loaded his piece, and it was fired with the charge. On attempting to reload he was unable to ram home the cartridge. Two of the enemy were making their appearance above the crest, within six feet of him; clubbing his rifle he flung it at them, but failed to hit either. No other piece was within reach, his companions were busy with their own work; the enemy were nearly upon him; time was precious. Looking hastily about he espied an axe; it was but the work of a moment to seize it, swing it above his head, and hurl it at the approaching foe. It hit and knocked one down, while the other fell at the same instant, pierced by a bullet.

It was now apparent that the enemy had enough, for their main attacking force had been driven back under the protection of the depression just in front of the bastion of the fort, and those in the ditch could not stand the havoc which the shells that were thrown over the parapet were making, so one of them stuck a piece of cloth on his gun and poked it up in front of the embrasure, a signal that they surrendered.

Sergt. Gray stepped into the embrasure and commenced to pass what men there were left through. In taking their arms and equipments he soon found some men with artillery equipments on, who, when questioned, allowed they had been sent up to work our guns; but as we were not in need of recruits, they were sent to the rear with the rest of the prisoners.

About this time the enemy's artillery again opened on the fort, but ceased in a few minutes, when Gen. Burnside offered the enemy an armistice lasting until noon, to allow them to care for their wounded and to bury their dead, which was promptly accepted.

How thankful they were to be relieved from their terrible position may be imagined when it is remembered that for fully an hour most of them had been exposed to as terrific and deadly a fire as ever fell to the lot of a soldier to endure. Every stump within the northern and western glacis of the fort yielded from one to two rebels, while those in the ditch still alive and not too severely wounded, made haste to get within the fort.

"Yanks" and "Rebs" were soon fraternizing, discussing the events of the past few weeks. It was then we learned that our enemy had been told they had only new troops opposed to them, who would run at the first fire, and could be swept away from their front with very little effort. Their confidence in this story had been somewhat shaken after their encounter with us at Campbell's Station, when they discovered the old Ninth Corps was in their front. They were as familiar with the fighting qualities of this corps as we were with theirs, and began to realise that our encounters would very likely resemble the traditional one "*when Greek meets Greek.*" They had been told that Fort Sanders was garrisoned only by Tennessee conscripts, and all they had to do was to yell like devils and they would run. Considerable bluffing was indulged in on both sides. They informed us that they were coming again soon, and when they did the boot would be on the other leg. We assured them that we would be glad to see them at any time, and guaranteed them a warm reception.

When noon arrived it was found that the work was not nearly completed, and the time was extended until five o'clock. On the arrival of that hour each side retired within its lines, our pickets occupying the rifle-pits from which they had been driven the night before.

The loss of the enemy in their attack upon Fort Sanders, as taken from their own reports, was 129 officers and men killed, 458 wounded, and 228 prisoners, an aggregate loss of 815. Besides this we captured three battle-flags, and between five and six hundred stand of small arms.

Monday, Nov. 30th, the thirteenth day of the siege, opened with much less firing from the pickets. It was said that during the armistice of Sunday the soldiers on both sides had entered into an agreement not to fire on each other's pickets.

Tuesday, Dec. 1st, sometime before daylight an alarm sent every man to his post, where they remained until sunrise, when, as there was no demonstration on the part of the enemy, the men were dismissed. During the afternoon there were indications from within the enemy's lines of another attack. We made ready to receive them, but happily it did not materialise.

Wednesday, Dec. 2nd, the enemy pushed forward their lines, their pickets very nearly reaching the advanced position occupied by them on the morning of the 19th. They could be seen erecting a new battery on a hill near the Clinton road. We sent a few shells at them, but the necessity of observing the closest economy in regard to our ammunition still continued, obliging us to use it very sparingly.

At daylight, Thursday, Dec. 3rd, it became evident to us that the enemy were leaving our front, and rumours of the abandonment of the siege were current in the fort, much to our relief. Probably for the purpose of deceiving us, a rattling picket fire was maintained by the enemy well into the night, which kept us at our posts, much to our disgust.

Friday, Dec. 4th, the news that Gen. Sherman was advancing with an army of forty thousand men, and that his advance had crossed the Tennessee River the day before, made us all very happy, and when, at one o'clock Saturday morning, our pickets reported that the enemy were leaving our front, our joy knew no bounds. At daylight our skirmish line advanced and found that the enemy had departed.

The siege of Knoxville was over.

It is customary to date the commencement of this struggle between the Union and Confederate forces, on the 17th of November, that being the date on which the Union army entered Knoxville and began the erection of the defences.

A careful consideration of the movements occurring a few days just previous to that date, will convince anyone that the siege practically commenced on the 13th, the date upon which Gen. Longstreet reached Loudon, attacked our pickets, and moved down the Tennessee River to Hough's Ferry. From that moment until midnight Dec. 5th, there was no cessation, day or night, from deadly encounters, varying from the picket or skirmish fire, to that of the pitched battle, in which record will show as many men lost in killed, wounded and missing, as in any battle of the war where the numbers engaged were equal.

Commencing also on the 13th, the soldiers of this army were called upon to endure an amount of physical and mental strain such as men have seldom been called upon to pass through. Battery D's experience during this trying time was an average one. The record of its daily participation in the struggle of those three weeks is one of which its officers and men are justly proud. Not only were the members of the battery complimented by the commanding general for the excellence of their service, but individual members were specially complimented and praised in reports by other officers.

The faithful and intelligent serving of the fourth gun, in its two positions at the northwestern bastion of Fort Sanders, was acknowledged to have been of greater service in repelling the enemy from that section than any other piece of artillery; and when Gen. Burnside visited the fort with his staff soon after the flag of truce had been accepted, he personally shook hands with every member of the fourth piece, and thanked them for the gallant manner in which they had done their duty, and directed Capt. Buckley to apply at once to the Governor of Rhode Island for a commission for Sergt. Gray.

The first piece, under Lieut. Rhodes, had done excellent work from Battery Noble; the second and sixth, under Lieut. Parker, had done themselves proud in preventing the enemy from entering our works by the ravines at Second Creek, while the third and fifth, under Lieut. Chase, had as usual, done efficient service in their respective positions. The battery had certainly added much during the siege to its excellent record as a fighting battery.

Battery D entered East Tennessee well supplied with clothing, the men having replenished their wardrobes at Camp Nelson, but the long journey over the Cumberland Mountains had been so rough, and so filled with difficulties, in the way of climbing the rocky and precipitous roads, the lifting necessary in order to get the heavy carriages over the rough places, had, to say the least, entirely destroyed that appearance of newness which the cloth had possessed a month before. Then came the twice-repeated march, almost from one end of East Tennessee to the other, and it began to dawn upon some of us that the time was not far distant when we should be obliged to draw clothing to hide our nakedness. We were told that a train was then upon its way over the mountains, and promised that as soon as it arrived clothing would be issued. That was a train which was longingly looked for, but never came.

During the three weeks siege the men had no time to give any attention to their persons, and as may be imagined, they were, at the close of the siege, in a deplorable condition. Daily the expected clothing train was looked for, but it did not materialise. Fortunate was it for us that we could not see into the future, and have known that it would be more than two months before we would see that clothing, and realise fully what suffering we would have to endure from the extreme poverty of our condition in regard to clothing and food.

Up to the appearance of Gen. Longstreet, before we had been deprived of the privilege of foraging, our army had been able to live upon the country. His coming altered that condition of things immediately. As soon as Gen. Burnside became assured of the approach of the enemy, he ordered Col. Goodrich, Chief Commissary, to collect all the beef cattle, hogs, etc., and drive them into Knoxville. The hogs were killed and salted; the cattle were collected in two droves, one located near Temperance Hill, the other near Second Creek, in close proximity to Battery D's caissons.

Orders were at once issued to reduce rations. The commissary, hoping, I suppose, to impress the men's minds with the fact that they were after all getting a fair amount of food, stretched his conscience as much as he could, and called the amount given us one-fourth rations; but the old soldiers that he was trying to deceive were too well posted upon the size of a ration to be thus taken in. They were perfectly certain that a piece of fat pork about the size of their hand, together with a quart of flour or corn meal—ground cob and all—issued to last three days, but frequently made to last four, which could be eaten at one meal without the least sensation of fullness or the slightest indication of indigestion, was not only not a fourth ration, but was not even an eighth. Small rations, such as coffee, beans, etc., were discontinued entirely, the supply being so small that it was found necessary to reserve them all for the hospitals.

Our flour ration was not a popular one, from the beginning, in consequence of the difficulties attending the getting it into edible condition. Before we were shut in we succeeded in getting along fairly well, because we were able to secure from our lady friends a supply of those rather essential articles for making good bread—leaven and salt. After we were shut in we found it impossible to procure those articles, and our efforts at bread-making yielded only a cake of burnt dough, which required a good appetite to enable us to eat.

The enemy found it impossible to extend their line on the northwest much beyond the Taswell road, and on the south the excellent work of a division, aided by the cavalry of the Twenty-third Corps, prevented the rebels from extending their lines much beyond their works, which left open to us the free use of our bridges and enabled us to forage along the French Broad River and out on to the Louisville road, both of which were kept open to our foraging parties during the principal part of the siege. The loyal citizens sent down the French Broad River a large amount of grain and meat in flats, and Capt. Doughty maintained a small force up the river during the whole siege directing the efforts of the people in our behalf.

On our arrival at Knoxville on the 17th, we had a mixed motive power consisting of mules and horses, but as soon as we had been assigned positions in the works, we gave up our mule teams. They had helped us out of a bad hole on the road from Loudon, but we had not taken kindly to them, and were glad to see them go.

Our caissons were parked in the ravine near Second Creek, and all our horses but the wheel teams on the pieces, were picketed in a small grove of pine trees near the caissons. Forage was short, and it was soon found that it was an impossibility to keep them hitched, as they would chew up every piece of leather that they could get at, and in a few days there were no halters to be had, and the picket ropes went with the halters. They ate up all the pine boughs, and finally we had to shoot quite a number of them, as they were so near starved it was a mercy to put them out of their misery.

The departure of the enemy was very satisfactory to us. A person who has never passed through the experience of being confined within very narrow limits for a considerable time, under an almost constant fire from artillery and infantry, can hardly realise what a strain it produces on one's nervous system.

To be continually upon the alert, prepared to dodge a shell, never forgetting to keep your head down and your body out of sight, lest some sharpshooter should get a bead upon you which would certainly end your earthly career; the constant screaming of the shells and the whirring of the minie balls, all have such a wearing effect upon the nerves of a man that he wishes something would happen that would make the other fellow quit and give him a rest. With us something had happened—the other fellow had gone, and for the first time in weeks we could straighten our backs and walk erect.

Among the very few pleasant recollections of that disagreeable time is the writer's remembrance of the affection entertained by the men of the Army of the Ohio for their commanding general. His appearance at any time, day or night, along the rifle-pits, or in the forts, always aroused their enthusiasm to the highest pitch. His interest in, love and sympathy for them in their sufferings, conveyed to them in orders, conversations and kindnesses, quite won their hearts.

Many are the stories in circulation illustrative of the kindness of his heart towards his army; true or not, they found ready believers among the men. Personally, the stories were accepted as truthful by my young mind, and today I would not willingly listen to any argument or story which had for its object the lessening of my faith in the great humanity of my beloved general, Ambrose E. Burnside.

On Dec. 6th the battery was paid, and for the first time in our experience we took no interest in receiving money. We had received pay more frequently since entering Tennessee than at any previous time during our service. There was very little to buy, and our stock of greenbacks had accumulated. It was said that the government's liberality toward us was occasioned by the fact that our paymasters had found themselves at the beginning of the siege with a large supply of money, and desiring to be relieved of part of the responsibility, allowed the men to share it with them.

After a careful searching for information, I am fully assured that the following brief account of the Confederates' movements from ten o'clock on the evening of the 28th to half-past eight on the morning of the 29th, is substantially true:

At dark on the 28th, Gen. Longstreet sent a dispatch to Gen. McLaw ordering him to double his pickets, and as soon as the moon had risen sufficiently to throw a little light upon the movement, to press our pickets back as far as possible. After having successfully accomplished this, he was to move the three brigades of his division chosen for the assault, to a depression occurring in the topography of the glacis in front of the northwestern bastion of Fort Sanders, where they were to lie down until the signal gun should be discharged.

At daylight Anderson's brigade, of Hood's division, was ordered to take position about one hundred yards to the left—our right—of the fort, and in case of the success of McLaw's column, to break over our breastworks, wheel to the left and force their way through the ravine of Second Creek to the rear of Fort Sanders. If, however, McLaw was unsuccessful, Anderson was to wheel to the right after passing our breastworks, and take the fort by an attack in reverse.

At the appointed time, as we have seen, the signal gun was fired. Wofford's brigade sprang to their feet, closely followed by Bryan's and Humphrey's brigades; the Seventeenth Mississippi, of Humphrey's, and Phillips Georgia, of Wofford's brigade, leading the assaulting column, dashed forward to the fort.

Wofford, who was to attack the northwest bastion, with his left well extended along the northern face of the fort, was so disturbed by the physical difficulties, including the wire entanglement through which he was obliged to pass, that he took so much distance to the right that the attack extended only about twelve feet upon the northern face, or to the first embrasure, occupied on that side by the fourth gun of Battery D.

Humphrey's brigade, with Bryan on his right, moved to the assault on the right of Wofford's, meeting with all the physical difficulties of the last-named, in their endeavour to get to the ditch.

Anderson's brigade, of Hood's division, which had been ordered to attack the rifle-pits upon the left of Fort Sanders, became so excited and exasperated over the terrible treatment their comrades were receiving, that they rushed with impetuosity toward the fort, and were into the ditch and suffering the same treatment, before orders which had been sent them to retire from in front of the fort, could reach them, leaving many of their number in the ditch dead or wounded.

As to the number of Confederates engaged in the assault on Fort Sanders, it can only be approximated. Four brigades participated. Wofford's contained six, Humphrey's four, Bryan's four, and Anderson's five regiments.

Gen. Jenkins, who commanded Hood's division upon this occasion, gives us the only clue, when he states that Anderson's brigade, which had been greatly reduced by details for picket duty, contained only about one thousand rifles. This would seem to make the statement truthful, that four thousand men of the Confederate army marched to the assault of Fort Sanders on Sunday morning, Nov. 29th, 1863, and out of that number, less than two hundred and eighty Union soldiers obliged nearly twelve hundred in killed, wounded and prisoners, to remain.

Of this bloody work Battery D did its full share. The fourth piece did the largest part, because of its situation, but the third and fifth did a work which caused the rebel Gen. McLaw to complain of the damage done to Wofford's brigade by guns on his left—our right—in the fort. The second and sixth pieces won this compliment from a rebel source:

> That two guns, mounted in a redoubt on the left (our right) of Second Creek, fired so rapidly and accurately as to prevent his column from penetrating the ravine at that point.

The first piece, in its position at Battery Noble, was too far removed from the scene of active operations to take a prominent part.

Dec. 7th we were ordered to prepare as many of our guns as possible and be ready to start in pursuit of the enemy. In consequence of losing so many of our horses, we found it impossible to equip more than four guns. These, with about three-fourths of our army, started at noon for Strawberry Plains. Capt. Buckley, Lieuts. Rhodes and Chase accompanied us. The other two pieces, with the battery wagon and forge, were left at Knoxville, under command of Lieut. Parker.

Following the enemy as fast as our impoverished condition would allow, we reached Rutledge about two o'clock on Dec. 9th, where we remained until late in the evening of Dec. 15th, and then began a retrograde movement towards Knoxville. Our enemy had been encamped during this time about nine miles beyond Rutledge. He had now turned upon us. and rumour had it that an attempt was being made to flank us at Strawberry Plains, and Thursday, Dec. 17th, quite a brisk engagement occurred at that place, which quieted down toward evening, and some prisoners captured upon that evening gave us the information that the rebels were retiring from our front.

We encamped for the night, and next day started for Knoxville, arriving on the 20th, and went into camp on the south side of the city. After a rest of a day or two the order came to have fifty men detailed each day to work on fortifications. This was a duty which the men did not relish, and being still short of rations, and having very little clothing, it was a physical impossibility for the men to do even a half day's work.

The weather was very cold, and many of the men left the prints of their toes on the snow as they walked. This was by far the hardest winter that we had seen in the service, and when, about the first of March, we had a chance to draw clothing and shoes, it was appreciated, and when a few rations of coffee and some "hardtack" was issued, the members of the battery thought they had struck a bonanza.

Notwithstanding the privations we had passed through, nearly two-thirds of the battery re-enlisted, and on March 10th we turned in our guns and horses, and on the 12th started for Rhode Island, on a thirty days furlough. The men that did not re-enlist were left at Knoxville.

We marched to the depot at two o'clock in the morning on the 12th, and took cars for Loudon; crossed the Ferry at eight o'clock that forenoon, and boarded cars for Chattanooga; from there we went to Stevenson, Ala., Nashville, Louisville, Jefferson, Cincinnati, Pittsburg, Harrisburg, New York, and finally reached Providence on March 20th. We had been eight days on the road, having had several delays, but as we were going toward home, we found no fault.

It was quite a change to us when we were told that we could now go to our respective homes for thirty days. It is needless to add that we made the most of our leave of absence. I think most of us rather appreciated our change of diet, and it seemed as if those thirty days passed off very quickly; but notwithstanding the good times we were having, on April 20th, every man but one reported in Providence to Capt. Buckley, ready to again go to the front.

CHAPTER 8

Battles of the Wilderness and Spottsylvania

Leaving Providence at quarter past seven o'clock, on April 20th, 1864, we took the steamboat train *en route* for Washington, where we arrived at dark on the 23rd, and went to the "Soldiers' Res" barracks.

On the 24th we took in the Capitol and other sights about Washington, and the next daywent into camp about a mile east of the Capitol.

The 26th we drew two government wagons, ambulance, and horse equipments for the officers. The men who did not reenlist, and were left in Knoxville, joined the battery at this camp.

On the 27th we drew horses, a battery of six Napoleon guns, ammunition, etc., and were now ready for the field; and on the morning of the 30th we were ordered to Alexandria, and arrived there in the afternoon, and went into camp near the city.

May 2nd, loaded the battery on cars and started for Warrenton Junction, arriving there at three o'clock in the afternoon, and were assigned to the artillery brigade of the Ninth Army Corps.

The whole Army of the Potomac was in our immediate vicinity, under command of Gen. Meade; the Ninth Corps, under Gen. Burnside, reporting direct to Gen. Grant, who was in command of the entire Army of the United States, and was personally directing the movements of the campaign against Richmond, and at this time, May 2nd, had about completed his plans to cross the Rapidan and attack Lee's army.

On May 4th, the Fifth and Sixth Corps crossed at Germania Ford, and the Second Corps and Sheridan's cavalry crossed at Ely's Ford; Burnside's Corps was at the crossing of the Rappahannock River and

Alexandria Railroad, to hold that position until our troops had crossed the Rapidan.

On May 3rd we got everything in shape for a forward movement, and on the 4th moved toward Brandy Station, and encamped near the railroad bridge for the night.

May 5th, broke camp early in the morning, and moved with the corps across the Rapidan, at Germania Ford, and continued our march until late in the evening. Since early in the forenoon we had heard the incessant roar of artillery and musketry in our front, and during the last part of the march had passed large numbers of wounded men going to the rear.

On the morning of the 6th we hitched up at three o'clock, and awaited orders. At five o'clock we started with Benjamin's battery, and marched about four miles and went into position near some woods. There had been a constant roar of musketry since five o'clock. Our position was such that we could see but a very small part of the field, and we wondered why we were put in such a position, as the underbrush in the woods just in our front was so thick that we could not see an enemy until they were right on our guns.

We remained in this position until nine o'clock in the evening without firing a shot. All day long the roar of battle had continued; large numbers of wounded had been passing our position all day; occasionally a stray shot would come our way, but nothing of any account.

At nine o'clock in the evening we had orders to limber up, and moved about live miles out on the Chancellorsville road, and went into camp at three o'clock in the morning.

On the 7th we hitched up at eight o'clock in the morning, but did not move until dark: then we marched by the Chancellorsville House, and at daylight went into camp. From this until the 15th, we remained near this camp, going into position once or twice, but not firing a shot; in the meantime the infantry and cavalry with some artillery, had been having some very hard fighting, but the large amount of woods and the contour of the ground was such that a small amount of artillery was used in the battles of the Wilderness and Spottsylvania, so that on the 15th a large number of batteries were sent back to the rear.

We hitched up at four o'clock on the morning of the 15th, and started for Fredericksburg, where we arrived in the evening, and encamped; remained in camp the 17th, crossed the Rappahannock on the 18th, and next day marched to Belle's Landing, and remained there until the 24th, when we started for Port Royal, where we arrived on the 26th.

On the morning of the 27th we received orders to send forty horses and twenty men to the front.

On the 28th we turned over the balance of our horses, and loaded guns and caissons on steamer and started for Washington, landing at the Navy Yard on the night of the 31st, and turned in our battery, then marched to Fort Lincoln, about four miles north of the city, and went into barracks. We remained there doing garrison duty and having drills on both light and heavy artillery until July 5th.

On the morning of the 5th we started for Fort Sumner, on the northwest of the city near the Potomac, arriving there in the afternoon, and went into barracks. In the fort was a battery of six thirty-two pound rifled guns, and we were given charge of these. The infantry in the fort were all one hundred day men.

On the 7th Gen. Augur visited the fort and ordered Capt. Buckley to draw muskets for the men. We did not like this move, but had to "*take our medicine.*" We had to smile when we saw some of the hundred-day men out on drill; but when we went out on our first drill with muskets I guess it must have been rather amusing to the spectators.

We appeared on dress parade with the infantry the same night we received our muskets, and it wasn't a success as far as we were concerned. Quite a large number of our men had been in the service long enough to get quite a good idea of infantry tactics, but on this occasion they failed to remember "just a little bit" of them.

The next morning we sent a detail of thirteen men and a sergeant up the Potomac on picket. That night at about one o'clock we heard firing on our picket-line, and in a short time some of the infantry pickets reached the fort and reported that the rebel cavalry were driving in our whole line.

Everybody was turned out, and there was considerable excitement. We waited for some of our men to show up, but they did not come, and we came to the conclusion that it was a scare.

In the morning our relief went out, and when our men came in we found that two farmers had come down the road with a wagon and some led horses. Our men halted them, but some of the led horses got away and started on. The infantry pickets opened on them, and our men tried to stop their firing, but the more they halloed the faster came the bullets. For self-protection, our men opened on the pickets, firing high, and in a few minutes everything was quiet on the picket-line.

Perhaps a slight history of the situation of affairs at this time will be of interest. The Army of the Potomac was before Richmond; Gen. Hunter, commanding forces in the Shenandoah Valley, had moved up the valley and had met with good success, destroying the Central Virginia Railroad at Goshen Springs and at Staunton, also destroying at Staunton the enemy's depot, woollen factory, government stables, and large quantities of army material, and captured fifteen hundred prisoners and three pieces of artillery.

Here Hunter was joined on June 8th by the troops of Crook and Averell, who had marched from West Virginia by way of Warm Springs and Goshen, making his available force about eighteen thousand men. On the 10th Hunter started with his whole army for Lynchburg. Two days marching brought him to Lexington, Va., where he remained until the 14th, waiting for his expected wagon train, and then continued his march. Averell reached Lynchburg on the afternoon of the 17th, and Hunter's main force the same evening.

On the 18th Hunter attacked with all his available force, but was repulsed. From some prisoners taken Hunter found that Breckenridge had been re-enforced during the night by the corps of Gen. Early (Stonewall Jackson's old corps).

Hunter was now in a tight place, and could not retreat up the Shenandoah Valley, as the enemy had repaired the railroad and could now send troops by rail and hold Rockfish Gap, so Hunter resolved to retreat by way of Bulford's Gap to Charlestown, in the Kanawha Valley. Early hurried him along for a time, but soon turned back. By this move the Shenandoah Valley was left open, and Gen. Lee immediately started Early and Breckenridge down the valley and into Maryland, and on the 11th of July Early was in front of Washington.

Things remained quiet in our front until the afternoon of the 11th, when our pickets reported that our cavalry was falling back under quite a brisk fire from the enemy's cavalry. We had our muskets piled up and at once took our positions on the thirty-two pound rifle battery, thinking we could do more execution with them than we would be apt to with the muskets. At about five o'clock in the afternoon our men out on picket were relieved by some cavalry.

We did not fire a shot from our battery, and only one shot was fired from the fort, and that was at a squad of our own cavalry. The shot did no harm, as it went wide of its mark. The major commanding our fort wanted us to open on this same party, but Capt. Buckley refused to do so until he was satisfied who we were going to fire on.

We felt rather blue over our situation, as all in our immediate vicinity were new troops or clerks from the city, and we did not have much confidence in them, but we soon heard that the Sixth Corps and a part of the Nineteenth had arrived, and we felt that Washington was safe.

The night of the 11th was quiet in our front, and on the 12th only a little picket firing. Before dark Early had been driven back by Wright's Sixth Corps, and things had quieted down.

About noon time we received orders to turn in our muskets and report at Camp Barry. Nobody objected to this order, and soon we were on the march. Capt. Buckley and Lieuts. Bonn and Gray started ahead, and when the men under command of Lieut. Chase arrived at Camp Barry, they had requisitions for a four-gun battery of three-inch rifles. We did not get our complement of horses, baggage wagons, ambulance, etc., until the next morning, but at five o'clock on the afternoon of the 13th we marched in pursuit of Early.

We reached Tenallytown and went into camp, but the next morning we found that many of our horses were lame, and we had to stay there two days, working night and day to get them shod.

On the 16th we started for Snicker's Gap. Marched twenty miles, and went into camp at Edwards' Ferry. Hitched up early in the morning, crossed the Potomac, and marched to Leesburg, and joined the Nineteenth Corps.

Early in the morning on the 18th, we were on the road; passed through Snicker's Gap and went into camp near the Shenandoah River, but later crossed the river and marched about four miles and went into position, where we remained until about nine o'clock in the evening, when we received orders to recross the river and report at Washington with the Nineteenth and Sixth Corps.

This movement was by order of Gen. Grant, he supposing that Early had started for Richmond, and wanting the Sixth and Nineteenth Corps forwarded *via* Washington to join the Army of the Potomac, then in front of Petersburg.

We marched nearly all night, stopping at Leesburg to feed, and then continued on to Goose Creek, where we went into camp, having marched about twenty-four miles. Our march was continued for three days, starting early in the morning and making camp at dark.

The 23rd we started at daylight and arrived at Chain Bridge in the afternoon and went into camp, remaining there two days, which gave the men and horses a rest. The weather had been very warm, and the dust on the march was almost suffocating.

On the 26th we had orders to start back to Harper's Ferry, and we broke camp early in the morning and hurried along, arriving at our destination on the evening of the 29th and went into camp, the men and horses being pretty well tired out. We omitted the evening roll-call so as to allow the men to go to sleep early; but we were just a little vexed to get orders in the evening to be ready to move at three o'clock in the morning—where? Right back over the road we had just come!

"Boots and saddles" were blown at half-past two the next morning, and we moved out of camp promptly at three o'clock. It was reported that someone in the battery, on being woke up and told that we were to retrace our steps over the same ground that we had covered twice since the 16th, made a very profane remark, but on investigation the culprit could not be found.

We marched that day until late in the evening, when we encamped in a lot alongside of the pike. Starting early next morning we passed through Frederick City and went into camp on the Gettysburg pike, where we remained one day, and then started back, making twenty-four miles, and again went into camp. We remained there until Aug. 6th, when we started at daylight and reached Knoxville, having marched twenty-three miles.

On the 7th we crossed the Potomac at Harper's Ferry, and en-camped at Halltown.

There were various reasons for the marches and counter-marches we had been making for the past fifteen days. Early had not started up the valley as was supposed, but was holding on to some of the fords, and his whole force was in the lower part of the Shenandoah Valley. There were a number of generals commanding certain sections of the country in the vicinity of Washington, and each thought that Early was sure to attack him, and if a small cavalry force showed up in his vicinity, he immediately wired to Washington that Early's whole force was after him, and then everything had to "hustle;" but at last Gen. Grant insisted that one man should take command of the whole, and Gen. Philip H. Sheridan was sent from his command of the Cavalry Corps of the Army of the Potomac to take command of all troops on the Upper Potomac. Gen. Grant, on the 6th of August, ran down to Monocacy Bridge, in Maryland, and met Gen. Sheridan at that point, and gave him his final instructions.

Gen. Hunter had just arrived from his long trip down the Kanawha Valley, and his troops were at or near Harper's Ferry, having been delayed by low water in the Ohio River, and also by various breaks on the Baltimore & Ohio Railroad, from reporting as soon as expected.

Gen. Halleck had sent one or two sharp telegraph orders to Hunter, hurrying him up, so Hunter, as soon as he had his troops at the Ferry, sent his resignation to Washington, and it was accepted, and the army lost a good general.

Sheridan's army consisted of the Sixth Corps, commanded by Maj. Gen. Wright, its three divisions by Gens. Russell, Getty and Rickets; one division of the Nineteenth Corps, Maj. Gen. Emory commanding corps, Gen. Dwight commanding division (the second division of the Nineteenth Corps, Gen. Grover, arrived on the 18th of August); Army of West Virginia (Eighth Corps), Gen. Crook commanding, Gens. Thoburn and Duval as division commanders. The cavalry consisted of Gen. Torbert's division and Averell's; Torbert was appointed as Chief of Cavalry, with Merritt and Averell commanding divisions.

The rebel force in the valley consisted of "Stonewall" Jackson's old corps, now commanded by Early, with Gens. Rodes, Ransom and Gordon commanding divisions. Breckenridge's division, three battalions of artillery and one corps of cavalry commanded by Gen. Lomax, with Vaughn, Johnson, McCausland and Imboden as brigade commanders.

I quote from Sheridan's *Memoirs* the following description of the Shenandoah Valley, that the reader may have a better idea of the different movements of the army:

> The valley has its northern limit along the Potomac between McCoy's ferry at the eastern base of the North Mountain, and Harper's Ferry at the western base of the Blue Ridge. The southern limit is south of Staunton, on the divide which separates the waters flowing into the Potomac from those that run to the James. The western boundary is the eastern slope of the Alleghany Mountains, the eastern, the Blue Ridge; these two distinct mountain ranges trending about southwest enclose a stretch of quite open, undulating country varying in width from the northern to the southern extremity, and dotted at frequent intervals with patches of heavy woods.
>
> At Martinsburg the valley is about sixty miles broad, and on an

east and west line drawn through Winchester about forty-five, while at Strasburg it narrows down to about twenty-five. Just southeast of Strasburg, which is nearly midway between the eastern and western walls of the valley, rises an abrupt range of mountains called Massanutten, consisting of several ridges which extend southward between the North and South Forks of the Shenandoah River until, losing their identity, they merge into lower but broken ground between New Market and Harrisonburg. The Massanutten ranges, with their spurs and hills, divide the Shenandoah Valley into two valleys, the one next the Blue Ridge being called the Luray, while that next the North Mountain retains the name of Shenandoah.

A broad macadamized road, leading south from Williamsport, Maryland, to Lexington, Virginia, was built at an early day to connect the interior of the latter State with the Chesapeake and Ohio Canal, and along this road are situated the principal towns and villages of the Shenandoah Valley, with lateral lines of communication extending to the mountain ranges on the east and west. The roads running toward the Blue Ridge are nearly all macadamized, and the principal ones lead to the railroad system of eastern Virginia through Snicker's, Ashby's, Manassas, Chester, Thornton's, Swift Run, Brown's and Rockfish Gaps, tending to an ultimate centre at Richmond. These gaps are low and easy, offering little obstruction to the march of an army coming from eastern Virginia, and thus the Union troops operating west of the Blue Ridge were always subjected to the perils of a flank attack; for the Confederates could readily be brought by rail to Gordonsville and Charlottesville, from which point they could move with such celerity through the Blue Ridge that, on more than one occasion, the Shenandoah Valley has been the theatre of Confederate success, due greatly to the advantage of possessing these interior lines.

As before stated, our battery arrived at Halltown on the 7th of August. We put our guns in position and remained there three days.

On the 9th, Lieut. Gray was detailed as Ordnance Officer, Artillery Brigade, Nineteenth Army Corps.

The 10th we moved with our corps to Berryville, and on the morning of the 11th we made a forward movement, Sheridan intending to force Early into a fight. Early was not willing to accept a battle, and moved his army up the valley.

We followed as far as Cedar Creek, and on the afternoon of the 13th had quite a lively brush with Early's rear guard, we only firing a few shots. We remained there until the evening of the 15th, when we moved out of camp at ten o'clock, and reached Winchester at daylight, and went into position, where we remained until the morning of the 17th, when we moved back to Berryville.

Next morning we retired about four miles and formed line-of-battle, Crook on the left, Emory in the centre, and Wright on the right. This retrograde movement was caused by Sheridan receiving notice that Kershaw's division of infantry and two brigades of Fitzhugh Lee's cavalry were on the way to re-enforce Early, and at that time, the 16th, had reached Front Royal, where Merritt, with his cavalry, was disputing their advance.

Early, as soon as he found that Sheridan had fallen back, put his force in motion, and lost no time in following us down the valley, and from this until the 19th, our army was on the defensive. We were at or near Halltown, where several skirmishes occurred, we firing only a few shots, however.

On the 3rd of September all the three-years men who had not re-enlisted were mustered out at Charlestown, and went home under the charge of Capt. Buckley.

Sheridan learned on the 16th that Kershaw's division of infantry and Cutshaw's artillery had been returned to Richmond, and he immediately made preparations for a forward movement; and on the morning of the 19th his cavalry forced the Berryville crossing of the Opequon, followed by the Sixth, Eighth and Nineteenth Corps. The enemy was posted in line-of-battle, and in a short time the engagement became general. It was nearly dark before Early was fairly beaten and sent "whirling through Winchester."

Our part in this important victory may be seen in part from the report of Capt. E. D. Taft, Chief of Artillery, Nineteenth Army Corps:

> Battery D, First Rhode Island Artillery, by my direction, took position in a skirt of woods on the right of the Nineteenth Army Corps, and immediately opened fire on one of the enemy's batteries, then enfilading our lines on the right, when the enemy opened fire from two guns in the wood with canister, about two hundred yards distant and in rear of our line of infantry. The battery soon silenced these two guns, and then

renewed the fire on the battery enfilading our line, silencing it for a short period, but the infantry falling back for want of ammunition rendered the position unsafe for artillery. The battery had whilst in this position, although under a severe fire front and left oblique, been gallantly fought. The support having retired, and the battery having lost four men and six horses and one wheel broken, I ordered it to withdraw, which was done in good order. This closed the operations of these batteries for the day.

Capt. Taft's report is wrong in one particular. When our infantry fell back, Capt. Taft did ride up to our battery and tell the commanding officer to hold his position as long as possible, but look out and not lose his pieces, and then rode away. We soon had orders to limber up.

At this time some infantry in our front was showing up rather near our position. As we were afraid they would get at us before we could get through the woods, we thought that a few rounds of canister, rightly distributed, would give them a check and allow us to retire.

Lieut. Bonn was in command of the right section, and Lieut. Gray of the left. Lieut. Gray was still on detached duty, but came up while we were halted in the woods and took his section into the fight. We promptly commenced to distribute canister among the infantry in our front, and they soon took shelter under the bank of Red Bud Run. Just at this time Lieut. Gray's left piece was disabled by a shot, and he sent it to the rear, but retained the cannoneers to help on the other pieces. It was now decided that we could pull out.

The right section pulled out, and the right piece of the left section was about to limber up, when a shot from a twenty-pound Parrott that was across the Red Bud Run passed entirely through the swing horses. We had to stay then, and Sergt. Tucker and his men needed no orders to commence firing again.

We soon expended all our canister, and had to use solid shot as our shell had given out some time before. The infantry that was under the bank to our right and front now commenced to give us some trouble, and we began to think that we had staid too long; but we would shy a shot along the bank and they would lay low; meantime we were hurrying to get our dead horses on the limber clear, but it was a slow job.

About this time an officer rode out of the woods in our rear and gave us the welcome news that a brigade of the Eighth Corps was close at hand; and in a minute or two we saw them coming on the double-quick. When they arrived we ceased firing and limbered up, and taking the harnesses from our dead horses, we soon joined the rest of the battery. When our lines advanced, we were ordered to move with them, and we had quite a good view of the final rout of Early's army. We went into camp for the night just outside of Winchester.

On the morning of the 20th we started early in pursuit of the enemy, and on arrival at Strasburg went into camp. Gen. Early was found in position just in our front at Fisher's Hill, strongly fortified. His position was almost impregnable from an attack in front, so Sheridan sent the Eighth Corps around his left to take the position by flanking it. It took until the afternoon of the 23rd to get the Eighth Corps into position, as they had to make most of the movements through thick woods, and keep out of sight of the rebels' signal stations. On the afternoon of the 23rd the Eighth Corps charged down on to Early's left flank and routed it. The movements in our front were to help carry out this project.

On the morning of the 23rd our corps was advanced, and at three o'clock in the afternoon Grover's division drove in the skirmish line in our front and formed in line-of-battle. Some two hundred yards in our front was a ridge, and the rebel sharpshooters took up their position on this ridge, and made it very uncomfortable for us. The third brigade, second division, Nineteenth Corps, soon made a charge and captured this position, which was within three hundred yards of the enemy's fortifications.

Gens. Sheridan and Grover were at the right of our battery when the infantry carried the hill. Sheridan wanted a piece of artillery sent out there, and Gen. Grover came and asked Lieut. Chase if he could put a piece on that ridge. Lieut. Gray was sent to see if it was possible to do so. Dismounting just before the top of the ridge was reached, he left his horse in charge of an orderly and took to all fours to do the rest of the distance.

There was quite a depression on the top of the ridge, and just on the other edge was a slight rifle-pit that had been hastily thrown up by the enemy. Our skirmishers were occupying this, and it was quite necessary to keep well down, as the enemy's infantry and artillery were within short range, and were giving this particular spot very close attention.

Becoming convinced that if a piece could be put into this depression it would do good execution, Lieut. Gray gave the signal, and

Sergt. Tucker with his piece started on the gallop and was soon there, the piece being halted before the top of the ridge was reached. The pickets kept up a sharp fire so as to have the smoke hide our movements, and we ran the piece by hand into the depression and filled both haversacks with ammunition and loaded. We had a sure mark, and when we sent that shell into the earthwork in our front, it made things jingle. The enemy was not slow in returning the compliment, and as they had eight or ten guns in our immediate front, we laid low, but just as soon as we thought they had fired everything, we repeated the experiment before they had loaded.

We had been in this position about fifteen or twenty minutes when Gens. Sheridan and Grover ran over the ridge and took shelter in the depression just to our right. Sheridan was anxious to see the whole situation, and crawled up to the skirmish line, some ten feet in advance of us. Gen. Grover soon joined him, and just about this time a shot from a twenty-pound Parrott ploughed through the slight ridge within a foot of Sheridan's head, covering him with dirt. He rolled over on his side, and we thought he was wounded, but he was only getting the dirt out of his ear and neck; he came back, though, and took his position by the side of our piece.

In a few minutes we heard cheers on our right and soon saw the enemy breaking all along the line. We sent shot after shot in quick succession, but were told to stop firing. Soon our corps came sweeping over the ridge and down the other side.

Sheridan now wanted his horse, but could not see it, so Lieut. Gray let him take his, but regretted it in a moment, as Sheridan went dashing down the hill over stumps and fallen trees, and we expected to see horse and rider take a tumble, but they were soon out of sight.

We limbered up and went back to where the remainder of the battery was, and then started over to the pike and joined our division. We marched nearly all night and then went into camp at Woodstock, to get a little sleep and some rations.

At two o'clock in the afternoon we started again and reached Edenburg, where toward night we fired a few shots and then encamped. In the morning we were away early, and marched all day, going into position two or three times and firing a few shots, but apparently doing the enemy no great harm. The next day we marched to Mount Jackson, having quite a skirmish in the afternoon.

On the morning of the 29th we started at nine o'clock, and on reaching Harrisonburg, went into camp, remaining there until the 6th of October, occupying the time in foraging for our horses.

On the morning of the 30th Lieut. Gray took nine mounted men from the battery, armed with revolvers, and started out into the country to secure some horses that he had seen the day before, but on arriving where he had seen the horses he found the natives had run them off to the mountains. Following the trail for about seven miles we ran across a few straggling rebel cavalrymen, several of whom were captured, and also a number of horses.

We continued on until we were about fifteen or sixteen miles from camp, when we stopped at a farmhouse and had dinner and fed our horses. We then started toward camp again, but by a different road than that on which we came. We had two or three quite sharp skirmishes with squads of rebel cavalry, and about dusk Billy Mills, who was in the advance, rode back bringing the information that there was a company of rebel cavalry drawn up on the side of the road with the intention of obstructing our passage. We had at this time nine rebel cavalrymen as prisoners and twenty-three horses.

The line was immediately halted, and Lieut. Gray rode ahead to reconnoitre. When he arrived at the edge of the woods he found a company of rebels drawn up in line in a large field adjoining the road. On looking over the situation he found that the fence in the rear and on the left had been taken down, to allow egress from the lot, which gave him the impression that the force there had some doubt as to the number of our men.

Riding back, the column was started forward, following the road until close to the edge of the woods where we could be seen from the lots. We filed by twos from the road into the woods and made a short counter-march on to the road and into the woods again, which manoeuvre made it look as if we had two companies. On moving into the woods the second time, all the rebel cavalrymen were dismounted, their arms strapped to each other and ordered to sit down, and one man left as guard.

The darkies that had been confiscated to take care of the spare horses, twelve in number, were mounted on them, and a line was formed at the edge of the woods, consisting of twenty men, nine of us and eleven darkies sandwiched in, the other darkey being left to look after the horses. These arrangements were not quite satisfactory to some of the darkies; but they were told that when we started out of the woods they must keep well up in the line or get shot.

An order was given to charge, every man was told to halloo as loud as he could yell, and ride straight for the line of the rebel cavalry. The scheme worked like a charm. The rebel line soon broke and fled to the woods, we in hot pursuit, capturing three, two seriously wounded, while our loss was one darkey shot, and slight wounds on two horses. We soon collected our men together and sent them back to the woods under command of Sergt. Tucker.

Lieut. Gray and Mills rode down to the town to see if there were any rebels there, we having seen a squad of men leaving there a few minutes before we had our brush with the company of cavalry. Both Lieut. Gray and Mills had on rebel uniforms, and they soon had information that the body of men which had left the town a few minutes before were Yankees, which information was pleasing to them.

Mills was immediately sent back to have the line moved forward, and we soon entered the town. Lieut. Gray sat on his horse with a dozen people around him, who were giving what information they could, and urging him to hurry so as to capture some of the Yankees that had left a few minutes before. The squad of men we saw leaving the town was Lieut. Corthell and some men from Battery G, of our regiment. When our line came up there was a look of astonishment on the faces of some of the people when they found we were Yankees.

We arrived in camp about eight o'clock with twenty-eight horses and thirteen rebel cavalrymen, which we considered a good day's work for ten light artillerymen.

On the morning of the 6th Sheridan started his army down the valley having done all the damage with his cavalry that he could in this neighbourhood. We bivouacked at Mount Jackson, and started the next morning and reached Woodstock late in the evening.

On the morning of the 8th we hitched up early, but did not move. We soon learned that Sheridan had made up his mind to give the rebel cavalry another lesson.

Gen. Rosser had just arrived in the valley with his brigade, and he was put in command of all the cavalry. Since leaving Harrisonburg they had been annoying our rear guard, so Sheridan sent word to Torbert on the evening of the 7th to "give Rosser a drubbing in the morning, or get whipped yourself, and the infantry will be halted until the affair is over."

Torbert had the divisions of Merritt and Custer, and in the morning he attacked Rosser. After a hard fight of about two hours Rosser had received his "drubbing," losing eleven pieces of artillery, several wagons, and three hundred prisoners.

We started on our march at ten o'clock, and encamped near Strasburg, remaining there one day, and then moved to the north bank of Cedar Creek, and went into position just off the pike on the extreme left of the Nineteenth Corps. Crook (Eighth Corps) went into position on the left of the pike joining the left of the Nineteenth Corps, his right advanced some hundred and fifty yards beyond our position. The Sixth Corps had started for Port Royal, to rejoin the Army of the Potomac, while Merritt's cavalry was on the extreme right of our line.

Our cavalry destroyed all the mills and crops in the valley as we fell back, and gathered in all the live stock, so that Early could not subsist his army' in the valley. Early was at Fisher's Hill on the morning of the 13th, just the same, but probably brought his rations with him. We occupied this position until the morning of the 19th. In the meantime the Sixth Corps had come back and taken position in rear of the Nineteenth Corps. Sheridan had been called to Washington, which left Wright in command.

At break of day on the 19th, three of Early's divisions surprised Crook's camp and stampeded his whole command. Our battery, being on the extreme left of the Nineteenth Corps, were the first troops to receive their attention after the Eighth Corps had been swept away.

We had orders to have our battery hitched up at daylight, and we had just completed the task when we heard a volley of musketry on our left. We fired four rounds, just to make a noise and wake up the camp, not yet realising just what had happened on our left.

Lieut. Gray hurriedly gave orders to have the tents struck and everything in readiness to move. In a few minutes we saw a line coming over the hill on our left, and making sure they were not our troops, we opened on them, but after firing for a few minutes, Gen. Emory dashed up and ordered us to stop firing, as they were some of our men, and Lieut. Gray was told to always look out before he commenced firing. At this moment Lieuts. Chase and Bonn came up, and Chase took command.

In the two or three minutes that had elapsed since we had stopped firing, the line of infantry that we had driven behind the brow of the hill, now opened on us, and in a few seconds we had orders to "give it to them." We had just opened on them as Gen. Wright rode up. He asked Emory "What is the matter?" and Emory replied, "Early has surprised us—Crook's corps has gone." Wright quickly took in the situation, and started off.

We had warm work before us, the enemy's line of infantry on our left having a notion of charging us, but as they came over the ridge we had very nearly a complete flank fire on them, and our left section commenced using canister. The right of their line was driven back over the ridge, but the left was swinging up parallel with the pike, which gave them a flank fire on our battery. We were lucky in having three or four loads of hay piled up just in rear of the limbers and on a line with the caissons on the extreme left of the battery, this pile of hay stopping many of the bullets from our left.

At this time the fourth brigade, second division, Nineteenth Corps, swung into position on our left. The smoke and fog was quite thick, and they did not open fire for some minutes thinking that the line in their front was some of the Eighth Corps falling back. Their mistake was discovered, and none too soon, for the enemy made a dash for our guns, but the line on our left had their guns loaded, and poured a volley at them which checked their onward rush.

We were firing very rapidly and doing good execution, as we kept the line on our left (or in front of our left section, which had swung to the left) back to the brow of the ridge; but it now became apparent that we must fall back, as the right of our support had given way and the troops on the left of the battery were only hanging on so as to give us a chance to get out; and to add to our troubles, the line of infantry on our left, which we had until now been able to keep back to the ridge, was joined by Wharton's rebel division which had moved up the pike, and they were pouring in a nasty fire.

When we received the order, "Limber to the rear," we were not long in executing it, as the rebels were now very close to us. All the pieces were taken off but the left piece of Lieut. Gray's section—three of the limber horses being down, and in a minute every horse on the limber was shot. It was impossible to take the piece by hand to the rear, and the caisson had started some minutes before. The pike had been in the hands of the rebels for the last fifteen minutes, so Lieut. Gray told the three or four cannoneers who had been trying to get the limber clear, to join the battery.

Maj. Hart, of Gen. Emory's staff, wanted to save this piece, and told Lieut. Gray to fix the prolong and he would have the infantry haul it off. It was simply sacrificing men to make the attempt under the circumstances. Maj. Hart lost his life, also Capt. Watson and Lieut. Quay, both of the Eighth Indiana, and Lieut. Col. Kenny, commanding the Eighth Indiana, was severely wounded, and four others. Lieut.

Gray was the only one who escaped from the attempt to get the piece away.

The following is from Vol. XLIII of the Official Records of the War;

> Hdqrs. Fourth Brig., Second Div., 19th Army Corps,
> Cedar Creek, Va., October 24, 1864.

Captain: I have the honour to submit the following report of operations of my command in the engagement on the 19th of October, instant:

> . . . . . the right regiment (Eighth Indiana) supporting Battery D, First Rhode Island Artillery. In consequence of the dense fog, which existed at the time, the enemy advanced on the battery and were within a short distance of it before we could distinguish whether they were friends or foes, the more so, as we supposed them to be a portion of the Eighth Corps, and notwithstanding we received a very heavy fire from that direction, we did not reply to it until they charged directly on the battery. Five pieces were withdrawn successfully, and while attempting to save the last one Major Hart (of General Grover's staff), Capt. William D. Watson, and Lieut. George W. Quay (both of Eighth Indiana) were killed, and Lieut. Col. A. J. Kenny (commanding Eighth Indiana) severely wounded. . . . .

I cannot close this report without referring to the bravery of the lamented Major Hart (of General Grover's staff), who was killed while cheering on the men in their attempt to save the last gun of Battery D, First Rhode Island Artillery. In him we have lost a noble, brave, efficient officer.

I am, very respectfully, your obedient servant,

David Shunk,
Colonel Eighth Indiana, Commanding.

Capt. E. A. Fiske,
Adg. Asst. Adjt. Gen.,
Second Div., Nineteenth Army Corps.

> Hdqrs. Third Brig., Second Div., 19th Army Corps,
> Near Cedar Creek, Va., October 24, 1864.

Sir: In obedience to orders, I have the honour to make the following report of the operations of this brigade in the action of the 19th instant:

..... the left of the One Hundred and Seventy-sixth New York reached nearly to and supported Battery D, First Rhode Island Artillery.

These dispositions had scarcely been made, and orders given to the men to reserve their fire until the enemy was near enough to make the fire effective, when we began to receive a heavy fire of musketry from the advancing, but still hidden, enemy. The fire came from our front, our right, and our left, with a heavy, but random fire of artillery from the heights formerly occupied by General Crook's command. The enemy's lines were not developed until they were within one hundred and fifty yards of our lines, and then were but dimly visible through the fog. At this time they opened a furious and destructive fire upon us, still advancing, which was vigorously and effectively returned, checking to some extent their advance. The enemy's lines, as now developed, were nearly at right angles with the main brigade line, and facing the One Hundred and Seventy-Sixth New York and the three companies of the One Hundred and Fifty-Sixth New York, which had changed front. The left of their lines extended very nearly to Cedar Creek, while their right extended as far as the eye could reach through the fog and smoke. In a very few moments they were on us in force, their left swinging to the right, while their right poured heavy volleys in our rear. A desperate hand-to-hand fight ensued on the left of the brigade line. The enemy had planted their colors on our works and were fighting desperately across them, meeting with a stubborn resistance, while they swarmed like bees round the battery on our left and rear. .....

I have the honour to be, very respectfully,

your obedient servant,

Alfred Neafie,
Lieutenant Colonel, Commanding Brigade.

Capt. E. A. Fiske,
Acting Assistant Adjutant General.

When the battery retired, we moved to the right and rear of our position, crossed Meadow Brook, passing to the west of the Bell Grove house (Sheridan's headquarters) and joined some infantry about one thousand yards to the rear, and went into position, firing at a line of infantry on the pike, and then fell back just beyond Middletown, and again went into position behind some light breastworks that had been thrown up. We remained there until three or four in the afternoon, firing occasionally when we could see anything to fire at.

Gen. Sheridan joined his command at about half-past ten in the morning, from Winchester. At this time Getty's division, of the Sixth Corps, was holding a position about one mile north of Middletown, his left near the pike. Col. Lowell's cavalry extended from Getty's left to near Middletown. The other two divisions of the Sixth Corps, the Nineteenth, and part of the Eighth Corps, were just south of Newtown.

Our army had lost twenty-four pieces of artillery, a large amount of camp equipage, ambulances, wagons, and thirteen hundred prisoners.

Sheridan's arrival gave our men confidence. He had the two divisions of the Sixth Corps, also the Nineteenth, and part of the Eighth Corps put in line on the right of Getty's division. The enemy tried to break this line, but Emory handsomely repulsed the charge.

At about a quarter of four o'clock Sheridan advanced his whole line, which was met by a stubborn resistance; but soon the enemy was obliged to give way, and in a short time it was a complete rout.

Our infantry followed the enemy until their old camps were reached at Cedar Creek, and then the cavalry took up the chase. All of our guns were recaptured, and twenty-four of Early's (just the number we lost in the morning), besides about all of the ambulances and wagons that were lost in the morning were in our hands that night, with a large majority of Early's.

Our battery followed the infantry when the advance was made, and on arrival at Cedar Creek, went into our position of the morning. We had lost one gun and one limber and all of our camp equipage (our teams, having taken the pike when they fell back, were captured); notwithstanding, we felt happy at the way things had turned out. We also experienced just a little regret that we had no blankets, tents, or anything else in fact, but what we had on.

Not a man of the battery had had a morsel to eat since the night before, and no show for rations getting to the front that night. We could get along without tents or blankets, but the day's excitement had given us a good appetite. We built up two large camp fires and sat around discussing the events of the day.

About nine o'clock Lieut. Gray (who had left the battery shortly after we arrived in our old position) rode into camp escorting a four-mule team which he had captured. The contents of the wagon were soon spread out, disclosing three boxes of "hard-tack" as a part of the capture. This was issued at once, and we had a good supper.

The following is Lieut. Gray's report of his two hours' absence:

When we arrived in our old position just at dusk, there was a rebel battery on the hill beyond the bridge, and quite a piece to the right. A few shells came over our camp, and I knew they were from a three-inch rifle; having lost one of that kind in the morning, I thought I would ride over and see if I could find it.

I rode down toward our right, crossed a small stream in the woods, and came out near a small plateau where some two or three hundred rebel infantrymen were trying to hold our cavalry from coming up the hill. I swung back and joined the head of our cavalry line, which proved to be the First Vermont, Col. Bennett. He was waiting for his men to close up.

I crossed the stone wall and rode a few yards to the left, when Gen. Custer, with the Fifth New York came up, and both regiments charged. I was carried along with the crowd, but before we had gone fifty yards the rebel infantry broke. I made friends with a sergeant, and suggested that we shove ahead and get the guns of the battery that had been firing but a minute or two before.

He fell into the scheme, and we gathered about a dozen of his command and struck out for the battery, but they had limbered up, and were quite a piece from where we expected to find them. We were riding at a sharp trot, passing through quite a number of rebel infantry, who paid not the least attention to us. I soon made out the battery, which was bearing off to the right.

I rode to the head of the battery and ordered them to halt. The officer in command told me that he had orders to go to the rear as quick as possible. I explained to him who I was, and ordered him to counter-march. As soon as the battery was halted three or four of the mounted men rode up to see what the matter was, and heard the conversation. I heard the click of two or three revolvers, and wished I was at home, as my friend the sergeant and his men had stopped to take some of the rebel infantry into camp, leaving me entirely alone.

I rode directly in front of the commanding officer of the battery, holding my Colt's navy revolver very close to him, and told him it was no use making a fuss, as our cavalry was some distance in our front, and it was impossible for him to get away.

He finally gave the order to counter-march, and we were nearing the pike when some of our cavalry came up, and they demanded our surrender. I explained to them how things stood, and that they could have all the pieces but one, but I wanted one at least. The officer in command allowed I had no business out there anyway, and he would take charge of the guns. We had quite an argument, but I had to let him have his own way.

I now came to the conclusion that I didn't want any guns, so I rode up the pike, where I soon got into their infantry, which was scattered over the lots on each side of the pike. On the pike were three lines of vehicles going at a slow trot, the lines being composed of pieces of artillery-, wagons, ambulances, and caissons, all mixed in together.

I rode alongside the pike until I came to a place where there was a down grade, and I then took a whip from one of the drivers and his "jerk-line" and swinging his lead mules over against the next team to him, I put the whip to them, and it was fun to see those mules try to climb over that team. In a few seconds there was a mix-up, mules, horses, wagons and drivers, being piled up, completely blocking the road.

I went back down the pike asking different drivers what they had in their wagons. I soon struck one that said he had three boxes of Yankee hard-tack, a wall tent, blankets, and the mess-kit of the surgeon of the Fourth Georgia. I asked him to pull out out into the lot, but he allowed that he would lose his place in line if he did; but as the line was halted, I persuaded him to do as I suggested, telling him I would answer all questions if anyone asked them.

I remained there some fifteen or twenty minutes, meanwhile there were hundreds of men going along, but no organisation to them. One small squad of four or five came by and they had two flags. I started to capture the flags, but saw a squad of mounted men coming, and waited for them to pass. One of them asked what I had the team there for, and I told him that the captain was wounded, and I was waiting to put him in the wagon, as I could not find an ambulance. He advised me to hurry up, as the Yankees were right near.

I followed up the flags for a minute or two, but finally weakened, and gave it up. When our cavalry came up I was again ordered to surrender, and I had quite a task to keep my wagon, but I soon led it down the pike, and at about nine o'clock I arrived at our camp. The driver of the team I had, as soon as he found I wasn't going to harm him, told me he was glad to get away from the rebel service.

Major DeForrest, aid on Gen. Emory's staff, in his letter published in *Harper's Monthly Magazine*, of February, 1865, gives the following:

Lieut. Gray, Company D, First Rhode Island Artillery, galloped up to a retreating battery and ordered it to face about. "I was told to go to the rear as rapidly as possible," remonstrated the sergeant in command. "You don't seem to know who I am," answered Gray. "I am one of those d——d Yanks. Counter-march immediately!" The battery was countermarched, and Gray was leading it off alone, when a squadron of our cavalry came up and made the capture a certainty.

As soon as we had eaten our hardtack, we made ourselves as comfortable as possible, and tried to get some sleep; but the night was chilly, and most of the men were up at daylight. We rather envied our officers, who had wall-tents and plenty of blankets (part of the contents of the captured wagon).

About nine o'clock in the morning we drew rations, and soon had hot coffee, which put us all right again; but it was nearly noon before we could obtain grain for our horses, by which time they were very hungry, having had nothing to eat for about forty-two hours.

Capt. Buckley arrived in camp at about five o'clock in the afternoon on the 18th, from his visit to Providence with the men that were mustered out. He did not take part in the proceedings of the battery on the 19th, and was mustered out Oct. 23rd.

Nov. 7th Elmer L. Corthell, who had established an excellent military reputation by long service on various fields, joined the battery and took command, having been promoted from First Lieutenant of Battery G, to Captain of Battery D. We found him a very efficient and conscientious officer.

We remained in camp in our old position at Cedar Creek until Nov. 9th, when we moved to near Newtown, and went into winter quarters.

On the 9th Early, hearing that Sheridan had fallen back, immediately advanced, and on the 11th crossed Cedar Creek. On the morning of the 12th Sheridan sent his cavalry out on both flanks and they had quite a sharp brush with Early's cavalry, and with the usual result. Dudley's brigade of the Nineteenth Corps, and a small force from the Sixth Corps, were advanced up the pike to assist the cavalry. Early soon found that Gen. Sheridan was still in the valley, and promptly retreated to his old camp at New Market. This was Early's last advance in the Shenandoah Valley.

We built shelter for our horses, and quite good quarters for the men; but we had not more than completed our quarters before we had orders to move nearer our base of supplies, so on Dec. 12th we broke camp and marched through Winchester to within a short distance of Stephenson Station.

This march was very hard on both men and horses, as it commenced to snow soon after we started, and when we arrived at camp there was about six inches of snow. It cleared up at night, and came out cold, the ground freezing up, making it quite a job to pitch our tents. There was very little sleep that night.

The next day we had time to log up our tents, and at once began to build shelters for our horses. We soon had a very comfortable camp, where we remained until the 10th of March, 1865, with no hard duty to perform.

By the middle of December Gen. Sheridan had sent all of the Sixth Corps to the Army of the Potomac, then in front of Petersburg. One division of the Eighth Corps was sent to City Point, and the other to West Virginia, the cavalry and the Nineteenth Corps remaining in the valley. The cavalry made a raid through Luray Valley and destroyed all the forage and wheat; they also drove off about three thousand sheep, one thousand hogs, and hundreds of cattle and horses.

On the 19th of December Torbert started up the valley with eight thousand cavalry, to strike the Virginia Central Railroad and destroy the James River Canal. This enterprise was not a success, and on the 27th he returned to Winchester, many of his men frost-bitten by the excessive cold.

This ended all movements until February 27th, when Gen.

Sheridan started with ten thousand cavalrymen and two sections of artillery on his successful trip up the valley, through to Grant's army before Petersburg. At Waynesboro he captured all of Early's command, and the valley was clear of any large force of the enemy.

On the 10th of March we broke camp and moved near Winchester, remaining in this camp a short time, and then moved to the east of Winchester about a mile and went into camp. Our duties there were light. We fired a salute of one hundred guns on Lee's surrender. Knowing that the war was about over, we had very short drills, both mounted and the manual.

On the 4th of July we received orders to turn in our battery and other government property, and proceed to Rhode Island. It is needless to say that this order was received by the men with every conceivable manifestation of joy; some hugged each other, while others shouted and threw their hats in the air, and when "water call" was blown it took fifteen minutes to form the line, but after that things quieted down, and on the morning of the 10th we started for home, under command of Capt. Corthell, taking the cars as far as New York, and then the steamer *John Brooks*, which landed us at Fox Point wharf on the morning of July 13th.

The officers accompanying Capt. Corthell and belonging to the battery were First Lieuts. Frederick Chase and Charles F. Bonn, and Second Lieut. Charles C. Gray. The men numbered ninety-five, and presented a remarkably fine appearance, having nearly new uniforms.

We were received by the Mechanic Rifles and a detachment of the Marine Artillery, and escorted to Washington Hall, where we found a bountiful collation prepared for us by L. H. Humphreys. The collation was soon over, and the men dismissed with orders to report at the Revenue Office, on South Main Street, on the 17th for final pay and muster out.

On the 17th of July, 1865, the battery was mustered out by Capt. Joseph S. York, of the Fifteenth United States Infantry, and Battery D, First Rhode Island Light Artillery, was no more; but we all felt that the battery had made a record that was honourable alike to itself and the State.

Roster

Aldrich, Halsey A., Corp., Providence, R. I. Sept. 4, 1861, enrolled; Sept. 4, 1861, mustered in. Originally served as private; Sept. 3, 1864, mustered out at Charlestown,Vn.

Andrews, Robert H., 1st Sergt.; Warwick, R. I. Sept. 4, 1861, enrolled; Sept. 4, 1861, mustered in. Originally served as Corp.; Nov. 12, 1861, promoted Sergt.; Aug. 30, 1862, wounded in action and borne as absent sick in hospital until April, 1863; Jan. 30, 1864, re-enlisted as Vet. Vol. Borne on furlough of fifteen days from April 29, 1865; June 25, 1865, promoted 1st Sergt.; July 17, 1865, mustered out.

Arnold, George E., Priv., Warwick, R. I. Sept. 4, 1861, enrolled; Sept. 4, 1861, mustered in; Aug. 29, 1862, captured at Bull Run, Va.; Sept. 1, 1862, released at Bull Run, Va., and reported at Camp Parole, Md. Borne as absent on detached service at Knoxville, Tenn., from Dec. 8, 1863, until Jan., 1864; Sept. 3, 1864, mustered out at Charlestown, Va.

Arnold, Olney, Priv., Lonsdale, R. I. Sept. 4, 1861, enrolled; Sept. 4, 1861, mustered in. Borne as absent sick in hospital, from May 21, 1863, until Oct. 8, 1863, when transferred to 74th Co. 2nd Bat.V. R. C; Sept. 4, 1864, mustered out as of 74th Co. 2nd Bat.V. R. C.

Austin, Allen, Priv., Warwick, R. I. Sept. 4, 1861, enrolled; Sept. 4, 1861, mustered in; April, 1864, absent sick in hospital, and so borne until Sept., 1864; Sept. 3, 1864, mustered out at Charlestown, Va.

Ballou, Stephen, Priv. Sept. 4, 1861, enrolled at Providence, R. I.; Sept. 4, 1861, mustered in; Sept. 3, 1864, mustered out at Charlestown, Va.

Barber, Robert F., Priv. Oct. 22, 1864, enrolled at Providence, R. I.; Oct. 22, 1864, mustered in; July 17, 1865, mustered out.

Bates, Daniel J., Priv. Dec. 22, 1862, transferred from Battery H. Borne as absent sick in hospital, from Feb. 7, 1863, until May, 1863.

Borne as absent sick in hospital, from Aug. 12, 1863, until Oct 15, 1863, when transferred to 83rd Co. 2nd Bat.V. R. C; May 15, 1865, mustered out as of 83rd Co. 2nd Bat.V. R. C.

Bennett, George, Priv. Dec. 4, 1862, enrolled at Providence, R.I; Dec. 4, 1862, mustered in. Probably recruited for Battery H. Re-enlisted as a Vet.Vol.; Jan., 1864, granted furlough of forty-five days; March 7, 1864, deserted at Providence, R. I.

Bennett, William R., Priv., Warwick, R. I. Sept. 4, 1861, enrolled; Sept. 4, 1861, mustered in. Relieved from duty as Corporal, by request; Sept. 17, 1862, missing in action; Dec. 22, 1862, joined from missing in action; Aug. 10, 1863, deserted at Cincinnati, Ohio. Bezely, John F., Priv., Coventry, R. I. Sept. 4, 1861, enrolled; Sept. 4, 1861, mustered in. Borne on detached service at Knoxville, Tenn., from Dec. 8, 1863, until Jan., 1864. Borne as absent sick in hospital, from Feb. 23, 1864, until March, 1864; Sept. 3, 1864, mustered out at Charlestown,Va.

Biglan, John, Priv., Woonsocket, R. I. Sept. 4, 1861, enrolled; Sept. 4, 1861, mustered in; Sept. 3, 1864, mustered out at Charlestown,Va. Mustered in as Biglow.

Billen, Michael, Priv. Oct. 26, 1864, enrolled at Providence, R. 1.; Oct. 26, 1864, mustered in; July 17, 1865, mustered out.

Bizburger, John, Artificer. Providence, R. I. Sept. 4, 1861, enrolled; Sept. 4, 1861, mustered in; Dec. 23, 1861, transferred to Battery G. Blush, Curtis A., Priv. July 9, 1863, enrolled at Camp Nelson, Ky.; July 17, 1865, mustered out.

Bonn, Charles E., 1st Lieut. April 26, 1864, commissioned. Mustered in to date from May 4, 1864. Promoted from 1st Sergt. Battery H, to 2nd Lieut. Battery D. Borne on leave of absence from Oct. 24, 1864, until Nov., 1864; Nov. 24, 1864, ordered on detached service as A. A. A. G. at Hdqrs. Art. Brig. 19th Army Corps, and so borne until July, 1865; April 3, 1865, commissioned 1st Lieut., and mustered in as such April 11, 1865; July 17, 1865, mustered out. Brevet Captain, for bravery and good conduct in the field, to date from March 13, 1865.

Botter, Erich P., Priv., North Kingstown, R. I. Oct. 20, 1862, en-rolled; Oct. 20, 1862, mustered in; July 17, 1865, mustered out.

Bourn, Samuel D., Priv. Nov. 30, 1864, enrolled at Providence, R.I.; March 12, 1865, discharged on Surgeon's certificate, at Stephenson's Station,Va.

Bowers, William R., Artificer, Providence, R.I. Sept. 4, 1861, enrolled; Sept. 4, 1861, mustered in; Dec. 23, 1861, transferred to Battery G.

Boyle, John, Priv. Dec. 7, 1864, enrolled at Providence, R. I.; Dec. 7, 1864, mustered in; July 17, 1865, mustered out.

Brady, Alexander, Priv., Pawtucket, R. I. March 25, 1864, enrolled; April 20, 1864, mustered in. Borne on furlough for fifteen days from May 23, 1865; July 17, 1865, mustered out.

Brand, William C, Priv., Coventry, R.I. Sept. 4, 1861, enrolled; Sept. 4, 1861, mustered in; March, 1862, in General Hospital; April 10, 1862, discharged on Surgeon's certificate, at camp near Bristoe, Va.

Brod, John, Artificer, North Kingstown, R.I. Oct. 20, 1862, enrolled; Oct.. 20, 1862, mustered in; July 17, 1865, mustered out.

Brown, Herbert M., Priv., North Providence, R. I. Aug. 8, 1862, enrolled; Aug. 8, 1862, mustered in; June 23, 1865, mustered out.

Brown, William W., Priv., Warwick, R. I. Aug. 14, 1862, enrolled; Aug. 14, 1862, mustered in; June 23, 1865, mustered out.

Buckley, Andrew, Priv., Pawtucket, R.I. March 14, 1864, enrolled; April 20, 1864, mustered in; Oct. 19, 1864, missing in action near Cedar Creek, Va. Gained and borne as absent sick in hospital, from Nov. 24, 1864, until Feb., 1865; July 17, 1865, mustered out.

Buckley, William W., Capt. Oct. 30, 1862, commissioned. Mustered in to date Nov. 1, 1862. Promoted from 1st Lieut. Battery C. Borne on leave of absence sick, from Jan. 18, 1863, until Feb. 28, 1863. Absent with leave from May 10, 1863, until June 8, 1863; March, 1864, absent with leave; Sept. 3, 1864, granted leave of absence; Oct. 23, 1864, mustered out; Brevet Major for faithful and meritorious services during the war, to date from March 13, 1865.

Budlong, Moses, Priv., Providence, R.I. Sept. 4, 1861, enrolled; Sept. 4, 1861, mustered in; Jan, 30, 1864, re-enlisted as a Vet. Vol.; July 17, 1865, mustered out.

Burdick, John C, Priv. Nov. 1, 1864, enrolled at Providence, R. I.; Nov. 1, 1864, mustered in; July 17, 1865, mustered out.

Burkhardy, Charles J., Priv. Dec. 19, 1864, enrolled at Providence, R. I.; Dec. 19, 1864, mustered in; July 17, 1865, mustered out.

Burns, Christopher, Priv., Pawtucket, R. I. March 14, 1864, enrolled; April 20, 1864, mustered in; July 17, 1865, mustered out.

Burt, Everett B., Priv., Providence, R. I. Sept. 4, 1861, enrolled;

Sept. 4, 1861, mustered in; Sept. 17, 1862, severely wounded at the battle of Antietam, and sent to hospital; borne as absent sick until June 27, 1863, when dropped from rolls. No further record.

Busby, John J., Priv., Pawtucket, R. I. Sept. 4, 1861, enrolled; Sept. 4,1861, mustered in; Jan. 30, 1864, re-enlisted as a Vet. Vol.; July 17, 1865, mustered out.

Caesar, Daniel, Priv., Smithfield, R. I. Sept. 4, 1861, enrolled; Sept. 4, 1861, mustered in; March 19, 1863, admitted to Chesapeake General Hospital, Fort Monroe, Va.; March 26, 1863, died of disease.

Caesar, Royal W., Priv., Smithfield, R. I. Sept. 4, 1861, enrolled; Sept. 4, 1861, mustered in; Sept. 17, 1862, injured by cannon shot at Antietam, sent to hospital and borne as absent sick until Dec, 1862; Sept. 6, 1864, mustered out at Providence, R. I.

Cahoone, Andrew J., Corp., Coventry, R. I. Sept. 4, 1861, enrolled; Sept. 4, 1861, mustered in. Originally served as private. Borne as absent on furlough for twenty days from June 14, 1863; borne on detached service at Knoxville, Tenn., from Dec. 8, 1863, until Jan., 1864; borne as absent sick in hospital, from Jan. 24, 1864, until Feb., 1864; Sept. 3, 1864, mustered out at Charlestown, Va.

Carrier, Andrew, Priv. Dec. 12, 1862, enrolled at Providence, R. I.; Feb. 10, 1863, deserted at Belle Plain Landing.

Card, Samuel A., Priv., Warwick, R. I. Sept. 4, 1861, enrolled; Sept. 4, 1861, mustered in. Borne as absent sick in hospital, from March 24, 1863, until March 7, 1864, when he deserted from hospital.

Carpenter, Christopher H., Priv., Providence, R. I. Sept. 4, 1861, enrolled; Sept. 4, 1861, mustered in; Sept. 3, 1864, mustered out at Charlestown, Va.

Carrigan, Thomas, Priv., Warwick, R. I. April 15, 1864, enrolled; Dec. 16, 1864, deserted near Opequon Creek, Va.

Carroll, Edward, Priv., Warwick, R. I. Sept. 4, 1861, enrolled; Sept. 4, 1861, mustered in; Sept. 17, 1862, killed in action at Antietam.

Carroll, James, Priv., Warwick, R. I. Feb. 21, 1862, enrolled; Sept., 1862, in General Hospital, and borne as absent sick until Nov. 21, 1862, when discharged on Surgeon's certificate at Mount Pleasant General Hospital, Washington, D. C.

Cary, Owen A., Priv., Providence, R. I. Oct. 28, 1864, enrolled; Oct. 28, 1864, mustered in; July 17, 1865, mustered out.

Chase, Frederick, 1st Lieut. Dec 4, 1862, commissioned. Promoted from Sergt. Battery F, to 2nd Lieut. Battery D. Borne on leave of absence for thirty days from Dec. 17, 1863; March, 1864, absent with leave; April 8, 1864, commissioned 1st Lieut., and mustered in as such to date April 8, 1864; Sept. 1864, commanding Battery, and so borne until Nov., 1864; borne on leave of absence from Nov. 20, 1864, until Dec, 1864; Jan., 1865, commanding Battery; June 12, 1865, commissioned Captain (never mustered); July 17. 1865, mustered out.

Collins, Alexander, Priv. Dec. 12, 1862, enrolled at Providence, R.I.; Feb. 10, 1863. deserted at Belle Plain Landing.

Corey, Augustus, Priv., Warwick, R. I. Sept. 4, 1861, enrolled; Sept. 4, 1861, mustered in; March 10, 1862, left in hospital at Upton's Hill, Va., having been run over by a caisson while in line of duty. April 24, 1862, discharged on Surgeon's certificate.

Corey, Joseph W., Priv., Providence, R. I. Sept. 4, 1861, enrolled; Sept. 4, 1861, mustered in; Jan. 30, 1864, re-enlisted as a Vet. Vol.; July 17, 1865, mustered out.

Cornell, Charles W., Priv., Coventry, R. I. Sept. 4, 1861, enrolled; Sept. 4, 1861, mustered in. Borne as absent sick in hospital from March 19, 1863, until Aug. I, 1863, when transferred to 30th Co., 2nd Bat. V. R. C; Nov. 28, 1865, mustered out as of 4th Co , 2nd Bat. V. R. C, to which transferred.

Cornell, Daniel B., Q. M. Sergt., Coventry, R. I. Sept. 4, 1861, enrolled; Sept. 4, 1861, mustered in. Originally served as Corp.; June 13, 1862, promoted Sergt. Borne on detached service at Knoxville, Tenn., from Dec. 8, 1863, until Jan., 1864; Jan. 30, 1864, re-enlisted as a Vet. Vol.; April 13, 1865, promoted Q. M. Sergt.; July 17, 1865, mustered out.

Cornell, Patrick, Priv., Smithfield, R. I. Sept. 4, 1861, enrolled; Sept. 4, 1861, mustered in. Borne as absent sick in hospital from Oct. 20, 1863, until March, 1864; Sept. 3, 1864, mustered out at Charlestown, Va.

Corthell, Elmer L., Capt. Oct. 21, 1864, commissioned; Nov. 2, 1864, mustered in. Promoted from 1st Lieut. Battery G. Borne on leave of absence for fifteen days from Jan. 21, 1865; July 17, 1865, mustered out.

Coyle, Olney. Priv., Providence, R. I. Nov. 19, 1864, enrolled; Nov. 19, 1864, mustered in; July 17, 1865, mustered out.

Crawford, William, Priv., Pawtucket, R. I. Sept. 4, 1801, enrolled; Sept. 4, 1861, mustered in; Sept. 3, 1864, mustered out at Charlestown, Va.

Cross, Benjamin, Corp. Dec. 22, 1862, transferred from private Battery H; Jan. 5, 1864, re-enlisted as a Vet. Vol.; Jan., 1864, granted furlough of forty-five days; Oct. 19, 1864, captured at Cedar Creek, Va.; April 1, 1865, escaped from Salisbury, N. C; May 2, 1865, reported at Camp Chase, Ohio; June 27, 1865, mustered out at Camp Chase, Ohio.

Cross, Henry C, Priv. Dec. 22, 1862, transferred from Battery H. Borne as absent sick in hospital from June 15, 1863, until Oct. 8, 1863, when transferred to 74th Co., 2nd Bat. V. R. C; Sept. 5, 1864, mustered out of the V. R. C. to accept commission as Capt. 115th U. S. C. Inf.; Feb. 10, 1866, mustered out as Capt. Co. D, 115th U. S. C. T.

Cullen, Patrick, Priv., Pawtucket, R. I. March 12, 1864, enrolled; April 20, 1864, mustered in. Borne as absent sick in hospital from Sept. 4, 1864, until Dec, 1864; July 17, 1865, mustered out.

Curigan, Thomas, Priv., Pawtucket, R. I. March 21, 1864, enrolled; April 20, 1864, mustered in. Borne on furlough for fifteen days from April 29, 1865; July 17, 1865, mustered out.

Currie, William, Priv., Westerly, R. I. Feb. 24, 1802, enrolled. Borne as absent sick from Dec. 30, 1862, until Feb. 9, 1863, when discharged on Surgeon's certificate, at Providence, R. I.

Daniels, William, Priv. Dec. 22, 1864, enrolled at Providence, R. I.; Dec. 22, 1864, mustered in; July 17, 1865, mustered out.

Darcy, Thomas, Priv., Pawtucket, R. I. March 16, 1864, enrolled; April 20, 1864, mustered in; July 17, 1865, mustered out.

Dearnley, James, Priv. Nov. 30, 1864, enrolled at Providence, R I.; Nov. 30, 1864, mustered in; July 17, 1865, mustered out.

Deming, Richard H., 1st Sergt., Providence, R. I. Sept. 4, 1861, enrolled; Sept. 4, 1861, mustered in; Dec. 4, 1861, discharged for disability, at Camp Dupont, Va.

DeSilvey, John W., Priv. July 30, 1863, enrolled; July 30, 1863, mustered in; July 17, 1865, mustered out. Dixon, John, Priv., Apponaug, R. I. Sept. 4, 1861, enrolled; Sept. 4, 1861, mustered in; Dec. 27, 1862, deserted at Falmouth, Va.

Dodge, Reuben D., Priv., Block Island, R. I. Sept. 4, 1861, enrolled; Sept. 4, 1861, mustered in; Sept. 17, 1862, wounded at the battle of

Antietam, sent to hospital and borne as absent sick until Dec, 1862; April 14, 1863, discharged on Surgeon's certificate, at Armory Square Hospital, Washington, D. C.

Dolan, Joseph, Priv. Dec. 12, 1862, enrolled at Providence, R. I. No further record.

Donnelly, James, Corp., Warwick, R. I. Sept. 4, 1861, enrolled; Sept. 4, 1861, mustered in. Originally served as private. Jan. 30, 1864, re-enlisted as a Vet. Vol. Borne on furlough of fifteen days from May 23, 1865; July 17, 1865, mustered out.

Doran, Hugh, Priv., Apponaug, K. I. Sept. 4, 1861, enrolled; Sept. 4, 1861, mustered in; Aug. 30, 1862, killed in action at Bull Run.

Doyle, Patrick, Priv. Dec. 12, 1862, enrolled at Providence, R. I. No further record.

Duddy, Thomas C. , Priv., Westerly, R I. Aug. 7, 1862, enrolled; April 20, 1864, deserted at Providence, R. I.

Edwards, Edwin, Priv., Warwick, R. I. Sept. 4, 1861, enrolled; Sept 4, 1861, mustered in; July, 1862, absent sick, and so borne until Oct., 1862; Dec. 13, 1862, discharged on Surgeon's certificate, at Providence, R. I.

Egan, John, Priv. Dec. 1, 1864, enrolled at Providence, R. I.; Dec. 1, 1864, mustered in; July 17, 1865, mustered out.

Eldred, George A., Corp., Coventry, R. I. Sept. 4, 1861, enrolled; Sept. 4, 1861, mustered in; Aug. 30, 1862, killed in action at Bull Run.

Elliott, Daniel. W., Priv., Smithfield, R. I. Sept. 4, 1861, enrolled; Sept. 4, 1861, mustered in; Jan. 30, 1864, re-enlisted as a Vet. Vol. Borne on furlough of fifteen days from Jan. 21, 1865; July 17, 1865, mustered out.

Ellis, Leonard G., Priv. Transferred from Battery A; Nov. 16, 1863, wounded at battle of Campbell's Station, Tenn.; June 23, 1865, mustered out.

Esser, Philip, Priv., Pawtucket, R. I. Sept. 4, 1861, enrolled; Sept. 4, 1861, mustered in; Dec. 3, 1861, admitted to General Hospital, Baltimore, Md.; Jan. 14, 1864, discharged at Providence, R. I. , to date Jan. 20, 1862.

Fairbrother, James H., Corp., Warwick, R. I. Sept 4, 1861, enrolled; Sept. 4, 1861, mustered in. Originally served as private; Sept. 3, 1864, mustered out at Charlestown, Va.

Finley, Roger, Priv., Providence, R. I. Sept. 4, 1861, enrolled; Sept. 4, 1861, mustered in; Oct., 1862, in General Hospital, and so borne until Dec, 1862; Oct. 12, 1863, discharged on Surgeon's certificate at Lovell General Hospital, Portsmouth Grove, R. I.

Fisk, Stephen W., 2nd Lieut., Providence, R. I. Sept. 7, 1861, commissioned; Sept. 9, 1861, mustered in; Dec. 4. 1862, promoted 1st Lieut. Battery C.

Fisk, William H., Priv. Sept. 4, 1861, enrolled at Providence, R. I.; Sept. 4, 1861, mustered in; Sept. 3, 1864, mustered out at Charlestown, Va.

French, Joseph B., Priv., Providence, R. I. July 18, 1862, enrolled; July 18, 1862, mustered in; June 23, 1865, discharged at Winchester, Va.

French, Joseph S., Priv., Providence, R. I. July 21, 1862, enrolled; July 21, 1862, mustered in; Oct. 24, 1862, died of disease at hospital, Smoketown, Md.

Galindo, Peter, Priv. Jan. 2, 1863, enrolled at Providence, R. I; Feb. 10, 1863, deserted at Belle Plain Landing.

Gallagher, Charles, Priv., Warwick, R. I. Sept. 4, 1861, enrolled; Sept. 4, 1861, mustered in. Borne as absent sick in hospital from July 15, 1863, until Aug., 1863; Sept. 3, 1864, mustered out at Charlestown, Va.

Galloughly, John, Priv., Providence, R. I. Sept. 4, 1861, enrolled; Sept. 4, 1861, mustered in; Sept. 17, 1862, killed in action at Antietam.

Gilmore, Solomon, Priv., Providence, R. I. Sept. 4, 1861, enrolled; Sept. 4, 1861, mustered in; Jan. 30, 1864, re-enlisted as a Vet. Vol.; July 17, 1865, mustered out.

Gladding, Henry R., 1st Lieut., Providence, R. I. Sept 7, 1861, commissioned; Sept. 9, 1861, mustered in; Nov. 30, 1862, mustered out. at Brooks Station, Va.; Aug. 1, 1863, commissioned 1st Lieut. Fifth Rhode Island Heavy Artillery. Never mustered in nor served under commission.

Glassey, John, Priv., Lonsdale, R. I. Sept. 4, 1861, enrolled; Sept. 4, 1861, mustered in; May, 1862, received injury, sent to hospital, and borne as absent sick until Oct. 7, 1862, when discharged on Surgeon's certificate, at Providence, R. I.

Goff, Bernard, Priv., Pawtucket, R. I. March 12, 1864, enrolled:

April 20, 1864, mustered in; July 17, 1865, mustered out.

Goodwin, Terrence, Priv., Pawtucket, R. I. March 14, 1864. enrolled; April 20, 1864, mustered in; Sept. 19, 1864, wounded at Battle of Winchester, Va., sent to hospital, and borne as absent sick until May 20, 1865, when discharged on Surgeon's certificate, at U. S. General Hospital, York, Pa.

Gordon. James, Priv., Pawtucket, R. I. March 18, 1864, enrolled; April 20, 1864, mustered in; July 17, 1865, mustered out.

Gorton, Erastus, Priv., Coventry, R. I. Sept. 4, 1861, enrolled; Sept. 4, 1861, mustered in. Borne on extra duty as teamster from March 1, 1863, until May, 1863; Jan. 30, 1864, re-enlisted as a Vet. Vol.; July 17, 1865, mustered out.

Gorton, John S., Priv., Coventry, R. I. Sept. 4, 1861, enrolled; Sept. 4, 1861, mustered in; Jan. 30, 1864, re-enlisted as a Vet. Vol. Borne as absent sick in hospital from Aug. 1, 1864, until Oct., 1864; July 17, 1865, mustered out.

Gray. Charles C., 2nd Lieut., Providence, R. I. Sept. 4, 1861, enrolled; Sept. 4, 1861, mustered in. Originally served as Corporal. Promoted Sergeant; Jan. 30, 1864, re-enlisted as a Vet. Vol; May 26, 1864, commissioned 2nd Lieut.; May 26, 1864, discharged as Sergeant to accept promotion. Mustered in as 2nd Lieut. to date May 27, 1864. Borne on detached service as Acting Ordnance Officer 19th Army Corps from Aug. 9, 1864, until Sept., 1864; June 12, 1865, commissioned 1st Lieut., never mustered; July 17, 1865, mustered out.

Green, John T., Priv., Coventry, R. I. Sept. 4, 1861, enrolled; Sept. 4, 1861, mustered in; March 6, 1863, died of disease at Newport News, Va.

Grey, John, Priv., Smithfield, R. I. Aug. 2, 1862, enrolled; May 18, 1863, discharged on Surgeon's certificate, at Providence, R. I.

Grinnell, Robert A., Priv., Warwick, R. I. Sept. 4, 1861, enrolled; Sept. 4, 1861, mustered in. Borne on detached service at Knoxville, Tenn., from Dec. 8, 1863, until Jan., 1864; Jan. 30, 1864, re-enlisted as a Vet. Vol.; July 17, 1865, mustered out.

Handy, Otis G., Priv. Sept. 4, 1861, enrolled at Providence, R. I.; Sept. 4, 1861, mustered in; Jan. 30, 1864, re-enlisted as a Vet. Vol.; July 17, 1865, mustered out.

Harkness, George C, 1st Lieut., Providence, R. I. Sept. 7, 1861, commissioned; Sept. 9, 1861, mustered in; Jan., 1862, on leave of absence; Aug. 30, 1862, wounded in action at Bull Run, and borne as absent sick until Nov., 1862; Nov., 1862, commanding Battery; March 3, 1863, discharged on lender of resignation.

Hathaway, Charles B., Priv. Sept. 4, 1861, enrolled at Providence, R.I.; Sept. 4, 1861, mustered in; April 24, 1863, deserted at Parkersburg, Va.

Havens, William, Priv., Warwick, R. I. Sept. 4, 1861, enrolled; Sept. 4, 1861, mustered in. Borne as absent sick in hospital from Jan. 21, 1864, until Sept., 1864; Sept. 3, 1864, discharged at Charlestown, Va.

Hawkins, George N., Priv., Coventry, R. I Sept. 4, 1861, enrolled; Sept. 4, 1861, mustered in; Jan. 30, 1864, re-enlisted as a Vet. Vol.; July 17, 1865, mustered out.

Hawkins, Richard) S., Priv., Coventry. R. I. Sept. 4, 1861, enrolled; Sept. 4, 1861, mustered in; Dec, 1861, absent sick in hospital, and so borne until Feb. 11, 1862, when discharged on Surgeon's certificate, at Georgetown, D. C.

Hayward, James S., Priv., Pawtucket, R. I. Sept. 4, 1861, enrolled; Sept. 4, 1861, mustered in. Borne as absent sick in hospital from July 13, 1862, until Oct., 1862; Sept. 3, 1864, mustered out at Charlestown, Va.

Hicks, Otis F., Priv., Providence, R. I. Sept. 4, 1861, enrolled; Sept. 4, 1861, mustered in; Aug. 30, 1862, killed in action at Bull Run.

Hollihan, Thomas, Priv., Warwick. R. I. Sept. 4, 1861, enrolled; Sept. 4, 1861, mustered in. Borne as absent sick in hospital from March 24, 1863, until April 26, 1864; Sept. 3, 1864, mustered out at Charlestown, Va.

Hood, William H., Priv., Warwick, R. I. Sept. 4, 1861, enrolled; Sept. 4, 1861, mustered in; Sept. 26, 1861, deserted at Camp Sprague, Washington, D. C.

Hopkins, Daniel, Priv., Foster, R. I. Feb. 24, 1862, enrolled; Aug. 28, 1862, missing in action, taken prisoner; date of parole not shown; Nov. 10, 1862, died of disease at Military Hospital, Camp Parole, Annapolis, Md.

Hopkins, Henry H., Priv., South Scituate, R. I. Sept. 4, 1861, enrolled; Sept. 4, 1861, mustered in. Borne as teamster from April 1, 1862, until Jan., 1863. Borne as absent sick in hospital from Jan. 25, 1863, until Sept. 3, 1864, when mustered out.

Hopkins, Henry W., Bugler, Foster, R. I. Sept. 4, 1861, enrolled;

Sept. 4, 1861, mustered in. Originally served as private; Jan. 30, 1864, re-enlisted as a Vet. Vol. Borne as absent sick in hospital from July 27, 1864, until Oct., 1864; July 17, 1865, mustered out.

Hopkins, Jeremiah D., Priv., Coventry, R. I. Sept. 4, 1861, enrolled; Sept. 4, 1861, mustered in; Nov., 1861, absent sick; Dec. 27, 1861, returned to duty; Sept. 17, 1862, wounded in action at Antietam, and borne as absent sick until Dec. 29, 1862, when discharged on Surgeon's certificate, at Frederick, Md.

Hopkins, John, Priv., West Greenwich, R. I. Sept. 4, 1861, enrolled; Sept. 4, 1861, mustered in; Jan. 12, 1862, discharged on Surgeon's certificate, at Camp Dupont, Va.

Hopkins, John W., Priv., Coventry, R. I. Sept. 4, 1861, enrolled; Sept. 4, 1861, mustered in; Sept. 17, 1862, wounded at the Battle of Antietam, and borne as absent sick in hospital until Dec, 1862; April 2, 1863, discharged on Surgeon's certificate.

Hopkins, Thomas W., Priv. Sept. 4, 1861, enrolled at Providence, R.I.; Sept. 4, 1861, mustered in; April 2, 1863, discharged on Surgeon's certificate, at Antietam Hospital, by reason of gun shot wound.

Howard, Martin L., Priv., North Scituate, R. I. Jan. 2, 1865. enrolled; Jan. 2, 1865, mustered in; July 17, 1865, mustered out. I

Hoxsie, Joseph W., Priv., West Greenwich, R. I. March 14, 1864, enrolled. Borne as absent sick in hospital from July 6, 1864, until August 13, 1864, when discharged for disability, at Judiciary Square Hospital, Washington, D. C.

Hunter, Samuel, Priv., Pawtucket, R. I. Nov. 17, 1864, enrolled; Nov. 17, 1864, mustered in; July 17, 1865, mustered out.

Jackson, Charles O., Priv. Sept. 4, 1861, enrolled at Providence, R. I.; Sept. 4, 1861, mustered in. Borne on detached service at Hdqrs. Chief of Arty., Dept. of the Ohio, from March 7, 1864, until Sept., 1864; Sept. 14, 1864, discharged at Providence, R. I , to date Sept. 3, 1864.

Jencks, Hezekiah, Artificer. Sept. 4, 1861, enrolled at Providence, R.I.; Sept. 4, 1861, mustered in; Jan., 1862, transferred to Battery B.

Jenkins, Samuel, Priv., Warwick, R. I. Sept. 4, 1861, enrolled; Sept. 4, 1861, mustered in; April, 1864, sick in hospital, and so borne until Sept., 1864; Sept. 3, 1864, discharged at Charlestown, Va.

Jerrold, Frederick L., Priv. Aug. 13, 1862, enrolled at Providence, R. I.; Aug., 1862, mustered in. Reported as having been transferred from

Battery B; June 23 1865, mustered out at Winchester, Va. Also borne as Jerraulds.

Johnson, Hugh, Priv., Providence, R. I. Nov. 25, 1864, enrolled; Nov. 25, 1864, mustered in; July 17, 1865, mustered out.

Johnson, Willett A., Priv., Warwick, R. I. Sept. 4, 1861, enrolled; Sept. 4, 1861, mustered in. Borne as absent sick from Sept. 2, 1862, until Dec. 29, 1862, when discharged on Surgeon's certificate, at Philadelphia.

Jones, Thomas Lloyd, Priv. Nov. 30, 1864, enrolled at Providence, R. I.; Nov. 30, 1864, mustered in; July 17, 1865, mustered out.

Keables, Thomas A., Priv., Westerly, R. I. Feb. 24, 1862, enrolled; June 4, 1862, discharged on Surgeon's certificate.

Keach, Jesse D., Priv., Smithfield, R. I. Oct. 27, 1864, enrolled; Oct. 27, 1864, mustered in; July 17, 1865, mustered out.

Kehoe, James, Priv., Pawtucket, R. I. March 12, 1864, enrolled; April 20, 1864 mustered in; July 17, 1865, mustered out.

Kelly, Patrick, Priv. July 27, 1864, enrolled at Providence, R. I.; July 27. 1864, mustered in. Transferred to Battery B.

Kennison, Charles H., Priv., Providence, R. I. Sept. 4, 1861, enrolled; Sept. 4, 1861, mustered in. Borne as absent sick from March 24, 1863, until Aug. 3, 1863, when discharged on Surgeon's certificate, at United States General Hospital, Baltimore, Md.

Kenyon, Joseph B., Priv., Warwick, R. I. Sept. 4, 1861, enrolled; Sept. 4, 1861, mustered in. Borne on duty as teamster from March I, 1863, until May, 1863; Sept. 3, 1864, mustered out at Charlestown, Va. Mustered in as John B. Kenyon.

Kilburn, Bernard, Priv., North Providence, R. I. Aug. 6, 1862, enrolled; Sept. 17, 1862, missing in action at Antietam. No further record.

Kimball, Charles H., Sergt., North Scituate, R. I. Sept. 4, 1861, enrolled; Sept. 4, 1861, mustered in. Originally served as Corp. Borne as absent sick in hospital from Oct. 20, 1863, until Dec, 1863; Dec. 13, 1863, died of disease in General Hospital, at Knoxville, Tenn.

Knight, Edwin R., Corp., Warwick, R. I. Sept. 4, 1861, enrolled; Sept. 4, 1861, mustered in; Aug., 1862, in General Hospital, and so borne until Dec, 1862; Jan. 30, 1864, re-enlisted as a Vet. Vol.; July 17, 1865, mustered out.

Knowles, John B., Priv., Warwick, R. I. Sept. 4, 1861, enrolled; Sept. 4, 1861, mustered in; Oct. 12, 1861, discharged on Surgeon's certificate, at Camp Sprague, Washington, D. C.

Landry, Joseph, Priv. Nov. 5, 1864, enrolled at Providence, R. I.; Nov. 5, 1864, mustered in; July 17, 1865, mustered out.

Lee, Royal Henry, 1st Sergt., Pawtucket, R. I. Sept. 4, 1861, enrolled; Sept. 4, 1861, mustered in. Originally served as Sergt.; Nov. 12, 1861, promoted 1st Sergt.; Dec. 25, 1862, discharged to accept promotion as 2nd Lieut., Battery C.

Lewis, Clark, Priv., Richmond, R. I. Jan. 2, 1865, enrolled; Jan. 2, 1865, mustered in; July 17, 1865, mustered out. Linn, Peter, Corp., Pawtucket, R. I. March 12, 1864, enrolled; April 20, 1864, mustered in. Borne on furlough of fifteen days from Jan. 21, 1865; March 25, 1865, promoted Corp.; July 17, 1865, mustered out.

Locke, James W., Priv. Sept. 4, 1861, enrolled at Providence, R. L; Sept. 4, 1861, mustered in. Borne on detached service at Knoxville, Tenn., from Dec. 8, 1863, until Jan., 1864; Jan. 30, 1864, re-enlisted as a Vet. Vol.; July 17, 1865, mustered out.

Loper, Peter, Priv. Transferred from Battery H; April 24. 1863, deserted at Baltimore, Md. Also borne as Lopez.

Lopez, Manuel, Priv. Jan. 2, 1863, enrolled at Providence, R. I. Feb. 10, 1863, deserted at Belle Plain Landing, Va.

Lynch, Daniel, Priv., Pawtucket, R. I. March 16, 1864, enrolled; April 20, 1864, mustered in; July 17, 1865, mustered out.

Lyon, Lewis, Priv. Dec. 22, 1862, transferred from Battery H; Sept. 14, 1863, deserted at Loudon, Tenn.

Matthews, Albert N., Corp. Sept. 4, 1861, enrolled at Providence, R. L; Sept. 4, 1861, mustered in. Originally served as private. Borne as absent sick in hospital from March 21, 1863, until Dec, 1863; Jan. 30, 1864, re-enlisted as a Vet. Vol.; Sept , 1864, absent sick in hospital; Nov. 30, 1864, detached for service at Hdqrs. Arty. Brig., 19th Army Corps; July 17, 1865, mustered out.

Mattison, Anson, Sergt., Warwick, R. I. Sept. 4, 1861, enrolled; Sept. 4, 1861, mustered in. Originally served as private. Promoted Corp.; Jan. 30, 1864, re-enlisted as a Vet. Vol.; July 17, 1865, mustered out.

Mattison, Edmund H., Priv., Warwick, R. I. Sept. 4, 1861, enrolled; Sept. 4, 1861, mustered in; Jan. 30, 1864, re-enlisted as a Vet. Vol.; July 17, 1865, mustered out.

May, Charles E., Bugler. Sept. 4, 1861, enrolled at Providence, R.I.; Sept. 4, 1861, mustered in. Borne as absent sick from Nov. 16, 1862, until June, 1863; June, 1864, in hospital, and so borne until Sept., 1864; Sept. 20, 1864, mustered out at Providence, R. I.

McCann, John, Priv. July 22, 1862, enrolled at Providence, R. L; July 22, 1862, mustered in. Probably recruited for Battery E; June 23, 1865, discharged at Winchester, Va.

McCausland, Alexander, Priv., Warwick, R. I. Aug. 13, 1862, enrolled; Aug. 13, 1862, mustered in. Borne on detached service at Knoxville, Tenn., from Dec. 8, 1863, until Jan., 1864; Nov. 30, 1864, detached for service at Hdqrs. Arty. Brig., 19th Army Corps; June 23, 1865, discharged at Winchester, Va.

McCausland, Norman L., Priv. Sept. 4, 1861, enrolled at Providence, R. 1; Sept. 4, 1861, mustered in; March, 1862, in General Hospital; April 10, 1862, discharged on Surgeon's certificate, at camp near Bristoe, Va.

McCormick, James P., Jr., Priv., Pawtucket, R. I. Sept. 4, 1861, enrolled; Sept. 4, 1 86 1, mustered in; Dec. 27, 1862, deserted at camp near Falmouth Station, Va.

McGinnity, John, Priv., Pawtucket, R. I. March 12, 1864, enrolled; April 20, 1864, mustered in; July 17, 1865, mustered out.

McGovern, John, Priv., Providence, R. I. Sept. 4, 1861, enrolled; Sept. 4, 1861, mustered in; Sept. 17, 1862, killed in action at Antietam.

McKearnan, Edward, Priv., Warwick, R. I. Sept. 4, 1861, enrolled; Sept. 4, 1861, mustered in; Jan. 30, 1864, re-enlisted as a Vet. Vol.; July 17, 1865, mustered out.

McKenna, James F., Priv., Pawtucket, R. I. Sept. 4, 1861, enrolled; Sept. 4, 1861, mustered in. Borne as absent sick in hospital from July 29, 1863, until Aug., 1863; Jan. 30, 1864, re-enlisted as a Vet. Vol. Borne as absent sick in hospital from Aug. 24, 1864, until Feb., 1865. Borne as absent sick in hospital from April 6, 1865, until June 7, 1865; July 17, 1865, mustered out.

McKenna, John, Priv., Warwick, R. I. Aug. 13, 1862, enrolled; Aug. 13, 1862, mustered in; Dec. 8, 1863, detached for service at Knoxville, Tenn.; June 23, 1865, discharged at Winchester, Va.

McKenna, John, 1st, Priv., Warwick, R. I. Sept. 4, 1861, enrolled; Sept. 4, 1861, mustered in; Sept. 3, 1864, mustered out at Charlestown, Va.

McLaughlin, John, Priv. Nov. 25. 1864, enrolled at Providence, R.I.; Nov. 25, 1864, mustered in; July 17, 1865, mustered out.

McMannus, James, Priv. Nov. 30, 1864, enrolled at Providence, R.I.; Nov. 30, 1864, mustered in; July 17, 1865, mustered out.

McQuade, Patrick, Priv. Oct. 22, 1864, enrolled at Providence, R.I,; Oct. 22, 1864, mustered in; July 17, 1865, mustered out.

Means, Joseph F., Priv., North Providence, R. I.; Nov. 23, 1864, enrolled; Nov. 23, 1864, mustered in; July 17, 1865, mustered out.

Mendosa, Raphael, Priv. Dec. 12, 1862, enrolled at Providence, R.I.; Dec. 12, 1862, mustered in. Originally assigned to Battery H; Feb. 1, 1863, deserted at Falmouth, Va.

Mills, William T., Priv., Warwick, R. I. Sept. 4, 1861 enrolled; Sept. 4, 1861, mustered in; Jan. 30, 1864, re-enlisted as a Vet. Vol. Borne as sick in hospital from May 15, 1865, until June, 1865. Borne on furlough of twenty days from June 10, 1865; July 17, 1865, mustered out.

Milne, William O., Sergt. Sept. 4, 1861, enrolled at Providence, R.I.; Sept. 4, 1861, mustered in. Promoted Corp. Absent on furlough for fifteen days from July 24, 1863; Jan. 30, 1864, re-enlisted as a Vet. Vol.; July 17, 1865, mustered out.

Moore, Frederick, Priv., Westerly, R. I. Feb. 20, 1862, enrolled; Feb. 25 1864, mustered out by virtue of re-enlistment; Feb. 26, 1864, re-enlisted as a Vet. Vol.; July 17, 1865, mustered out.

Monroe, J. Albert, Capt., Providence, R. I. June 6, 1861, commissioned; June 6, 1861, mustered in. Originally served as 1st Lieut. Battery A; Sept. 7, 1861, commissioned Captain, mustered in as such to date from Sept. 7, 1861, and assigned to Battery D; Oct. 24, 1862, promoted Major; Oct. 29, 1862, resigned as Captain to accept promotion.

Moore, John, Priv., Westerly, R. I. Feb. 24, 1862, enrolled; Feb. 25, 1864, mustered out by virtue of re-enlistment; Feb. 26, 1864, re-enlisted as a Vet. Vol. Borne as absent sick in hospital from July 27, 1864, until Oct., 1864; July 17, 1865 mustered out.

Morgan, Edward, Priv., North Kingstown, R. I. Oct. 13, 1862, enrolled; Oct. 13, 1862, mustered in. Deserted, date not shown.

Morgan, Michael, Priv., Richmond, R. I. Oct. 13, 1862, enrolled; Oct. 13, 1862, mustered in. Deserted, date not shown.

Morrell, Joseph, Priv. Nov. 5, 1864, enrolled at Providence, R. I.;

Nov. 5, 1864, mustered in; July 17, 1865, mustered out.

Mulick, Charles A., Priv., Providence, R. I. July 19, 1862, enrolled; Dec. 6, 1862, discharged on Surgeon's certificate, at Providence, R. I.

Nicholas, Lyman, Priv., Coventry, R. I. Sept. 4, 1861, enrolled; Sept. 4, 1861, mustered in; Feb. 19, 1864, ordered on special duty as teamer. Borne as absent sick in hospital from July 16, 1864, until Sept., 1864; Sept. 3, 1864, discharged at Charlestown, Va.

Nickerson, David R., Priv., Coventry, R. I. Sept. 4, 1861, enrolled; Sept. 4, 1861, mustered in; Nov., 1861, on extra duty at hospital, and so borne until May, 1862. Borne as absent sick in hospital from July 13, 1862, until Nov. 16, 1862, when discharged on Surgeon's certificate, at Fort McHenry.

Nichols, Edward L., Sergt. Aug. 11, 1862, enrolled at Falmouth, Va.; Aug. 11, 1862, mustered in. Originally served as private; June 1, 1863, promoted 1st Lieut. Va. Arty.; June 14, 1863, discharged by reason of promotion.

Norris, Bradley J., Priv. Dec. 22, 1862, transferred from Battery H. Borne as absent sick in hospital from Dec. 28, 1863, until Jan. 3, 1864, when he (lied of disease at camp near Blaine's Cross Roads, Tenn.

Cakes, William A., Priv., Providence, R. I. Sept. 4, 1861, enrolled; Sept. 4, 1861, mustered in; Aug. 30, 1862, wounded and borne as absent sick until Dec, 1862; borne as absent sick in hospital, probably wounded, from Nov. 27. 1863, until March, 1864; Sept. 3, 1864, mustered out at Charlestown, Va.

Oglesby, Samuel S., Priv., Providence, R. I. Sept. 4,1861, enrolled; Sept. 4, 1861, mustered in; Jan. 30, 1864, re-enlisted as a Vet. Vol. Borne as absent on furlough of fifteen days from Jan. 21, 1865; July 17, 1865, mustered out. Also borne as Samuel I.

O'Rourke, John, Priv., Providence, R. I. Sept. 4, 1861, enrolled; Sept. 4, 1861, mustered in; April 10, 1862, discharged on surgeon's certificate, at Camp near Bristoe, Va.

O'Rourke, Mathew, Priv., Providence, R. I. Sept. 4, 1861, enrolled; Sept. 4, 1861, mustered in; May 10, 1862, left in hospital at Upton's Hill, Va.; May 26, 1862, discharged on Surgeon's certificate.

Parker, Ezra K., 2nd Lieut., Coventry, R. I. Sept. 7, 1861, commissioned; Sept. 9, 1861, mustered in; Nov. 30, 1862, mustered out and re-commissioned 2nd Lieut., by Governor of Rhode Island same day; again mustered in to date Dec. 15, 1862. Borne on detached service at Knoxville, Tenn., from Dec. 8, 1863, until Jan., 1864; March, 1864, absent with leave; April 23, 1864, mustered out by reason of promotion to 1st Lieut. Battery E.

Parmenter, Orange S., Corp., Providence, R. I. Sept. 4, 1861, enrolled; Sept. 4, 1861, mustered in; Jan. 10, 1862, discharged on surgeon's certificate, at Camp Dupont, Va.

Peckham, William S., Priv., Wakefield, R. I. Sept. 4, 1861, enrolled; Sept. 4, 1861, mustered in; June, 1862, on extra duty as teamster, and so borne until Oct., 1862. Borne as absent sick from Oct. 30, 1862, until Dec, 1862; Feb. 28, 1863, discharged on Surgeon's certificate, at Providence, R. I.

Perez, Joseph, Priv. Jan. 2, 1863, enrolled at Providence, R. L; Jan. 2, 1863, mustered in; July 12, 1863, deserted at Nicholasville, Ky.

Phetteplace. David, Priv. Dec. 21, 1864, enrolled at Providence, R.I., Dec. 21, 1864, mustered in; July 17, 1865, mustered out.

Phillips, George G., Priv., Providence, R. I. July 21, 1862, enrolled; Sept. 13, 1862, deserted at New Market, Md. Also borne as George V.

Phinney, Thomas R., Priv., Providence, R. I. Sept. 4, 1862, enrolled; Sept 19, 1864, wounded in action near Winchester, Va., sent to hospital and borne as absent sick until May 19, 1865, when mustered out from United States General Hospital, West Philadelphia, Pa.

Pickering, Daniel, Priv., Scituate, R. I. Sept. 4, 1861, enrolled; Sept. 4, 1861, mustered in. Borne as absent sick in hospital from Sept. 2, 1862, until Dec. 6, 1862, when discharged on Surgeon's certificate, at Philadelphia.

Pierce, William T. Priv., Providence, R. I. Sept. 4, 1861, enrolled; Sept. 4, 1861, mustered in; Jan. 30, 1864, re-enlisted as a Vet. Vol.; July 17, 1865, mustered out.

Pinkham, Charles H., Priv., Providence, R. I. Nov. 7, 1864, enrolled; Nov. 7, 1864, mustered in; July 17, 1865, mustered out.

Pitcher, Joseph S., Priv., Providence, R. I. July 12, 1862, enrolled; April 21, 1864, discharged on Surgeon's certificate, at Lovell General Hospital, Portsmouth Grove, R. I. , by reason of injuries received while on duty at Fredericksburg, Va., Dec, 1862.

Place, John E., Priv., Warwick, R. I. Sept. 4, 1861, enrolled; Sept. 4, 1861, mustered in; Nov. 20, 1863, transferred to Co. G, 1st Regt. V. K. C; Nov. 14, 1865, mustered out as of Co. G, 1st Regt. V. R. C.

Place, Joseph B., Priv., West Greenwich, R. I. Aug. 13, 1862, enrolled; Aug. 23. 1862, mustered in. Transferred to Battery B, previous to Oct. 31, 1862.

Pollard, John, Jr., Priv., Cranston, R. I, Feb. 20, 1862, enrolled. Borne as absent sick in hospital from June 29, 1862, until July 31, 1862, when discharged on Surgeon's certificate, at Fredericksburg, Va.

Potter, Frank A., Priv., Providence, R. I. Sept. 4, 1861, enrolled; Sept. 4, 1861, mustered in; Sept. 17, 1862, missing in action at Antietam. No further record.

Pratt, Albert F., Q. M. Sergt. Sept. 4, 1861, enrolled at Providence, R. I.; Sept. 4, 186 1, mustered in. Originally served as Corp.; promoted Sergt. Borne on detached service at Knoxville, Tenn., from Dec. 8, 1863, until Jan., 1864; Jan. 30, 1864, re-enlisted as a Vet. Vol.; Oct. 19, 1864, wounded at Cedar Creek, Va., and borne as absent sick in hospital until April 13. 1865, when discharged on Surgeon's certificate, at Baltimore, Md.

Pratt. Henry B., Priv. Sept. 28, 1861, transferred from Battery C; Oct. 7, 1863, transferred to 19th Co., 2nd Bat. V. R. C; Oct. 25, 1864, mustered out as of the same.

Ragan, William H., Priv. Oct. 26, 1864, enrolled at Providence, R.I.; Oct. 26, 1864, mustered in; July 17, 1865, mustered out.

Rathbone, John, Priv., West Greenwich, R. I. March 4, 1864, enrolled; March 4, 1864, mustered in; Oct. 19, 1864, captured at Cedar Creek, Va.; March, 1865, released at N. E. Ferry, N. C; subsequently reported at Camp Parole, Md.; May 3, 1865, sent to Camp Distribution, Va.; June 23, 1865, mustered out at Winchester, Va.

Rawson, Samuel G., Priv. Sept. 4, 1861, enrolled at Providence, R.I.; Sept. 4, 1861, mustered in; Dec. 5, 1861, discharged at Regimental Hospital. Rector, John H., Priv., North Kingstown, R. I. Sept. 13. 1862, enrolled; Sept. 13, 1862, mustered in. No further record.

Remington, Charles R., Priv., Providence, R. I. Aug. 25, 1861, enrolled; Aug. 27, 1861, mustered in; Aug. 25, 1864, mustered out at Halltown, Va.

Reynolds, Thomas J., Corp. Sept. 4, 1861, enrolled at Providence, R. I.; Sept. 4, 1861, mustered in. Borne on furlough of twenty days from June 14, 1863. Borne on detached service at Knoxville, Tenn.. from Dec. 8, 1863, until Jan., 1864; Jan. 30, 1864, re-enlisted as a Vet. Vol.; July 17, 1865, mustered out.

Rhodes, Francis W., Priv., Warwick, R. I. Sept. 4, 1861, enrolled; Sept. 4, 1861, mustered in; Jan. 12, 1862, discharged on Surgeon's certificate, at Camp Dupont, Va.

Rhodes, William B., 1st Lieut. Dec. 26, 1862, transferred from Battery G. Commanding Battery from May 10, 1863, until June, 1863; March, 1864, absent with leave. Mustered out to date April 7, 1864, to accept promotion as Captain Battery E.

Rice, John E., Priv., Warwick, R. I. Sept. 4, 1861, enrolled; Sept. 4, 1861, mustered in; March, 1862, in General Hospital, and so borne until May 12, 1862, when discharged on Surgeon's certificate.

Rice, William T., Priv., Warwick, R. T. Sept. 4, 1861, enrolled; Sept. 4, 1861, mustered in. Borne as absent sick in hospital from Dec. 10, 1861, until March 25, 1862, when discharged on Surgeon's certificate, at General Hospital, Alexandria, Va.

Richardson, James A., Priv. Sept. 4, 1861, enrolled at Providence, R.I.; Sept. 4, 1861, mustered in. Borne as absent sick in hospital from May 21, 1863, until Aug., 1863. Borne on detached service at Knoxville, Tenn., from Dec. 8, 1863, until Jan., 1864; Jan. 30, 1864, re-enlisted as a Vet. Vol.; July 17, 1865, mustered out.

Rider, Hugh, Priv., Providence, R. I. Sept. 4, 1861, enrolled; Sept. 4, 1861, mustered in. Borne on detached service at Knoxville, Tenn., from Dec. 8, 1863, until Jan., 1864; Jan. 30, 1864, re-enlisted as a Vet. Vol. Borne on furlough of ten days from June 27, 1864; July 17, 1865, mustered out.

Robbins, Duty, Priv., Warwick, R. I. Aug. 14, 1862, enrolled; Sept. 17, 1862, missing in action at Antietam. No further record.

Rober, John, Priv. Transferred from Battery H; March 10, 1863, deserted at Newport News, Va.

Ross, David G., Priv., Warwick, R. I. Sept. 4, 1861, enrolled; Sept. 4, 1861, mustered in; Sept. 3, 1864, mustered out at Charlestown, Va.

Ross, John M., Priv. Oct. 18, 1864, enrolled at Providence, R. I.; July 17, 1865, mustered out. Also borne as John M. Rose.

Russell, Francis, Priv. Sept. 4, 1861, enrolled at Providence, R. I.; Sept. 4, 1861, mustered in; Sept. 17, 1862, missing in notion at Antietam. No further record.

Russell, Isaac D., Priv., South Kingstown, R. I. Sept. 4, 1861, enrolled; Sept. 4, 1861, mustered in; Jan. 30, 1864, re-enlisted as a Vet. Vol.; July 17, 1865. mustered out.

Samaniego, Joseph, Priv. Dec. 30, 1862, enrolled at Providence, R.I.; Feb. 10, 1863, deserted at Belle Plain Landing.

Schmidt, I. Jacob, Priv., Providence, R. I. Sept. 4, 1861, enrolled; Sept. 4, 1861, mustered in. Borne as absent sick in hospital from June 22, 1863, until Oct. 31, 1863, when transferred to 43rd Co., 2nd Bat. V. R. C; re-transferred to Battery D, by order dated Aug. 8, 1864; Sept. 3, 1864, mustered out at Charlestown, Va.

Shaw, David, Priv., Providence, R. I. Sept. 4, 1861, enrolled; Sept. 4, 1861, mustered in. Borne as absent sick in hospital at Falmouth, Va., from May 18, 1862, until Aug., 1862; Sept. 3, 1864, mustered out at Charlestown, Va.

Sheldon, Charles B., Priv., Warwick, R. I. Sept. 4, 1861, enrolled; Sept. 4, 1861, mustered in; Aug. 30, 1862, wounded in action, and borne as absent sick until Jan. 16, 1863, when discharged on Surgeon's certificate, at Philadelphia, Pa.

Shourdon, Robert, Priv., Lonsdale, R. I. Sept. 4, 1861, enrolled; Sept. 4, 1861, mustered in. Borne as absent sick in hospital from March 24, 1863, until Jan. 25, 1864, when discharged on Surgeon's certificate, at Lovell General Hospital, Portsmouth Grove, R. I.

Slocum, Isaac P., Priv., Westerly, R. I. Feb. 24, 1862, enrolled; June 7, 1862, left in hospital at camp near Haymarket, Va., and borne as absent sick until Oct. 10, 1862, when dropped from rolls. No further record.

Smith, David, Priv., Westerly, R. I. Aug. 16, 1862, enrolled; Sept. 17, 1862, missing in action at Antietam. No further record.

Smith, Henry W., Bugler, North Providence, R. I. Sept. 4, 1861, enrolled; Sept. 4, 1861, mustered in. Borne as absent sick from March 21, 1863, until May, 1863; Jan 30, 1864, re-enlisted as a Vet. Vol.; July 17, 1865, mustered out

Smith, Israel S., Priv., Providence, R. I. Nov. 22, 1864, enrolled; Nov. 22, 1864, mustered in; July 17, 1865, mustered out.

Smith, William G., Priv. Dec. 22, 1862, transferred from Battery H; Sept. 19, 1864, wounded in action near Winchester, Va., sent to hospital and borne as absent sick until June 19, 1865, when mustered out from United States Army Hospital, York, Pa.

Smith, William R., Priv. Sept. 4, 1861, enrolled at Providence, R. I.; Sept. 4, 1861, mustered in. Borne as absent sick in hospital from March 21, 1863, until Sept., 1864; Sept. 3, 1864, mustered out at Charlestown, Va.

Spear, John W., Priv., Richmond, R. I. Aug. 9, 1862, enrolled. Borne as absent sick from April 5, 1863, until May 26, 1863, when he deserted from United States Hospital, Cincinnati; July 17, 1863, returned from desertion; Jan. 14, 1864, deserted at Blaine's Cross Roads, Tenn.

Spencer, Gideon, Sergt., Warwick, R. I. Sept. 4, 1861, enrolled; Sept. 4, 1861, mustered in. Originally served as private; Jan. 30, 1864, re-enlisted as a Vet. Vol. Discharged to date April 28, 1864, by reason of promotion to 2nd Lieut. Battery B.

Stalker, William, Priv., Providence, R. I. Sept. 4, 1861, enrolled; Sept. 4, 1861, mustered in; Aug. 30, 1862, wounded at the battle of Bull Run; Sept. 3, 1864, mustered out at Charlestown, Va.

Steinhaur, Kirby, 1st Lieut. Feb. 8, 1863, commissioned; April 14, 1863, promoted from 2nd Lieut. Battery H. Borne on leave of absence for thirty days from Oct. 22, 1863; March, 1864, absent with leave; April 19, 1864, resigned.

Stickney, Daniel, Priv. Regimental return for Dec, 1862, reported him "Dropped Dec. 21, 1862, by G. O. 15, 1st A. C." No additional information found.

Stillman, Gideon S., Corp., Warwick, R. I. Sept. 4, 1861, enrolled; Sept. 4, 1861, mustered in. Originally served as private. Borne on extra duty as teamster from March 1, 1863, until May, 1863; Jan. 30, 1864, re-enlisted as a Vet. Vol.; July 17, 1865, mustered out.

Stinson, James, Priv. Transferred from Battery B, by order dated Jan. 1, 1862; Sept. 13, 1862, deserted at New Market, Md.

St. John, John, Corp., Providence, R. I. Sept. 4, 1861, enrolled; Sept. 4, 1861, mustered in. Originally served as private; Jan. 30, 1864, re-enlisted as a Vet. Vol.; July 17, 1865, mustered out.

Stollard, George F., Priv. October 31, 1864, enrolled at Providence, R. I.; Oct. 31, 1864, mustered in; July 17, 1865, mustered out.

Sullivan, Jeremiah, Priv., Warwick, R. I. Sept. 4, 1861, enrolled; Sept. 4, 1861, mustered in. Borne as absent sick in hospital from Aug. 7, 1863, until March 1864; Sept. 3, 1864, mustered out at Charlestown, Va.

Sullivan, John, Priv. Sept. 4, 1861, enrolled at Providence, R. I.; Sept. 4, 1861, mustered in; Sept., 1862, in General Hospital; Oct., 1862, on detached service at Div. Hdqrs., and so borne until March, 1863; April, 1863, deserted.

Sumner, George C, Priv., Providence, R. I. Sept. 4, 1861, enrolled;

Sept. 4. 1 861, mustered in; Sept. 3, 1864, mustered out at Charles-town, Va.

Sunderland, Henry A., Corp., Warwick, R. I. Sept. 4, 1861, en-rolled; Sept. 4, 1861, mustered in; Dec. 5, 1862, discharged on sur-geon's certificate, at Washington, D. C, by reason of injuries received when entering battle of Antietam.

Sutton, Henry L., Priv., Bristol, R. I. Dec. 31, 1864, enrolled; Dec. 31, 1864, mustered in; July 17, 1865, mustered out.

Swan, William, Priv., Providence, R. I. Sept. 4, 1861, enrolled; Sept. 4, 1861, mustered in. Borne as absent sick in hospital at Fredericks-burg, Va., from July 13, 1862, until Sept. 22, 1862, when discharged on Surgeon's certificate, at Cranch Hospital, Washington, D. C.

Taft, Anthony, Priv., Woonsocket, R. I. Nov. 28, 1864, enrolled; Nov. 28, 1864, mustered in; July 17, 1865, mustered out.

Taft, Charles CJ., Priv., Providence, R. I. Sept. 4, 1861, enrolled; Sept. 4, 1861, mustered in; April 24, 1863, deserted at Lexington, Ky.

Tanner, David B., Priv., Warwick, R. I. Sept. 4, 1861, enrolled; Sept. 4, 1861, mustered in. Borne .ns absent sick in hospital from Oct. 15, 1861, until March, 1862; April 7, 1862, discharged on Surgeon's cer-tificate, at Washington, D. C.

Tanner, James, Priv., Warwick, R.I. Sept. 4, 1861, enrolled; Sept. 4, 1861, mustered in. Borne on detached service at Knoxville, Tenn., from Dec. 8, 1863, until Jan. 1864; Jan. 30, 1864, re-enlisted as a Vet. Vol. Borne on furlough of ten days from March 20, 1865; July 17, 1865, mustered out.

Thornley, William H., Artificer, Providence, R. I. Sept. 4, 1861, en-rolled; Sept. 4. 1861, mustered in. Borne as absent sick in hospital from July 13, 1862, until Oct. 30, 1862, when discharged on Surgeon's cer-tificate, at Fort McHenry

Therber, Edwin I., Priv., Johnston, R. I. Sept. 4, 1861, enrolled; Sept. 4, 1861, mustered in; Sept. 28, 1861, transferred to Battery C Mustered in as Edward J. Thurber.

Tibbetts, J. R., Priv., Warwick, R. I. Sept. 4, 1861, enrolled; Sept. 4, 1861, mustered in; Nov. 12, 1861, discharged at Camp Dupont, Va.

Troutay, Alexander, Priv. Nov. 5, 1864, enrolled at Providence, R. I.; Nov. 5, 1864, mustered in; July 17, 1865, mustered out.

Tucker, Frank M., Sergt. Sept. 4, 1861, enrolled at Providence, R.I.;

Sept. 4, 1861, mustered in. Originally served as Corp.; Jan. 30, 1864, re-enlisted as a Vet.Vol.; June 12, 1865, commissioned 2nd Lieut., for gallant and meritorious service during the war; never mustered in; July 17, 1865, mustered out.

Tyson, John, Priv., Portsmouth, R. I. Aug. 6, 1862, enrolled; Aug. 6, 1862, mustered in; June 23, 1865, discharged at Winchester, Va.

Underwood, William J., Priv., Scituate, R. I.. Aug. 14, 1862, enrolled; Dec. 27, 1862, deserted at Falmouth, Va.; Jan. 10, 1863, joined from desertion, tried by G. C. M., and sentenced to be dishonourably discharged.

Vickery, William H., Priv., Warwick, R. I. Sept. 4, 1861, enrolled; Sept. 4, 1861, mustered in; Jan. 3. 1862, injured by a fall from his horse; May 3, 1862, discharged on Surgeon's certificate, at Philadelphia, Pa.

Wagg, Charles, Priv. Nov. 30, 1864, enrolled at Providence, R. I.; Nov. 30, 1864, mustered in. Borne as sick in hospital from June 3, 1865, until July, 1865; July 17, 1865, mustered out.

Walker, Clark, Artificer, Coventry, R. I. Sept. 4, 1861, enrolled; Sept. 4, 1861, mustered in. Originally served as private; Jan. 30, 1864, re-enlisted as a Vet.Vol.; July 17, 1865, mustered out.

Warner, John, Priv., West Greenwich, R. I. March 25, 1864, enrolled; April 20, 1864, mustered in; July 17, 1865, mustered out.

Warren, Charles W., Sergt., Lonsdale, R. I. Sept. 4, 1861, enrolled; Sept. 4, 1861, mustered in. Originally served as private; Aug., 1862, in General Hospital, and so borne until Nov., 1862; Jan. 30, 1864, re enlisted as a Vet.Vol. Borne on furlough of fifteen days from Jan. 21, 1865; June 25, 1865, promoted Sergt. from Corp.; July 17, 1865, mustered out.

Waterman, Frank A., Sergt., Providence, R. I. Sept. 4, 1861, enrolled; Sept. 4, 1861 mustered in; Jan. I, 1862, promoted Corp. Borne on detached service at Knoxville, Tenn., from Dec. 8, 1863, until Jan., 1864; Jan. 30, 1864, re-enlisted as a Vet.Vol.; July 14, 1864, discharged to accept promotion as 2nd Lieut. Battery G.

Watson, Charles H. Priv., Coventry, R. I. Sept. 4, 1861, enrolled; Sept. 4, 1861, mustered in; Dec. 27, 1862, deserted at Camp near Falmouth Station, Va.

Way. John, Priv., Westerly, R. I. Feb. 24, 1862. enrolled; Feb. 25, 1864, mustered out by virtue of re-enlistment; Feb. 26, 1864, re-enlisted as a Vet.Vol. Borne as absent sick in hospital from June 24 1864, until Oct., 1864; July 17, 1865, mustered out.

Webb Edward J., Priv., North Providence, R. I. Aug. 8, 1862, enrolled; June 2, 1863, died at Somerset, Ky., of disease.

Weeden, Henry M., Priv., Bristol, R. I. March 30, 1864, enrolled; April 20, 1864, mustered in; Nov. 12, 1864, detached for service at Hdqrs. Art. Brig. 19th Army Corps; July 17, 1865, mustered out.

Weish, George, Priv. Aug. 14, 1863, enrolled. Borne as absent sick in hospital from March 5, 1864, until Oct. 5, 1864, when discharged on Surgeon's certificate, at Cincinnati, Ohio. Also borne as Weist.

Westcott, James, Priv. Dec. 22. 1862, transferred from Battery H. Borne as sick in hospital from April 6, 1865, until June 19, 1865, when mustered out at Jarvis United States General Hospital.

Whipple, Benjamin N., Corp., Providence, R.I. Sept. 4, 1861, enrolled; Sept. 4, 1861, mustered in. Originally served as Artificer; Aug. 30, 1862, wounded; Sept. 17, 1862, wounded in action at Antietam and borne as absent sick until Feb., 1863; Jan. 30, 1864, re-enlisted as a Vet. Vol.; Sept. 19, 1864, wounded near Winchester. Va.; July 17, 1805, mustered out.

Whittaker, Henry C, Priv., Cranston, R. I. Sept. 4 1861, enrolled; Sept. 4, 1861, mustered in. Borne as absent sick from Aug. 22, 1862, until Dec, 1862; Sept. 3, 1864, mustered out at Charlestown, Va.

White, Henry J., Priv., Lonsdale, R. I. Sept. 4, 1861, enrolled; Sept. 4, 1861, mustered in; March 10, 1862, left in hospital at Upton's Hill, Va., and borne as sick in hospital until April 24, 1862, when discharged on surgeon's certificate, because of injuries received while in service.

Wickes, Rice A., Priv., Warwick, R. I. Sept. 4, 1861, enrolled; Sept. 4, 1861, mustered in. Borne as absent sick in hospital at Fredericksburg, Va., from June 29, 1862, until Sept., 1862; March, 1863, absent sick in hospital and so borne until Aug. 21, 1863, when transferred to the 30th Co., 2nd Bat. V. R. C; Sept. 5, 1864, mustered out at Fort Monroe, Va. as Sergt. 30th Co., 2nd Bat. V. R. C.

Wilbur, George, W., Priv., Warwick, R. I. Sept. 4, 1861, enrolled; Sept. 4, 1861, mustered in; Nov., 1861, absent sick; Dec 15, 1861, returned to duty. Borne as absent sick in hospital from April 14, 1863, until Sept. 20, 1863, when transferred to Co. B, 20th Reg. V. R. C; Sept. 12, 1864, mustered out as of Co. B 20th Regt. V. R. C.

Woolley, John, Priv., Scituate. R. I. Sept. 4, 1861, enrolled; Sept. 4, 1861, mustered in. Borne as absent sick from Jan. 25, 1863, until Feb.,

1863; Jan. 30, 1864, re-enlisted as a Vet. Vol.; Oct. 19, 1864, wounded in action near Cedar Creek, Va., and borne as absent sick in hospital until July 26, 1865, when mustered out.

Woolley, Samuel, Priv. Nov. 25, 1864, enrolled at Providence, R. I.; Nov. 25, 1864, mustered in; July 17, 1865, mustered out.

Wrightington, James H., Priv. Sept. 4, 1861, enrolled at Providence, R. I. Sept. 4, 1861, mustered in; Oct. 1, 1861, discharged on Surgeon's certificate, at Camp Sprague, Washington, D. C.

★★★★★

This Roster was taken from the Revised Adjutant General's Report of this State. There were several members of the battery who were sergeants or corporals during part of their service.

Edward H. Matteson was First Sergeant for quite a long time;

Stephen Ballou was Corporal and Sergeant for at least two years of his service;

Reuben D. Dodge and Charles H. Kennlson were Sergeants.

Charles Gallagher, Edward McKennan, and Isaac D. Russell, served as Corporals.

Those above named are all that I can remember for a certainty. Without doubt there were others. The reason that they were not credited with that part of their service was (as before stated in this work) that all our books were captured at Cedar Creek, and the new books only showed those that were serving at the time.

COMMISSIONED OFFICERS, AND TIME OF SERVICE WITH BATTERY D.

J. Albert Monroe, Capt., Sept. 7, 1861, to Oct. 21, 1862.
William W. Buckley, Capt., Nov. 1, 1862, to Oct. 23, 1864.
Elmer L. Corthell, Capt., Nov. 23, 1864, to July 17, 1865.
George C. Harkness, 1st Lieut., Sept. 9, 1861, to March 3, 1863.
Henry R. Gladding., 1st Lieut., Sept. 9, 1861 to Aug. 1 1862.
William B. Rhodes, 1st Lieut., Dec. 26, 1862, to April 7, 1864.
Kirby Steinhaur, 1st Lieut., April 14, 1863, to April 19, 1864.
Frederick Chase, 2nd & 1st Lieut., Dec. 4, 1862, to July 17, 1865.
Stephen W. Fisk, 2nd Lieut., Sept. 9, 1861, to Dec. 4, 1862.
Ezra K. Parker, 2nd Lieut., Sept. 9, 1861, to April 23, 1864.
Charles E. Bonn, 2nd Lieut., May 4, 1864, to July 17, 1865.
Charles C. Gray, 2nd Lieut., May 27, 1864, to July 17, 1865.

1st Sergt. Henry Royal Lee, to be 2nd Lieut. Battery C.

Sergt. Gideon Spencer, to be 2nd Lieut. Battery B.

Sergt. Charles C. Gray, to be 2nd Lieut. Battery D.

Sergt. Frank A. Waterman, to be 2nd Lieut. Battery G.

Sergt. Edward L. Nichols, to be 2nd Lieut. First Virginia Art.

Sergt. Frank M. Tucker, commissioned but never mustered.

ROLL OF MEN TEMPORARILY ATTACHED.

Allen, Erasmus, Priv. Jan. 5, 1865, detached from Battery A, 1st Mass. L. A.; Feb. 16, 1865, transferred to 9th Mass. Battery.

Arnold, Philo, Priv. Detached from 35th N. Y. Inf., from May 29, 1862, until Dec. 31, 1862.

Austin, Edward G., Priv. Jan. 5, 1865, detached from Battery A, 1st Mass. L. A.; Feb. 16, 1865, transferred to 9th Mass. Battery.

Barber, Amos P., Priv. Detached from Co. C, 7th R. I. Vols. Borne on detached service at Knoxville, Tenn., from Dec. 8, 1863, until Jan, 1864; Dec. 10, 1864, returned to 7th R. I. Vols., by order dated Dec. 3, 1864.

Barker, Albert, Priv. Oct. 15, 1864, detached from 175th N.Y. Vols.; May 11, 1865, returned to his regiment at Winchester, Va., by order dated May 8, 1865.

Barney, Marshall, Priv. Oct. 15, 1864, detached from 175th N. Y. Vols. Borne as absent sick in hospital from Dec. 28, 1864, until Jan , 1865; May 11, 1865, returned to his regiment at Winchester, Va., by special order dated May 8, 1865.

Bashee, Eli, Priv. Oct. 15, 1864, detached from 175th N.Y. Vols.; May 11, 1865, returned to regiment at Winchester, Va., by order dated May 8, 1865.

Bauer, John C, Priv. May 4, 1864, detached from Co. M, 14th N. Y. H. A. Borne as absent sick in hospital from Aug. 4, 1864, until Dec, 1864; Dec. 10, 1864, returned to regiment by special order dated Dec. 3, 1864. Also borne as John C. Bonn.

Beardsley, Philo, Priv. May 4, 1864, detached from 14th N.Y. H. A. Borne as absent sick in hospital from July 12, 1864, until Dec, 1864; Dec. 10, 1864, returned to regiment by special order dated Dec. 3, 1864.

Beck, William, Priv. Feb. 18, 1864, temporarily detached from Battery I., 2nd N.Y. Art., by special order dated Jan. 16, 1864.

Bird, Charles, Priv. Jan. 5, 1865, transferred from Battery A, 1st Mass. L. A., by order dated Dec. 31, 1864; Feb. 16, 1865, transferred to 9th Mass. Battery by order dated Feb. 9, 1865.

Blanchard, John F., Priv. Jan. 15, 1863, detached from Co. E, 7th R.I.Vols.; Feb. 1, 1865, returned to regiment.

Bogardus, John, Priv. May 4. 1864, detached from 14th N.Y. H. A. Borne as absent sick in hospital from Aug. 24, 1864, until Dec, 1864; Dec. 10, 1864, returned to regiment by order dated Dec. 3, 1864.

Boon, John, Priv. Oct. 15, 1864, detached from 175th N.Y. Vols.; May 11, 1865, returned to regiment at Winchester, Va., by order dated May 8, 1865.

Boss, Joseph A., Priv. Jan. 15, 1863, detached from Co. G, 7th R.I. Vols.; Dec. 10, 1864, returned to regiment by order dated Dec. 3, 1864.

Brill, Christian, Sr., Priv. Feb. 18, 1864, temporarily detached from Battery L, 2nd N.Y. Art., by special order dated Jan. 16, 1864.

Brill, Christian, Jr., Priv. Feb. 18, 1864, temporarily detached from Battery L, 2nd N.Y. Art., by special order dated Jan. 16, 1864.

Burman, Ira, Priv. May 4, 1864, detached from 14th N.Y. H. A. Borne as absent sick in hospital from Aug. 4, 1864, until Oct., 1864; Dec. 10, 1864, returned to regiment by order dated Dec. 3, 1864.

Cameron, Donald, Priv. Jan. 15, 1863, detached from 12th R. I. Vols.; July 12, 1863, returned to regiment.

Capron, Alpheus, Jr., Priv. Oct. 15, 1864, detached from 175th N.Y. Vols.; May 11, 1865, returned to regiment by special order dated May 8, 1865.

Carbinan, John, Priv. May 4, 1864, detached from 14th N.Y. H. A. Borne as absent sick in hospital from Aug. 4, 1864, until Oct., 1864; Dec. 10, 1864, returned to regiment by special order dated Dec. 3, 1864.

Carman, Silas, Priv. April 18, 1802, detached from Co. E, 7th Wis. Inf.; March, 1864, returned to regiment.

Chandler, James C, Priv. Oct. 15, 1864, detached from 175th N.Y. Vols.; May 11, 1865, returned to regiment by special order dated May 8, 1865.

Chatterson, Jesse, Priv. Feb. 18, 1864, temporarily detached from

Battery L, 2nd N.Y. Art., by special order dated Jan. 16, 1864. Cleveland, Lundon, Priv. May 4, 1864, detached from 14th N.Y. H. A.; Dec. 10, 1864, returned to regiment by special order dated Dec. 3, 1864.

Cole, William, Priv. May 4, 1864, detached from 14th N.Y. H. A.; Dec. 10, 1864, returned to regiment by special order dated Dec. 3, 1864.

Collins, William, Priv. Jan. 15, 1863, detached from 7th R. I. Vols. Absent on detached service at Knoxville. Tenn., from Dec. 8, 1863, until Jan., 1864; May I, 1864, died in Asylum Hospital, Knoxville, Tenn.

Coons, David S., Priv. Oct. 15, 1864, detached from 175th N.Y. Vols., near Cedar Creek, Va.; Oct. 20, 1864, accidentally shot at Cedar Creek, Va.

Covel, Milo, Priv. Detached from Co. G 7th Wis. Inf., from April 18, 1862, until Aug., 1864. Borne as absent sick from Jan. 8, 1864, until Aug., 1864.

Cunningham, John, Priv. Oct. 15, 1864, detached from 175th N.Y. Vols.; May 11, 1865, returned to regiment at Winchester, Va.

Cushing, William S., Priv. Detached from Co. I, 6th Wis. Inf., from April 18, 1862, until Aug., 1863; Aug. 30, 1862, wounded in action and borne as absent sick from that time until June, 1863.

Davis, Albert C, Priv. Jan. 14, 1863, detached from the 12th R. I. Inf.; July 12, 1863, returned to regiment.

Davis, Thomas, Priv. Detached from Co. B, 6th Wis. Inf. Borne as absent sick in General Hospital from Aug. 31, 1862, until Dec. 12, 1862, when discharged on Surgeon's certificate.

Dehue, Fritz, Priv. Temporarily detached from Battery L, 2nd N.Y. Art., by order dated Jan. 16, 1864.

Dinkins, William T., Priv. Temporarily detached from Co. G, 20th Indp't Inf. Borne as absent sick from Jan. 25, 1863, until July, 1863; Nov. 10, 1863, slightly wounded at battle of Campbell's Station, Tenn.; Jan. 5, 1864, discharged and returned to regiment by reason of re-enlistment.

Doolan, Patrick, Priv. Jan. 5, 1865, detached from Battery A, 1st Mass. L. A.; transferred to 9th Mass. Battery by order dated Feb. 9, 1865.

Doremus, William, Priv. Temporarily detached from Battery L, 2nd N.Y. Art., by order dated Jan. 16, 1864.

Dorsay, John, Priv. Jan. 14, 1863, detached from 12th R. I. Inf.; Jan.

6, 1863, shot by a citizen at Camp Dick Robinson, Ky.

Dunn, James N., Priv. Jan. 5, 1865, detached from Battery A, 1st Mass. L. A.; Feb. 16, 1865, transferred to 9th Mass. Battery.

Dunwell, William, Priv. Jan. 14, 1863, detached from 12th R. I. Inf.; July 12, 1863, returned to regiment.

Dutcher, William, Priv. Detached from Co. A, 2nd Wis. Inf, from May 4, 1862, until June, 1864.

Fannon, Joseph, Priv. Jan. 5, 1865, detached from Battery A, 1st Mass. L. A.; Feb. 16, 1865, transferred to 9th Mass. Battery.

Fitzgerald, John F., Priv. Jan. 5, 1865, detached from Battery A, 1st Mass. L. A.; Feb. 16, 1865, transferred to 9th Mass. Battery.

Fogerrty, Michael, Priv. Feb. 18 1864, temporarily detached from Battery L, N.Y. Art.

Fox, Samuel W., Priv. Oct. 15, 1864, temporarily detached from 175th N.Y.Vols. Borne as absent sick from Nov. 5, 1864, until Nov. 22, 1864, when he died in hospital at Winchester, Va.

Gann, Isaac, Priv. Oct. 15, 1864, detached from 175th N. Y. Vols.; May 11, 1865, returned to regiment by special order dated May 8, 1865.

Gardner, John, Priv. Jan. 5, 1865, detached from Battery A, 1st Mass. L. A.; Feb. 16, 1865, transferred to 9th Mass. Battery by special order dated Feb. 9, 1865.

Graves, Leander W., Priv. Oct. 15, 1864, detached from 175th N.Y. Vols. near Cedar Creek, Va.; Dec. 21, 1864, died at Jarvis United States Army Hospital, Baltimore, Md., from effect of gunshot wound.

Griffin, Joseph H., Jr., Priv. Jan. 15, 1863, detached from 7th R. I. Vols.; Dec. 10, 1864, returned to regiment.

Griffiths, James, Priv. Oct. 15, 1864, detached from 175th N.Y.Vols. near Cedar Creek, Va.; May 11, 1865, returned to regiment at Winchester, Va., by special order dated May 8, 1865.

Gyett, Lewis, Priv. Oct. 15, 1864, detached from 175th N.Y.Vols., near Cedar Creek, Va.; May 11, 1865, returned to regiment at Winchester, Va., by special order dated May 8, 1865.

Harry, Charles E., Priv. Jan. 14, 1863, detached from 12th R. I.Vols. Borne as absent sick in hospital from March 19, 1863, until July, 1863; July 12, 1863, returned to regiment.

Hastings, John, Priv. Temporarily detached from Co. I, 7th Wis.

Inf.

Hawkins, Orlando S., Priv. Temporarily detached from Co. H, 2nd Wis. Inf. Borne as absent sick from Aug. 22, 1862, until Dec. 21, 1862, when dropped from rolls. Joined, and borne as absent on detached service at Knoxville. Tenn., from Dec. 8, 1863, until Jan., 1864.

Head, Henry P., Priv. Jan. 14, 1863, detached from 12th R. I. Vols.; July 12, 1863, returned to regiment.

Helme, Anthony, Priv. May 4, 1864, detached from 14th N.Y. H.A. Borne as absent sick in hospital from Oct. 19, 1864, until Dec, 1864; Dec. 10, 1864, returned to regiment by special order dated Dec. 3, 1864.

Henon, William, Priv. Jan. 5, 1865, detached from Battery A, 1st Mass. L. A., at Camp Sheridan, Va.; Feb. 16, 1865, transferred to 9th Mass. Battery by special order dated Feb. 9, 1865.

Hill, Eben, Priv. Jan. 5, 1865, detached from Battery A, 1st Mass. L. A., at Camp Sheridan, Va.,; Feb. 16, 1865, transferred to 9th Mass. Battery by special order dated Feb. 9, 1865.

Howes, George, Priv. Jan. 5, 1865, detached from Battery A, 1st Mass. L. A. at Camp Sheridan, Va.; Feb. 16, 1865, transferred to 9th Mass. Battery by special order dated Feb. 9, 1865.

Hubbard, Franklin D., Priv. Temporarily detached from Co. D, 6th Wis. Inf.

Hudson, William J., Priv. Jan. 5, 1865, detached from Battery A, 1st Mass. L. A., at Camp Sheridan, Va. Borne on furlough of fifteen days from Jan. 21, 1865; Feb. 16, 1865, transferred to 9th Mass. Battery by special order dated Feb. 9, 1865. Also borne as N. L. Hudson.

Johnston, Daniel, Priv. Feb 18, 1864, temporarily detached from Battery I,, 2nd N.Y. Art., at Knoxville, Tenn., by special order dated Jan. 16, 1864.

Kellogg, McKendry, Priv. May 4, 1864, detached from 14th N.Y. H.A.; Dec. 10, 1864, returned to regiment by special order dated Dec. 3, 1864.

Knecht, John, Priv. Jan., 1863, detached from 12th R. I. Vols.; July 12, 1863, returned to regiment.

LaFont, Louis, Priv. May, 1862, detached from Co. C, 2nd Wis. Inf.; June 8, 1863, killed by a fall at Lexington, Ky.

LaFountain, John, Priv. Oct. 15, 1864, detached from 175th N.Y.

Vols., near Cedar Creek, Va.; May 11, 1865, returned to regiment at Winchester, Va., by special order dated May 8, 1865.

Laich, John T., Priv. Feb. 18, 1864, temporarily detached from Battery L, 2nd N. Y. Art., at Knoxville, Tenn., by special order dated Jan. 16, 1864.

Lampe, Christian, Priv. May 4, 1864, detached from 14th N. Y. H. A.; Dec. 10, 1864, returned to regiment by special order dated Dec. 3, 1864.

Lance, Alfred, Priv. Oct. 15, 1864, detached from 175th N. Y. Vols., near Cedar Creek, Va.; May 11, 1865, returned to regiment by special order dated May 8, 1865.

LaRocke, John, Priv. Oct. 15, 1864, detached from 175th N. Y. Vols., near Cedar Creek, Va.; May 11, 1865, returned to regiment at Winchester, Va., by special order dated May 8. 1865.

LaRose, John, Priv. Oct. 15, 1864, detached from 175th N. Y. Vols., near Cedar Creek, Va.; May 11, 1865, returned to regiment at Winchester, Va., by special order dated May 8, 1865.

LeMay, Peter, Priv. Jan. 5, 1865, detached from Battery A, 1st Mass. Art., at Camp Sheridan, Va.; Feb. 16, 1865, transferred to the 9th Mass. Battery by special order dated Feb. 9, 1865.

Lewis, Frank, Priv. Feb. 18, 1864, temporarily detached from Battery L, 2nd N. V. Art., at Knoxville, Tenn., by special order dated Jan. 16, 1864.

Main, John W., Priv. Jan. 5, 1865, detached from Battery A, 1st Mass. L. A., at Camp Sheridan, Va.; Feb. 16, 1865, transferred to 9th Mass. Battery by special order dated Feb. 9, 1865.

Main, Joseph H.. Priv. Jan. 5, 1865, transferred from Battery A, 1st Mass. Art., at Camp Sheridan, Va.; Feb. 16, 1865, transferred to 9th Mass. Battery by special order dated Feb. 9, 1865.

Malone, John, Priv. May 4, 1864, detached from 14th N. Y. H. A. Borne as absent sick in hospital from Oct. 19. 1864, until Dec, 1864; Dec. 10, 1864, returned to regiment at Opequan Creek, Va., by order dated Dec. 3, 1864.

Maloney, Daniel., Priv. Feb. 18, 1864, temporarily detached from Battery L, 2nd N. Y Art., at Knoxville, Tenn., by special order dated Jan. 16, 1864.

Marshall, John, Priv. May 4, 1864, detached from 14th N. V. H. A.;

Dec. 10, 1864, rejoined his regiment at Opequan Creek, Va., by special order dated Dec. 3, 1864.

Matteson, Robert F. , Priv. Jan. 14, 1863, detached from 12th R. I. Vols.; July 12. 1863, returned to regiment.

Melvin, Edward, Priv. Oct. 15, 1864, detached from 175th N.Y. Vols., near Cedar Creek, Va.; May 11, 1865, returned to regiment by special order dated May 8, 1865, at Winchester, Va.

Miller, George, Priv. May 4, 1864, detached from 14th N.V. H.A.; Dec. 10, 1864, returned to regiment at Opequan Creek, Va., by special order dated Dec. 3, 1864.

Millett, George L., Priv. Jan. 5, 1865, detached from Battery A, 1st Mass. L. A., at Camp Sheridan, Va.; Jan. 22, 1865, died of disease at Stephenson, Va.

Mills, Leander F., Priv. Temporarily detached from Co. C, 19th Ind. Inf. Also borne as Frederick Mills.

Mitchell, Stephen D. W., Priv. Jan. 14, 1863, detached from 12th R.I. Vols.; July 12, 1863, returned to regiment.

Moffatt, George, Priv. Oct. 15, 1864, detached from 175th N.Y. Vols., near Cedar Creek, Va.; May 11, 1865, returned to regiment at Winchester, Va., by special order dated May 8, 1865.

Moore, George, Priv. Sept. 16, 1863, detached from 1st Tenn. Battery, at Knoxville; Sept. 19, 1863, deserted at New Market.

Moore, Ira, Priv. Jan. 5, 1865, detached from Battery A, 1st Mass. L. A., at Camp Sheridan, Va., and borne as absent on detached service at Hdqrs. M. M. Div., until Feb., 1865; Feb. 16, 1865, transferred to 9th Mass. Battery by special order dated Feb. 9, 1865.

Morse, George, Artificer. Jan. 5, 1865, detached as private from Battery A, 1st Mass. L.A., at Camp Sheridan, Va.; Feb. 16, 1865, transferred to 9th Mass. Battery by special order dated Feb. 9, 1865.

Mundon, Hosea, Priv. April 21, 1863, detached from Battery C, 7th Wis. Inf.; June, 1863, returned to regiment.

Murphy, David S., Priv. Jan. 5, 1865, detached from Battery A, 1st Mass. L. A., at Camp Sheridan, Va; Feb. 16, 1865, transferred to 9th Mass. Battery by special order dated Feb. 9, 1865.

Narrow, Joseph, Priv. Oct. 15, 1864, detached from 175th N.Y. Vols., near Cedar Creek, Va.; May 11, 1865, returned to regiment at Winchester, Va., by special order dated May 8, 1865.

Nash, Richard, Priv. Temporarily detached from Co. F, 19th Indpt. Inf.

Nott, Peter, Priv. Oct. 15, 1864, detached from 175th N.Y. Vols., near Cedar Creek, Va.; May 11, 1865, returned to regiment at Winchester, Va., by special order dated May 8, 1865. Also borne as Noll and Kott.

Palmer, Samuel, Priv. Feb. 18, 1864, temporarily detached from Battery L, 2nd N.Y. Art., at Knoxville, Tenn., by special order dated Jan. 16, 1864.

Parker. Horace I., Priv. May 4, 1864, detached from 14th N.Y. H.A.; Dec. 10, 1864, returned to regiment at Opequan Creek, Va., by special order dated Dec. 3, 1864.

Peterson, Thomas, Priv. Aug. 17, 1863, detached from 100th Ohio Vols., at Stanford; Feb., 1864, returned to regiment at Knoxville, Tenn.

Pettis, David, Priv. Jan. 17, 1864, temporarily detached from Battery L, 2nd N.Y. Art., at Strawberry Plains. Also borne as Pettit.

Pickett, Erastus, Priv. Oct. 15. 1864, detached from 175th N.Y. Vols, near Cedar Creek, Va. Borne as absent sick in hospital from Nov. 16. 1864, until Nov. 24, 1864, when he died at Winchester, Va.

Pollard, John, Priv. Jan. 15, 1865, detached from 12th R. I. Vols,; July 10, 1863, returned to regiment.

Potter, Franklin H., Priv. Dec, 1863, detached from 7th R. I. Vols.; Dec. 10, 1864, returned to regiment at Opequan Creek, Va., by special order dated Dec. 3, 1864.

Prouty, Robert A., Priv. Jan. 5. 1865, detached from Battery A, 1st Mass. L. A., at Camp Sheridan, Va.; Feb. 16, 1865, transferred to 9th Mass. Battery by special order dated Feb. 9, 1865.

Raney, John, Priv. Jan. 14, 1863, detached from 12th R. I. Vols.; July 12, 1863, returned to regiment.

Rathbone, George, Priv. Jan. 15, 1863, detached from 7th R. I. Vols.; Dec. 10, 1864, returned to regiment by special order dated Dec. 3, 1864, at Opequan Creek, Va.

Reed, Charles, Priv. Temporarily detached from Co. A, 6th Wis. Inf.

Rengie, Samuel, Priv. May 4, 1864, detached from 14th N.Y. H.A.; Dec. 10, 1864, returned to regiment at Opequan Creek, Va., by special order dated Dec. 3, 1864. Also borne as Resign.

Rhodes, Charles G., Priv. Oct. 15, 1864, detached from 175th N. Y. Vols. near Cedar Creek, Va; May 11, 1865, returned to regiment at Winchester, Va , by special order dated May 8, 1865.

Rue, Richard M., Priv. Oct. 15, 1864, detached from 175th N. Y. Vols, near Cedar Creek, Va.; May 11, 1865, returned to regiment at Winchester, Va., by special order dated May 8, 1865.

Richards, George, Priv. Feb. 18, 1864, temporarily detached from Battery L, 2nd N. Y. Art., at Knoxville, Tenn., by special order dated Jan. 16, 1864, and borne as absent sick in hospital until March, 1864.

Ridiker, Theodore, Priv. Aug. 16, 1863, detached from 103rd Ohio Vol. Inf, at Danville, Ky.; March 11, 1864, transferred to 104th Ohio Vol. Inf.

Rogers, Silas, Priv. Oct. 15, 1864, detached from 175th N. Y. Vols, near Cedar Creek, Va.; May 11, 1865, returned to regiment at Winchester, Va., by special order dated May 8, 1865.

Roselle, William, Priv. Oct. 15, 1864, detached from 175th N. Y. Vols, near Cedar Creek, Va. Borne as absent sick in hospital from Nov. 23, 1864, until Jan., 1865; May ii, 1865, returned to regiment at Winchester, Va., by special order dated May 8, 1865.

Rowley, George W., Priv. May 4, 1864, detached from 14th N Y. H. A.; Dec. 10, 1864, returned to regiment at Opequan Creek, Va., by special order dated Dec. 3, 1864.

Russell, John B., Priv. Oct. 15, 1864, detached from 175th N. Y. Vols., at Cedar Creek, Va.; May 11, 1865, returned to regiment at Winchester, Va., by special order dated May 8, 1865.

Schwamb, Charles, Priv. Jan. 5, 1865, detached from Battery A, 1st Mass. L. A., at Camp Sheridan, Va.; Feb. 16, 1865, transferred to 9th Mass. Battery by special order dated Feb. 9, 1865.

Seymour, John N. , Priv. Detached from Co. B, 2nd Wis. Inf., from May 2, 1862, until April 18, 1864. Borne as absent sick in hospital from Aug. 12, 1863, until Dec, 1863.

Shannon, Edward, Priv. Jan. 5, 1865, detached from Battery A, 1st Mass. L. A., at Camp Sheridan, Va.; Feb. 16, 1865, transferred to 9th Mass. Battery by order dated Feb. 9, 1865.

Smith, John H., Priv. Jan. 5, 1865, detached from Battery A, 1st Mass. L. A., at Camp Sheridan, Va.; Feb 16, 1865, transferred to 9th

Mass. Battery by special order dated Feb. 9, 1865.

Smith, Reuben, Priv. Aug. 17, 1863, detached from 103rd Ohio Inf Borne as in hospital from April 26, 1864, until May, 1864; June 19, 1865, returned to regiment at Winchester, Va., by order dated June 17, 1865.

Somers, John, Priv. Reported as temporarily detached from 12th R. I. Vols.; returned to regiment, term of service having expired. Name not borne on rolls of 12th R. I. Vols.

Stamford, William, Priv. Feb. 18, 1864, temporarily detached from Battery L, 2nd N.Y. Art., at Knoxville, Tenn., by special order dated Jan. 16, 1864.

Starkweather, Melvin M., Priv. Temporarily detached from Co. D, 7th Wis. Inf.

Steinberg, Surgen, Priv. Feb. 18, 1864, temporarily detached from Battery L, 2nd N.Y. Art., at Knoxville, Tenn., by special order dated Jan. 16, 1864.

Sullivan, Patrick, Priv. Temporarily detached from 19th or 20th Ind. Inf

Sutliff, James, Priv. Jan., 1863, detached from Co. C, 12th R. I. Vols.; July 12, 1863, returned to regiment.

Taylor, Charles, Priv. Oct. 15, 1864, detached from 175th N.Y. Vols, near Cedar Creek, Va. Borne as absent sick in hospital from Oct. 19, 1864, until Nov. 11, 1864, when he died at York, Pa.

Terry, Maurice, Priv. Jan. 15, 1863, detached from Co. H, 7th R. I. Vols. Borne as absent sick in hospital from Sept. 1, 1864, until Dec. 10, 1864 when returned to regiment by special order dated Dec. 3, 1864.

Therny, John, Priv. Jan. 17, 1864, temporarily detached from Battery L, 2nd N.Y. Art. Borne as absent sick in hospital from Feb. 20, 1864, until March, 1864.

Toland, John, Priv. Oct. 15, 1864, detached from 175th N.Y. Vols. near Cedar Creek, Va.; May 11, 1865, returned to regiment at Winchester, Va., by special order dated May 8, 1865.

Tuckerman, James F., Priv. Jan. 15, 1863, detached from Co. C, 7th R. I. Vols. Borne as absent sick in hospital from July 29. 1863, until Aug., 1863; Dec. 10, 1864, returned to regiment at Opequan Creek, Va., by special order dated Dec. 3, 1864.

Vosburg, Ira, Priv. May 4, 1864, detached from 14th N.Y. H. A.;

Dec. 10, 1864, returned to regiment by special order dated Dec. 3, 1864, at Opequan Creek, Va.

Wardbruger, Jacob, Priv. May 4, 1864, detached from 14th N.Y. H. A.; Dec. 10, 1864, returned to regiment at Opequan Creek, Va. Also borne as I. Waldberger.

Warner, Harmon, Priv. Oct. 15, 1864, detached from 175th N.Y. Vols, near Cedar Creek, Va.; May 11, 1865, returned to regiment at Winchester, Va., by special order dated May 8, 1865.

Warner, George, Priv. May 4, 1864, detached from 14th N.Y. H.A.; Dec. 10, 1864, returned to regiment at Opequan Creek. Va., by special order dated Dec. 3, 1864.

Weaver, George H., Priv. Jan. 15, 1863, detached from 12th R. I. Vols. Borne as absent sick from Jan. 25, 1863, until March 15, 1863, when discharged for disability from General Hospital.

Webb, George A., Priv. Jan., 1863, detached from 12th R. I. Vols.; July 12, 1863, returned to regiment.

Werner, Frederick, Sergt. Feb. 18, 1864, temporarily detached from Battery L, 2nd N.Y. Art., at Knoxville, Tenn., by order dated Jan. 16, 1864.

Wheelock, Charles C. , Priv. Jan. 5, 1865, detached from Battery A, 1st Mass. L. A., at Camp Sheridan, Va.; Feb. 16, 1865, transferred to 9th Mass. Battery, by order dated Feb. 9, 1865.

Whitney, Henry, Priv. May 4, 1864, detached from 14th N.Y. H.A.; Dec. 10. 1864, returned to regiment at Opequan Creek, Va.

Wick, George, Priv. April 24, 1862, detached from Co. K, 2nd Wis. Inf.; Feb. 2, 1865, mustered out by reason of expiration of term of service.

Wilhelm, John, Priv. Feb. 18, 1864, temporarily detached from Battery L, 2nd N.Y. Art., at Knoxville. Tenn., by order dated Jan. 16, 1864.

Wilson, Daniel G., Priv. Jan. 5, 1865, detached from Battery A, 1st Mass. L. A.; Feb. 16, 1865, transferred to 9th Mass. Battery by special order dated Feb. 9, 1865.

Winsor, Chauncey A., Corp. Temporarily detached from Co. A, 6th Wis. Inf.

Worden, Charles H., Priv. Jan. 15, 1863, detached from 7th R. I. Vols.; Feb. 18, 1863, died of disease in Hampton General Hospital.

Battery D, First Rhode Island Light Artillery, at the Battle of Antietam, September 17, 1862

J. Albert Monroe

BATTERY D, AT THE BATTLE OF ANTIETAM

Although Battery D had a good and widespread army reputation, it was probably less known at home, here in Rhode Island, than any other of the eight batteries that formed the First Regiment Rhode Island Light Artillery, for the reason that the men composing it, having been recruited mainly from the towns of Warwick, Coventry, West Greenwich and Foster, had fewer friends in the thickly settled cities and towns, to take pride in narrating their exploits in the newspapers of the day, or to call the attention of editors to their deeds. In common with many other officers of the army, though exercising no rudeness, the commanding officer gave no encouragement to newspaper men to make notes in his camp, preferring to succeed or fail through the official record made by his superior officers, rather than to depend for reputation upon the reports of irresponsible civilians whose kisses, it was well understood, more often were rewards for favours than otherwise.

Nearly every other battery, too, had among its members some one who acted as regular or occasional correspondent of at least one of the Providence daily papers, and who kept the doings of his particular battery before the public, while in Battery D there was not a single newspaper letter-writer. In a thorough search of the files of the *Providence Daily Journal* and the *Evening Press,* I have been unable to find a single letter from that organization, except one or two of my own, giving the names of men killed and wounded in action—nothing more.

167

However limited was its reputation at home, it was known in the corps of which it was a part, as one of the best of fighting batteries, and how well it merited such distinction it is the purpose of this paper to show.

While preparing the paper, I have come across the following in the *Providence Daily Journal* of September 23, 1862. The correspondent alluded to was a little mixed in his account, for there can be no question but that Battery D was entitled to at least a part of the credit given in his story, and it is by no means strange that a mistake should be made ; in fact, it is a wonder that war correspondents, particularly at this period of the war, got their accounts so nearly accurate as they did, for during and immediately after a battle one could not tell in the confusion one division, brigade or battery from another, unless personally acquainted with the officers connected with them, for the system of flags and badges by which different commands could be designated, had not then been adopted. It will be noticed that he falls into the natural error of connecting the battery with General Green's command, or rather that he leads one to infer that it was a part of it, whereas there was no Rhode Island battery whatever attached to that division.

The article, under the head *A Rhode Island Battery in the Battle*, reads:

The correspondent of the *New York Herald* says that the Third Rhode Island Battery was in General Green's Division, better known as General Augur's. We do not know which battery is meant. It was supported by General Geary's old brigade, commanded by Lieutenant-Colonel Tyndale, of the Twenty-Eighth Pennsylvania Regiment, and by General Prince's old brigade, commanded by Colonel Steinrook, of the One Hundred and Ninth Pennsylvania Regiment. The letter says:

The two brigades were at first posted as supports to the Third Rhode Island Battery. The battery was placed in position in front of a small Dunkard church. The guns, apparently without much infantry support at first, presented a tempting offer as trophies to the enemy, and consequently a large force soon advanced in splendid style, firing on the gunners, apparently determined to capture. But as they came within convenient distance, they found to their sorrow that these two brigades of

General Green's had been in the meantime getting into position and had formed on a line on the right and left of the Rhode Island battery. As the rebels came from the woods in splendid style, as mentioned, they were met, not only by the galling fire of the artillery itself, but by a simultaneous fire of the infantry, which until then, was unperceived by the enemy.

It is a comparatively easy undertaking for a large body of soldiers to capture a battery of artillery, however quick its fire, if undefended by infantry, because the advancing line soon shoots down the horses and the gunners, but it is quite another thing to capture guns and carry them from the field when they are well supported by infantry. And so in the present instance were those Rhode Island guns defended. The audacious rebels were driven back into the timber, where our infantry then advanced upon them, drove them out of it and occupied the woods themselves.

The battery then wheeled to the left and poured a most destructive fire upon those retreating rebels and upon other rebel troops appearing on the left. The Twenty-Seventh Indiana Regiment, which had been sent to participate in the last mentioned operation, fought fast and was compelled to retire before some of the other regiments, because the men had expended all their ammunition.

The Thirteenth New Jersey Regiment, which was present on a similar service, did excellent execution and remained in the woods until the command retired.

The rebel battery had been compelled to retire, the gunners leaving their limbers behind, and this position was held for a full hour, until, at nearly noon, the enemy came out in tremendous force in front of General Howard's command of Sumner's Corps, which had already got into action further to the left, and General Green's Division being partially outflanked and subjected to a disastrous enfilading fire, was compelled to withdraw from the woods about a quarter of a mile, and did not actively participate in the battle during the remainder of the afternoon.

With this as a sort of preface, I will try to tell the story of Battery D at the battle of Antietam, which will describe, in its recital, more in detail what took place, so far as the artillery was concerned, at the time the correspondent speaks of.

September 13, 1862, the Army of the Potomac passed through the city of Frederick, Maryland. Lee's army had but just left there, and we had understood that its presence had been warmly welcomed by the citizens generally If I remember correctly, Frederick was then looked upon as a sort of hot-bed of secession in that section, the stronghold of the copperheads, and we looked forward to our march through the city with considerable feeling of curiosity I did not observe any special manifestations, either of joy or of disappointment, on the part of the people as we passed through, but there was displayed, on every hand, intense interest in our movement. The sidewalks of the street through which we marched were well filled with people, though by no means crowded, but the windows of the houses were thronged with eager observers.

The next day, the fourteenth, occurred the battle of South Mountain. During this action, Battery D was ordered to take position where it would be available in case of necessity Although we were so situated as to be constantly under fire, the battery was not actually engaged at any time during the day, though firing an occasional shot ; but our position was such that we had an excellent view of General Reno's movements, and we witnessed with intense satisfaction his charging lines of infantry as they made their assaults through the timber upon the enemy, who, under its protection, felt secure in his position on the mountain side.

The afternoon of the sixteenth found us in the vicinity of the field where was to take place the great battle of Antietam. The division of which Battery D formed a part, Doubleday's Division, Hooker's Corps, crossed the Antietam just before dark, and it was quite dark when we halted for the night. We struck off to the left from the road soon after crossing the stream, and marching quite a distance went into park at reduced intervals, with a number of other batteries. Our position was on cleared ground and on the summit of a commanding ridge, as we discovered the next morning. To our left and front was a heavy growth of timber, and as our infantry advanced into it to establish a picket line, a heavy skirmish took place. It had grown very dark then, and the flashes from the discharges of the small arms presented a beautiful sight. This took place but a few yards from us, and we knew that we were in the immediate presence of the enemy in force, and that by early dawn we would be struggling with him in battle on that very field. As a matter of fact, our lines were only a few yards apart, and during the night we made prisoners of several rebel pickets who, in the darkness, stumbled upon our pickets.

The caissons, battery-wagon and forge of the battery were disposed of under cover of the hill, and quite a long distance to the rear of our bivouac. The officers' cook was directed to stay with the caissons and to bring up breakfast before daylight in the morning. The teams were not unhitched from the carriages, but the bridles of the horses were slipped, so as to give the animals a chance to feed. It was late when the horses were fed and the men had eaten their suppers. The officers contented themselves with a hasty bite that the cook brought up from the rear.

At length we were all stretched upon the ground, wrapped in our blankets, and everything was quiet except the snoring of the heavy sleepers, the munching of the horses as they ground the grain with their teeth, and the occasional firing of the pickets. At this period of the war, picket firing was very unpopular with both sides, and though the two lines might be only a little distance apart, it was not much indulged in. In the spring and early summer of 1864, when the army marched through the Wilderness and entered upon the campaign that ended with the investment of Petersburg, the pickets made lively music whenever the lines were in close proximity, and it was seldom that the picket line was established or relieved without a number of casualties.

We were awakened before daylight by the cook, who had brought up a pail of steaming coffee, some johnny-cakes and "fixins," together with cups, plates and other table ware. A blanket was spread on the ground for a tablecloth, on which was placed the breakfast, and the officers gathered around it on their haunches. It was the early gray light that appeared just before the sun rises above the horizon, and we could little more than distinguish each other. We had not half finished our meal, but it had grown considerably lighter, and we could see the first rays of the sun lighting up the distant hilltops, when there was a sudden flash, and the air around us appeared to be alive with shot and shell from the enemy's artillery. The opposite hill seemed suddenly to have become an active volcano, belching forth flame, smoke and scoriae.

The first shot apparently passed directly through our little breakfast party, not more than a foot or two above the blanket, and it struck the ground only a few feet from us. Every one dropped whatever he had in his hands, and looked around the group to see whose head was missing. So suddenly did the firing commence and so rapidly did shot follow shot, I felt lost for an instant.—I never knew how the others felt,—but I at once ordered Hugh Rider, my groom, to give me my mare, who was hitched only about ten feet distant, and by the time he got her to me I had fully recovered from my surprise.

At the first flash of the rebel guns the men sprang to their posts, the drivers adjusted the horses' bridles, the cannoneers took their equipments, and the only order necessary to give was "Action front!" which was quickly executed. Gibbons' Battery, Company B, Fourth United States Artillery, was on our left ; Battery L, First New York Artillery, Captain JA. Reynolds, was on our right, as was also Gerrish's Battery, the First New Hampshire, under command of First Lieutenant F. M. Edgell. As quickly as possible every gun, twenty-four in number, fired in reply to the enemy.

I have always thought that but one battery opened upon us, though others believe there were two or three opposed to us. Whatever number there was, they must have found their position a warm one, for the gunners of three of these (our batteries) could not be excelled for marksmanship, estimation of distances, and all the good qualities that go to make a skilful gunner. The winter previous they had been exercised by Captain Gibbon in firing at target, sighting, etc., and they had acquired great proficiency in these points, as stated in my paper, *Incidents of the War*. The fuses of the shell and case were accurately timed, and the projectiles burst where it was intended that they should—among the guns and limbers of the enemy, who had stirred up a hornets' nest, and the hornets proved too many for him, for after an hour or so he ceased firing and withdrew his guns.

Soon after the firing commenced, Gibbon's battery was ordered by General Hooker to a position in some ploughed ground in front of the wood at our left, where it was supported by General Gibbon's brigade, and before the enemy's guns in our front were silenced, Captain Reynolds' battery was ordered to take position very near to it, but two other batteries advanced to the ground that Captain Reynolds had left, so that our fire was not diminished in the least.

Being on the extreme right of our line and somewhat to the rear of it, we were not very much exposed after the artillery ceased firing, for the enemy's centre and the right of his left wing were so hotly pressed that he had neither the time nor the force to attempt the advance of his extreme left. He tried only to hold the ground that he already had possession of, and right manfully he resisted the assaults made upon him.

After the cessation of the artillery fire we had an easy time until about ten o'clock, when General Gibbon rode up to me and said: "Here, Captain; your men are good and fresh ; General Hooker wants to see you." I thought it pretty cool, this reference to the fresh condition of the men, for they had had but little sleep for several nights, and they had been hard at work since early daylight, for after working the guns they were kept busy replenishing the ammunition chests and at other necessary work; besides, we were very short-handed, owing to heavy losses in previous actions. First directing Lieutenant Fisk to limber the pieces, I reported to General Hooker, whom I found at the point where a little while after he received the severe wound that incapacitated him for further service that day. Said he:

"Captain, you see that cornfield; the second one, I mean?"

"Yes, sir."

"You see the one beyond that?"

"Yes, sir."

"Well, I want you to go through the second one into the ploughed ground, and into the cornfield beyond, if you can get there. Now go and look out for your support ; you will find some infantry there to support you."

The bullets were right thick where he gave me the order, for the position was an exposed one, just such as one would expect to find General Hooker in.

On the right was the Hagerstown turnpike, leading to Sharpsburg, running southerly and parallel with the line of vision. The ground was elevated and gave a fine view of a long stretch of open land that lay between two irregular lines of timber, the easterly one on the left, fringing the hills at the base of the South Mountain range, where the Antietam coursed along on its way to the Potomac ; the other at the right, on the further side of the turnpike and to the westward, more clear and more open than the other. The trunks of the trees on the right were bare of branches and foliage from ten to twenty feet or more above the ground, and the rebels were distinctly seen in all the various regular and irregular formations of a battlefield. The Dunker church was in plain sight, and down to that point our troops, apparently, had driven the enemy into or across the turnpike. As far as the church the ground appeared to be a descending plain of cultivated land, beyond which it seemed undulating and uncertain in character.

There lay before the eye two-thirds of the distance to the bridge where General Burnside had then already commenced his heavy assaults, for the purpose of carrying the bridge and effecting a lodgement of his corps on the west of the Antietam, so as to make a junction with our centre. Over this space the two lines had been putting forth all their energies since early light, and the ground was strewn with dead and wounded horses and men, clothing, knapsacks, canteens, muskets and side arms broken and twisted in every imaginable manner. The blue and the gray were indiscriminately mingled, either motionless and lifeless, or dragging their bleeding forms along in search of some less exposed situation.

And there were those whose life-blood was fast or slowly ebbing away, with only strength sufficient to raise a supplicating arm for assistance or relief. The stretcher-bearers were straining every nerve to succour the helpless wounded, but it would have required a force in itself equal to a small army to have immediately removed them all; nor would their situation have been materially improved by removal, except that they would have been carried from the midst of the noise and excitement of the field, for the hospitals were crowded to repletion, and hundreds were waiting their turns for the care of the surgeons. Down through this field of confusion went Battery D, closely followed by Lieutenant Edgell with the First New Hampshire battery.

Unless under great excitement horses will not step on the bodies of men, either alive or dead, but when attached to a battery they may go so close as to cause further injury to the wounded or mutilation to the dead by passing the wheels over them ; so we picked our way carefully, avoiding running over the bodies strewn around on every hand, and looking out for the wounded. At one point we were moving along quite briskly, when a poor wounded fellow, clad in the dingy yellow, the "butternut," as we called it, so common to the uniforms of the rebel soldiers, with a countenance expressive of all the terror of one who expected no consideration, raised himself on one elbow and cried out, "Oh, don't run over me!" I said, as some of the men quickly but carefully removed him aside, "You shan't be hurt, my man," and an expression of relief and gratitude overspread his face that spoke more plainly and loudly than would have a thousand words of thanks.

We finally entered the cornfield designated by General Hooker, pushed through it and reached our advanced line. A little distance to our left and front was a brigade or division of infantry lying on the ground as if awaiting an attack. As the battery halted, a rifled projectile came tumbling through the air, which indicated that the rebel artillery was watching our movement. From the position the infantry were in, I judged there must be a strong force of the enemy in our immediate front, and questioned within myself the judiciousness of going into battery in so advanced a position. Riding to the infantry, I asked whose brigade it was, and was answered General Greene's.

Looking around I saw the general approaching, and I asked him if he could support my battery. He answered in a low tone of voice that he was out of ammunition. I remember the thought coming into my mind that it was a mighty funny place for men without ammunition to be in, and that if they could hold their position with nothing in their cartridge-boxes, artillery surely ought to be able to hold theirs with limber chests well packed and good men to work the guns, so I gave the order, "In battery."

What happened here may be best told in general terms by an extract from my official report of the part the division artillery took in the action. Captain Campbell, of Gibbon's battery, was the ranking artillery officer in the division, but he was severely wounded in the shoulder in the early part of the day, and his injury was so severe that it necessitated his removal to the hospital, and the command of the artillery consequently devolved upon me, and the report of its doings. Giving in detail the part taken by the batteries as the day progressed, the report says relative to Battery D:

General Hooker directed the Rhode Island battery to move forward beyond the second cornfield, if practicable, and to take position as near to the woods as possible. The battery advanced, followed by Lieutenant Edgell's New Hampshire battery, to the position indicated, and went into battery about —— yards from the wood—(This space is not filled in the original draft, which I retained. Probably it was so left in the draft and filled in the report after further consideration)—the New Hampshire battery taking position at the left and about one hundred yards in rear. A battery of the enemy here opened on the Rhode Island battery, but no attention was paid to it, as their fire was perfectly ineffective.

The Rhode Islanders opened with one section upon a body of

the enemy that was seen retreating just to the left of their front, and about an hundred and twenty-five yards distant, throwing them into great confusion. The other four guns opened with canister and case upon a large force advancing through the wood, which was very open, and with the assistance of the other two guns, which in a short time had accomplished their object, and the New Hampshire battery, checked the enemy, and he retired out of sight. While the Rhode Island battery was engaged in forcing back the enemy in the wood a body of sharpshooters had crept unobserved along a little ridge that ran diagonally to the battery front, and they opened a most deadly fire, killing and disabling many horses and men.

As soon as possible a section was directed to open upon them with canister. Though this caused them no injury, as they lay down under cover of the ridge, it kept them almost silent, they firing only an occasional shot without effect. While this section was keeping the sharpshooters silent, the other four guns and the New Hampshire battery opened upon the enemy's battery that was still firing, and they soon silenced it. The Rhode Island battery was then ordered to limber to the rear. The sharpshooters took advantage of the opportunity thus afforded and opened upon the battery most briskly, killing and disabling a large number of horses.

My own horse was pierced by six bullets, and Lieutenant Fiske's horse was also shot. On one piece all the horses but one lead horse were either killed or disabled, and the piece was drawn away by hand, by means of the prolonge. We were obliged to leave the limber, but it was subsequently recovered.

The New Hampshire battery left at the same time, and went back to its original position. After securing to a caisson the piece belonging to the lost limber, the Rhode Island battery moved into the plot of ground between the second cornfield and the ploughed land beyond the first cornfield, and went into battery with five guns, shelling the woods in front. After firing a short time it retired to its original position.

As soon as I found what a difficult and dangerous position we were in, I sent to General Greene a request to keep the sharpshooters down, so that we could get our guns away, but the answer came back that he could not, for want of ammunition. The cannoneers were rapidly leaving their posts on account of wounds, and the drivers were constantly employed in relieving their disabled horses.

I realised that we must get our guns away then, or leave them where they were. Not the slightest doubt arose in my mind but that the men would stick to their pieces, for at the Second Bull Run battle their nerve and steadiness were tested in a severer trial than I had ever expected to see artillerymen subjected to. Twice the enemy tried to wrest their guns from them, and in one of the attempts they got in among the cannoneers, but with a pluck that excited the highest enthusiasm among the infantry and several general officers who witnessed it, they took their guns away in safety, although batteries both on their left and their right were abandoned on the field by the men serving with them. I knew my men, and I felt that we were making a needless sacrifice.

When the order "Limber to the rear" was given it was executed almost in the twinkling of an eye, but the men behind the ridge then had us at their mercy, and right well did they improve the time in showing the temper of it. They rose up in an unbroken line and poured their lead into us a perfect storm.

Lieutenant Parker took away four pieces with few losses, considering the fire we were under. One of Lieutenant Fiske's pieces had similar good fortune, but the other was less fortunate. As the horses made the turn to bring the limber to the trail of the piece, they seemed to melt like wax before a fire. Before a disabled horse could be disengaged from the team, another would fall. A pang of intense pain rushed over me as the thought forced itself upon my mind that the piece must be left, and the closing paragraph of a letter that I received from Governor Sprague the previous winter stood out before me as in letters of fire. He wrote:

> I am glad you speak so well for your command. We must rub out Bull Run, you know, in any action that takes place, and remember those guns must never be given up alive.

It is astonishing how much one can remember, of how much he can think and resolve upon in an incredibly short space of time. I said hurriedly: "Mr. Fiske, get some infantry, quick—I'll fix the prolonge," and away he went on his wounded horse like the wind. I turned to the piece and there were only "number eight" of the caisson, who had taken the place of the wounded gunner, and one cannoneer who had his head ducked beside the rim of one of the wheels of the carriage, supposing that he was shielding it from the bullets, but in fact he was doing nothing of the sort, for he was on the side of the wheel exposed to the enemy.

There was not a man in the company who was not perfectly familiar with every implement connected with the battery, their uses and with the prompt adjustment of them to their proper places. "Fix prolonge," I ordered. The gunner leaned over the trail to disengage the rope, but the cannoneer, hugging closer to the wheel, turned up his face and cried out, "We don't know how, sir." *Spang—spang*—the bullets were hitting my mare, and as they struck her side they seemed to explode directly beneath me. Quick as thought my sword was raised over his head, and with all the energy of desperation I ordered, " Fix that prolonge, you ——— ——!" It may seem to have been a strange place for the use of profanity: death on every side, the black fiend harvesting his victims by thousands, but the most appropriate language on such urgent occasions is that which will produce the desired effect. Many lives have been lost by the supercilious choice of polite language, when, if a little of the right kind of emphasis had been thrown in, they would have been saved.

Like lightning the cannoneer sprang to the trail, recovering in an instant his lost energies, and assisted the gunner in inserting the toggle of the prolonge. Just then Lieutenant Fiske returned with fifteen or twenty infantrymen, and the piece went to the rear amid the cheers of both friend and foe. Even our enemies arose in an unbroken line and gave us their cheers.

This was a severe ordeal for men to go through, but from the humblest private to the commissioned officers there was no flinching. The poor private who crouched by the wheel never for a moment thought of leaving his piece without orders, and his momentary self-forgetfulness was only what may happen to the stoutest heart at the very point of some sudden emergency.

My first officer, Lieutenant George C. Harkness, was absent on sick leave on account of injuries received during the Second Bull Run battle ; my second officer was off duty and took no part in the action. I had but two commissioned officers for duty, both second lieutenants—Lieutenant Stephen W Fiske and Lieutenant Ezra K. Parker. I had the utmost confidence in Lieutenant Fiske. He had ably seconded my efforts from the day that I assumed command of the company, and in every emergency I had found him to be self-sacrificing, prompt and true as steel. As he came up with those infantrymen and relieved us from our perilous position, he seemed to me for the moment to be endowed with more than human qualities, and I could have embraced him there and then in gratitude and admiration.

My junior officer, Lieutenant Parker, and I had never understood each other, and our relations had not been of mutual confidence. He had always executed his prescribed duties, but it seemed to me he did so simply because he was so ordered by his superior officer. His position when all the officers were present for duty was a trying one to a man possessing pluck, grit and ambition. As chief of caissons his duty kept him in the immediate vicinity of the cassions, out of the way of direct harm in time of action, and his only responsibility was to keep within communicating distance and to see that the proper kind and quality of ammunition were sent forward as requisitions were made upon him from the front. A laggard would have enjoyed the position and congratulated himself upon having a soft thing, and I was uncertain as to whether or no Lieutenant Parker so considered it.

At Groveton he had executed a difficult order to blow up a disabled caisson, to prevent its falling into the hands of the enemy, under circumstances of great danger and personal peril, and at the second Bull Run he had handled his caissons with great skill as the battery changed position from one portion of the field to another. Daring the march through Maryland he filled Lieutenant Harkness' place, and he had become more cheerful, apparently taking a decided interest in everything pertaining to the welfare of the command, but I was not prepared to see such consummate gallantry as he displayed on this occasion.

I had always had a doubt as to what his conduct would be should we get into close quarters, but here, in one of the greatest of emergencies, he stood up to the scratch without flinching, and proved beyond question that he was thoroughly reliable. All his latent energies seemed suddenly to have awakened, and he handled the four pieces with a skill that would have put to blush many an old veteran, and he inspired the men with the same enthusiasm that he evidently felt himself. From that moment forward, I cherished for him the kindest of feelings, and had the deepest admiration for his pluck and grit.

Lieutenant Parker had halted the five pieces some distance to the rear of the position that we had been driven from, and thither we repaired with the rescued piece, and halted to straighten out matters. My poor mare had kept on her feet through all the excitement, and she had borne me on her back thus far, but she could go no farther.

179

Changing the saddle and bridle to the horse of one of the buglers, the bugler went to the rear with the equipments of his horse on his back.

Corporal Gray (Charles C.) who heartily enjoyed the excitement of a fight, here entered into the action on his own account. Four of his "number ones" had been picked off by the sharpshooters, and he had got thoroughly mad. Picking up a musket and stripping a nearly full cartridge-box from a dead body, he lay down and commenced firing back at the men who had inflicted so great loss upon us. His position getting rather warm, he rolled up a couple of bodies near him for breastworks, and continued his fire until his ammunition was exhausted, when he rejoined his piece.

Whipple (Benjamin N.), the artificer, came to the front here and assumed the duties of a cannoneer, acting as "number one." He might have remained at the rear with his forge, and there performed all the duty that could have been expected of him, but he was not the man to let his comrades be sorely pressed and not lend a helping hand. His bravery cost him a severe wound across the back of one hand, and the loss of one or two fingers.

We arranged five pieces in fighting trim and went into position. Our line near the turnpike had just wavered, the field was filled with stragglers, and the utmost confusion prevailed. Men were fleeing to the rear in every direction, batteries were hastily moving in one direction and another, officers were riding hither and thither, endeavouring to check the fugitives, swearing and yelling like all possessed. I remember seeing Generals Gibbon and Griffin tearing about like mad men, though there seemed to be purpose in their madness. Our line had weakened, and if that human tide was not stayed, the day was lost.

General Gibbon was one of the most accomplished artillery officers in the army, and he saw at a glance the crippled condition of Battery D. He said: "I see you are badly crippled, Captain, but you must help us out. Go into battery with four pieces," but we put in all five. Steadily the men went at their work, and one not aware of the fact would never have supposed that they had but just emerged from a fire that could be compared only to hell itself. Discipline asserted its supremacy, however, order was established in a few minutes, and the rebels were held to the turnpike.

As soon as confidence appeared to be restored, I deemed it prudent to retire, that the men might get a breathing spell, so we returned to the position that we first occupied in the morning. During the short sleep that I had the night before, I dreamed that the action had come on, and that I lost my left leg. I was not in the least superstitious, and did not think of it until after we returned to the rear, when it struck me as a little singular that most of the bullets that had hit my mare had passed in front and rear of my left leg and close to it.

While the men were changing horses, regulating harnesses and refilling the boxes with ammunition, I sat down on the ground, under and against a good-sized tree, resting my head and back against its trunk. 'Twas then that I thought of the peculiarity of this circumstance, and instinctively drew my left leg around farther behind the tree. I had got into a little doze, when I was awakened suddenly by a shot that must have been sent with a peculiar twist, for it dodged behind the tree I was under and struck the ground close to that apparently ill-fated left leg.

I gave up my attempt at dozing, but did not lose much, for in a little while the enemy's artillery opened from the same hill that we had driven it from in the morning, and we had the most furious cannonade that had taken place up to that time since the commencement of the rebellion. A number of batteries, either by chance or by orders, had taken position both to the right and left of Battery D, and every gun belched forth its thunder until the enemy ceased his fire, long after dark. When hungry and weary we lay down that night, our aching frames were too tired to admit of sleep, and we had but a fitful rest. The morning dawned at last, and we lay there all day, expecting to renew the attack any moment, or to be called upon to repel an attack upon us. The first thing done was to send for our limber that was still on the field where we had left it.

While waiting and talking with my officers over the occurrences of the day before, an officer came up with two or three rebel prisoners under a proper guard. The officer halted his charge and saluting, said, "Captain, do you know either of the prisoners?" I scanned their features carefully, in the endeavour to recognise the face of some old acquaintance or friend, thinking, that perhaps some old chum of my boyhood days or college companion had embraced the Southern cause, and having been taken a prisoner, desired to make himself and his situation known to me, in order to secure gentler treatment than he expected ; but I failed to find a lineament in either countenance with which I had ever been familiar.

I told the officer that I did not know either of them, and he was about to move on, when one of them stooped over and after fumbling a moment or so about his trousers' legs, fished from beneath the lining of his boot leg a folded piece of paper which he held towards me, saying as he did so, " Perhaps, Cap'n, you will know this." I unfolded the paper, and sure enough I did know it. When we lay at Fredericksburg a man by the name of ————, who had been detailed from the Seventh Wisconsin Volunteers to serve with Battery D, came to me one day and asked if I would object if he could manage to get detailed upon special duty as a spy. I tried to dissuade him from the notion, but he appeared to feel that in such service he would be in his true sphere and better fulfil his mission. A few days after, I received an order from " Division Headquarters" detailing ———— upon special duty, and immediately after he presented himself with a pass which read

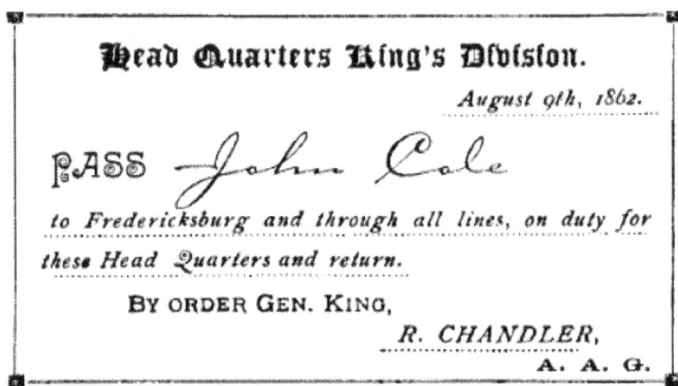

Head Quarters King's Division.

August 9th, 1862.

PASS ——— *John Cole*

to Fredericksburg and through all lines, on duty for

these Head Quarters and return.

BY ORDER GEN. KING,

R. CHANDLER,

A. A. G.

I had supposed that I would never hear from the man again, but here was the identical pass that he had shown me before leaving, and I then recognized him. The kind of uniform a man is dressed in, has a great effect upon his countenance.

I learned from him that he had either joined or was pressed into the rebel army after getting into the Confederacy, that he was able to send valuable information into our lines several times, and that he had contrived to be taken prisoner in order to rejoin his command, for he had become heartily sick of playing rebel soldier. In consideration of the perilous duty that he had performed, he was granted a furlough and allowed to go home to visit his friends.

There was considerable speculation among the men of the battery as to our execution upon the batteries opposed to us the morning and evening of the day previous, so some of them asked leave to go over to the position those batteries had occupied to see what had been the result of our fire upon them. On their return they reported that the effect of our shot had been all that was intended, for the ground was strewn with dead horses, and that a number of dead artillerymen were lying there.

Private Boss (David), accompanied by a number of men who had been with him to the place, brought me a letter that he found protruding from the knapsack of a dead artillerist, which had been sent to him by his wife. It was expressive of love, trust and confidence, and she was longing for the time to arrive when he would return home. A babe was born after he entered the army, and when she finished the letter in which she had told of the baby's cunning ways with all of a young mother's pride, she traced the baby's hand on the paper, by laying it on the portion unwritten upon and running a pencil around it, afterwards inking the lines with her pen. Within the hand was written: "Marthy Verginia, her hand sent to her paw," and in another place: "If you want to kiss the baby you must kiss this hand." The situation, the circumstances, the surroundings, all served to awaken emotions in the strongest and roughest hearts, even though unused to tender impulses, and this little hand so lovingly traced, reached way down into the stout soldier breasts and touched the wellsprings of pity and sympathy there, making fountains of the eyes that the trembling lids vainly endeavoured to conceal, while the quivering lips, more plainly than had they spoken in language, revealed the depth of the feeling that had been excited in their hearts.

What a subject for a painter—what a theme for a poet. The dead soldier lying there on the bare ground amid the desolation and havoc of a battlefield ; the rent knapsack containing all that had contributed to his comfort, his pleasure, and solace for sacrifice of home ; the letter, upon which was rudely traced his infant's hand, bearing in its tiny palm, as it were, all that it could of the strong affection cherished for and centred in him.

A group of soldiers gathered around their commanding officer— men accustomed only to the rough usages and associations of camp, inured to the privations, toils and hardships of the march ; men whose finer qualities of nature, whose tenderest impulses, had long since become blunted, dulled or almost altogether obliterated by the very nature of their duties ; with the wreck of battle, the results of bloody carnage surrounding them ; on every side and all about them nothing but the evidences of hate, revenge and the base qualities of human nature, made to overflow with emotion as tender, pure and sweet as ever displayed by sensitive woman. And why? None better than they knew that this was the most precious of the dead soldier's keepsakes ; none better than they knew that by the camp-fire's dim and flickering light, when all others, save the watchful sentries, were supposed to be wrapped in slumber, the poor fellow often had taken this letter from the knapsack that pillowed his head and imprinted a loving kiss upon its page, more for the sake of the mother than the child. To them it was a symbol of a priceless and holy affection such as each knew somebody had for him. They each had something just as precious, just as dear, to them just as sacred.

FACSIMILE OF THE TRACING.

I threw away the letter after cutting out the tracing. It must be borne in mind that throughout the South the common pronunciation of the contraction "pa" for papa, is "paw."

Thus the day was passed, loitering and lagging about ; the hospitals were visited to administer comfort and to sympathize with friends and acquaintances who had had the misfortune to receive injuries.

Cornie Welles (Cornelius Montague Welles), of Hartford, Connecticut, an old friend of mine, came upon the field and supplied us with some delicacies from the stores of the Christian Commission with which he was connected, and he also took pains to search in the hospitals for the wounded men of Battery D, to see that they had good care and received every comfort that the circumstances would admit of.

On the nineteenth we were ordered to move, and our march was over the turnpike that the rebels had so persistently held to on the seventeenth. The slaughter there had been fearful. The turnpike was very broad, and it must have been literally covered with dead men. They had been drawn aside from the travelled way, but only so as to leave sufficient space for the baggage wagons and the artillery to pass along. The entire space on either side of the column, between the carriages and the fences, or where the fences had been before the battle, was crowded with dead bodies, and in very many places they were piled one upon another, two and three deep. It was a sickening sight, for nearly all the faces were of African blackness, having been exposed to the sun since they fell. I do not remember how far we moved on the road, but so far as we went, the same evidence of the terrific struggle that had taken place presented itself.

When we halted, it was generally known that Lee had re-crossed the Potomac and that the great battle was over. The enemy was fleeing with shattered columns, to a great extent barefooted or nearly so ; as a resultant, according to all human reasoning, dispirited. And it was the universal expectation in the army, that we would pursue him and strike another blow while he was in a crippled condition. Great was the surprise that orders to that effect were not received.

Time disclosed the fact, however, according to the official correspondence discovered by the newspapers, that the major-general in command of the army learned through his inspectors that the shoes of his soldiers required mending before taking another long march, and the order was not issued.

Over thirty thousand men had been killed and wounded. Including the missing, the losses amounted to nearly forty thousand, and the important advantages that might have been secured, the great results that might have been attained, all failed to become a tangible reality because, figuratively speaking, the army was not provided with a corps of cobblers.

Note.—The *Providence Daily Journal* was furnished by me with a list of casualties, which I copy:

Casualties in Battery D.

The following is a correct list of casualties in Battery D at the late Battle of Antietam:

Killed.

Private John Galloughly,
  "   John McGovern,

185

"   Edward Carroll,
"   John Hopkins.
                    Wounded.
Artificer Benjamin N. Whipple, bullet across the back of hand—
    severe wound.
Private Reuben D. Dodge, bullet through the left arm—
    severe wound.
Private Jeremiah Sullivan, bullet through the shoulder—
    severe wound.
Private Jeremiah D. Hopkins, bullet through the leg—
    severe wound.
Private Everett Burt, bullet through the leg—
    severe wound.
Private Charles Reed, bullet through the leg—
    severe wound.
Private Royal W Cfesar, ankle injured by cannon ball—
    severe wound.
                    Missing.
Private Charles A. Mulick,
"   George Bennett,
"   Frank A. Potter,
"   Isaac D. Russell,
"   Jacob J. Schmidt,
"   Duty Bobbins,
"   Bernard Kilbarn,
"   David Smith, 2nd.

Besides the above there were some fifteen wounded, whose injuries were slight.

The newspaper correspondents afterwards reported Bennett and Kilbarn in hospital, wounded.

Recollections of Service in Battery D., First Rhode Island Light Artillery

George C. Sumner

The spring and summer of 1861 was full of excitement for the young men of that day. First, rumour of war, then actual war stirred their patriotism to its very depths. Then the enlistments began, and soon every armoury was filled with men and boys full of excitement; soldiers paraded day and night; the beating of drums could be heard at all times, and one could hardly pass along the streets without meeting companies out for drill, while train after train passed through the city filled with soldiers off to the war.

I was a boy of seventeen in those days, with perhaps the average amount of patriotism. At all events I imbibed my full share of the excitement, and it was with considerable effort that I repressed it sufficiently to prevent my enlisting, which I was unsuccessful in doing until the 2nd of September. On that day a friend and myself strolled over to the Marine Artillery armoury, on Benefit Street, and while there it was announced that Battery D needed only about a dozen men to finish its complement.

John said to George, "What do you say?"

George replied, "It is a go;" and down went our names for three years or the war.

The writer went immediately home and informed his people of his determination to go to the war, silencing all opposition by announcing that the deed had been done, as he had placed his name on the roll. We were mustered in on September 4th, and went to Camp Ames near Pawtuxet, where we were drilled in marching for a day or two. On the 13th boarded the cars, and were taken to Stonington, leaving that night on the boat for Elizabeth City, N. J., where we took the cars direct for Washington, arriving on the 15th, and went directly to "Camp Sprague," where we remained until October 12th. During this time we drew our guns and horses, did lots of drilling, had several reviews,—one by General Scott,—and numerous opportunities to look about the city I used frequently to go to the Capitol, climb to the top of the unfinished dome, and take a look over into Virginia, hoping to catch a glimpse of the rebels, but as my vision was limited to five or six miles, instead of the necessary fifty, I was of course unsuccessful.

On October 12th we were ordered to pack up and moved through Washington over Long Bridge into Virginia, marching five or six miles, and went into camp at a place called Hall's Hill. On the 14th we drew A tents, and pitched camp in the woods on a side hill.

The only thing I remember particularly about this camp is the immense camp-fires we used to have. The nights were rather cool, and we used to build these fires and then fell the trees over on to them, and as fast as the limbs burned off would pile them on, and soon had a fire that half the members of the battery could get around, and roast one side while the other froze.

On the 17th we moved our camp some three miles to Upton's Hill, and on November 2nd, to Munson's Hill. We remained here for a week or ten days, and then moved into what was thought to be a better location, and began to build our winter's camp. We parked the battery in regular style, pieces in front, caissons in the rear, and on either side of these we built stables for our horses, by first building a framework of poles and covering the top and sides with pine boughs. Our tents were pitched on a line with the stables, extending nearly to the officers' quarters, which left quite a commodious parade ground between the latter and the battery-park for inspections, guard-mountings, etc. These were Sibley tents, circular in form and quite large, with a stove in the centre.

I have forgotten whether we had one or two to a detachment; at any rate we had plenty of room. The bunks were built large enough to accommodate two, and were filled with straw, and as each man had two blankets, by bunking together we could lay two under and use two over us, with our feet towards the fire. The man from the tent who happened to be on guard made it his duty to see that the fire did not go out on cold nights. You may be sure that we slept just as comfortably as had we been on a feather bed at home.

We had as neighbours in this camp Battery B, Fourth United States Artillery, Captain John Gibbon, First New Hampshire, Captain Gerrish, and a Pennsylvania battery, Captain Durrell. Captain Gibbon of the regular battery, had command of the post. Quite a rivalry existed between the regular and volunteer company, and I recollect that some tall hustling used to be done to prevent their beating us in moving out of park, after "Boots and Saddles" had been sounded for drill or inspection. We seldom got left, but frequently had narrow escapes, and well do I remember how anxious we used to be on the left piece, sometimes, until we heard the order, "Right piece, forward!" fearing that it might please the fancy of the captain to move the battery out of park, left in front; as we were not quite ready, some kind-hearted cannoneer, at that moment, was finishing what the driver had not had time to do before the order to mount.

We used our time that fall and winter in drill, inspections, learning to ride, and the manual of the piece. I don't think I had ever mounted a horse before I became connected with Battery D, and well do I remember my experience in mastering the art of horsemanship. The method used for our instruction was heroic, with the single exception that we were allowed to put a blanket over the backbone of the horse, no saddles, no bridles were allowed. I should be sorry to attribute a wrong motive for the blanket consideration, but I am obliged to say that it was my opinion then, and is still, that the privilege was allowed us more from fear that without this protection we were liable to be incapacitated for guard and other duties, which we were obliged to do on foot, rather than our personal comfort.

We were obliged to control the horse as best we could with the halter, which was practically no control at all. The horse that I took my first lesson on was not a good saddle horse. He had only one easy gait, that was a walk. His trot was fearful. He could easily lift me four or five inches from his back every time he put his feet down; his running was not much better; lope he could not, and so sometimes when the rest of the battery were loping along easily, I was being pounded almost to death by his constantly changing gait from trot to run or run to trot, as he fell behind or gained on the rest of the column.

Many of us had the bad habit of holding on with our heels. We were cautioned time after time that we must not do so, but use our knees for that purpose, but the very next time we would forget and commit the same error; so some fertile brain among the officers conceived the horrible plan of placing spurs upon the heels of those who were troubled with this forgetfulness. I made up my mind that I would be sure and remember about those spurs, and succeeded very well so long as we remained at a walk; but when ordered to trot, and I commenced bounding all over that horse's back, I forgot, and hugged my horse with my heels. The effect was electrical. My horse darted ahead, and hitting the one in front, whose heels I was just able to dodge, started down the off side of the line on the dead run. I did some fine dodging on that trip. Seventy-five *per cent*, of the horses in that line tried to hit me, but not one succeeded.

All this time my poor horse was asking me, I suppose, to let up with those spurs; but I was so confused and astonished that I did not catch his idea, and he, despairing of my taking a reasonable view of the thing, and having reached a fence which barred his further progress, invited me in such an intelligent manner to dismount that I understood him, and complied, not in the graceful manner that I should have done if my will had governed it, but over his head and the fence into an adjoining field, all in a heap, and it was not until I had rubbed the pain out of my bruised head, arms and body, that I fully realized that the cause of my trouble had been those spurs.

Occasionally we would go out for target practice, and I remember on one occasion we had been firing in a direction, for example, towards the south, when soon up rides a colonel and desires to know why we were shelling his camp. The captain informed him that we had not been shelling in his direction at all, and pointed in the direction that we had been firing. The colonel said he did not care if we had been firing south, our shells had been going west. That lot of ammunition was speedily condemned.

About this time General McDowell, who commanded our corps, began to have his splendid reviews and sham fights. I had an experience at one of these sham fights that I must relate. The general would have the whole corps out, running them all over those plains, fighting an imaginary enemy, and firing blank cartridges. On one of these occasions I was driving the wheel team caisson, and we had been having a hard fight, when the general suddenly discovered the enemy had got around on our flank, and he gave orders to change our front, thereby giving the battery a run of about a mile, which would have been pleasant enough to us if it had not been for the fact that a large part of the way lay through what had been woods when the corps first went into camp, but it had been cut off by the soldiers, and the stumps left by them were of the usual irregular height that a soldier always left. No true soldier would ever bend his back in cutting down a tree, consequently the height of the stump varied according to the height of the man cutting it down. Well, we started on our run, and it was a fearful one for cannoneers. We would strike a stump and they would leave the box heavenward, meeting it again by the force of gravitation, and they had all they could do to remain on the boxes.

We made the journey, and arrived at a place where I thought we could come about, and held in my team, but my lead driver thought differently, seeing which, I let my team out again, and I had hardly done so when around he went, and the swing driver, who was a green one, instead of swinging out, as he should have done, did just the other thing, which brought his traces taut across the pole, and pulled my team around in spite of all they could do, and to add to our trouble, there happened to be a large stump in just the right place for the off wheels to hit it, which they did with great force, and over went the caisson, bottom side up, throwing both my horses and myself badly mixed up with them.

You may imagine my feelings as I saw that caisson going over, knowing that in the chests there were a dozen or more shells of the Parrott pattern, which were exploded by a percussion cap affixed to a plunger inside the shell, and needed only a severe concussion to explode them.

The mind works quickly at such times. I expected they would explode, and that being so near them I should probably be killed. I thought of home, friends, and a thousand other things during those few seconds; but fortunately they did not explode, although the cases were completely smashed. I managed to extricate myself from the debris, and was trying to arrange things, when General McDowell rode up with his grand staff and ordered a company of infantry to assist us in straightening out; but their help was in reality a hindrance, as they knew nothing about our work, and the first thing I knew they had unbuckled every buckle in the harnesses, and it took longer to buckle up again than to have straightened it out half a dozen times if left to ourselves; but finally we got fixed and went back into camp. Captain Monroe told me that night that the government would probably expect me to pay for that caisson, and I remember thinking that as I was working for thirteen dollars per month, and did not have any surplus, the government would probably have to take it on what would be called in these days the instalment plan. But nothing was ever said further about it, the government considering the claim worthless, I suppose.

March 10, 1862, we made our first march towards the rebels, and it was a memorable one from the fact of its being the most disagreeable of any I made during the war, save one. We broke camp early in the morning in a cold, drizzling rain, so cold that it froze as fast as it fell, and moved out near the Centreville pike, where, after waiting for an hour or so, we finally moved into the road and started towards Centreville. We made camp that night at Fairfax Court-House, and next day went as far as Centreville, and found the rebels had left. We remained here until the 15th, when we were ordered to inarch, and back we started towards Washington, turning off at Bailey's Cross-Roads towards Alexandria, and finally about seven in the evening drove into a farmyard at Cloud's Mill and went into camp, the most miserable lot of beings you ever saw, nearly frozen, hungry, and wet through.

My father had sent me a pair of rubber boots to march in, and I wore them on this march for the first and last time. I put them on in the morning, tucked my trousers nicely into them and mounted my horse. As soon as my clothing became saturated with water the surplus began to run down into those boots, and my misery commenced. I could not change them, as my shoes were back in my knapsack, and that was inaccessible; but you can imagine that I lost no time after we had unhitched in finding that knapsack and changing my footwear. By the time I had done this the boys had taken the fence in front of the dooryard and built a large fire, and we all hovered around it till morning. At some time during the next forenoon we moved back to our old camp.

April 4th we were ordered to prepare for another march, and we started over the same road. We made our first camp near Fairfax Court-House. On the 5th we reached Manassas, and on the 6th Bristoe Station. That night in camp at Bristoe Station it snowed and was rather cold. I remember I was on guard over horses. Did not have any trouble for the first two hours, but when I was aroused for my second trick, which came about an hour before daylight, I soon became cold and sleepy, and finally went to sleep, in which condition the relief found me. The sergeant entertained me with surmises of what would probably be done to me when it was reported at headquarters. He said that in ninety-nine cases out of one hundred the culprit was shot, and that I could take what comfort I could out of the chance that I might possibly be the one hundreth. I did not feel very happy that morning, and wished I had never become a soldier. I never heard any more from it, and a little later in my experience such small matters did not trouble me much.

We remained here until the 16th, then went to Cattlet Station. Started again on the 18th, and at night reached Falmouth, near Fredericksburg, and went into camp. The next day moved on a little further and went into camp opposite Fredericksburg, on the north bank of the Rappahannock, which proved to be our abiding place until May 25th. On the 26th of May our corps moved across the river and on towards Richmond, our battery remaining in Fredericksburg, camped on a common. The citizens were very bitter, and showed their hatred in various ways, the older ones being careful not to annoy us openly, but through children so small that we could not notice their acts, they sometimes made life almost a burden. I remember passing a tine place that abutted the street, with a high brick wall, on one of the main streets one clay, when three or four little fellows, the oldest not more than six, made it very warm for me by throwing gravel at my head as long as I remained within reach.

We left Fredericksburg on the 6th of August and marched to Rappahannock Station, reaching there late in the afternoon of the 8th. To accomplish this we were obliged to keep moving most of the time, halting occasionally for an hour to allow the men to lie down by the roadside and get a little rest.

My recollection of that campaign is, that for long-continued hard marching, and severe fighting, it exceeded anything in my experience. On our arrival at Rappahannock Station we went into position on the north bank of the river. We had heard heavy firing all the afternoon, and knew that a severe battle had been fought. This proved to be the battle of Cedar Mountain, the first in General Pope's campaign.

Sometime after dark we were ordered to limber, and pulled out into the road and started on our retreat toward Bull Run. From this time until the 28th we were on the march, moving here, there and everywhere. What it all meant at that time we did not know, but have since learned that we were tiding to find Stonewall Jackson, who had in some way become lost,—at least to our generals,—and they could not find him; but on the afternoon of the 28th, between five and six o'clock, we found him, or rather he found us. We were turning into the lots for a camp, and had some of the horses unharnessed. We were unaware that the rebels were anywhere near us, when all at once we were greeted with a tremendous volley from infantry, which was startling, to say the least.

We were immediately ordered to hitch up and go into position, and we had our first opportunity of showing how we could handle our guns in the presence of the enemy. For two hours or more we kept up a very rapid fire, and I think must have done considerable damage. We had the stock of one of our caissons broken by their fire, and the caisson was blown up under the direction of Lieutenant Parker. We lay in this position until about twelve o'clock, when word was passed that no one was to speak above a whisper, the drivers mounted, pieces were limbered, and we started silently away.

This battle was called Gainesville from its proximity to a village of that name. We had gone a little way beyond this village towards Groveton, but retraced our steps to the pike that ran to Manassas Junction, to which place we now marched, arriving early on the morning of the 29th. Late in the forenoon we started back, taking the road to Bull Run battlefield. We moved along very slowly, in consequence of the road being occupied by wagon trains. We could hear firing from the fight at Groveton, and were very impatient at our delay How I did fret over it! I was sure that we would be too late, and should have no chance to get at the Johnnies. I was never so anxious afterward; no amount of delay ever disturbed me after my experience of the next day.

About four o'clock we turned off the road, and were ordered forward on the run, and finally went into position on a hill overlooking quite an extent of country toward an unfinished railroad, where Jackson had been fighting our troops since noon. We could see the fighting very plainly from our position, but it was too far away for us to take any part.

I soon began to see the effect of war; wounded men began to pass through our battery, and I became convinced that this was serious business. I remember one poor fellow who passed through our lines three times within two hours on that afternoon, each time with a fresh wound. Twice he had them dressed and went back, but the third time he came back on a stretcher, and we saw no more of him.

We remained all night and until about two o'clock in the afternoon of the next day in our first position. We then moved back across the valley to a position a mile or so off to the rear and left of the old one.

We came into battery by the right flank, which placed my piece, it being the left of the battery, on the right of our line. Two other batteries were placed in position on our right in echelon, a brigade of infantry was brought up, and placed in our rear for support. I remember hearing the captain say to the general commanding the troops in our rear, all he wanted of him was to drive the Johnnies out if they got in between the guns, and to cover his limbering the pieces and taking them off. The general responded that he should stay there as long as the battery did. It is possible that he did stay, but his men did not, but dusted out long before the battery.

I think that Battery D, as it stood in position that afternoon, was as fine an organisation of the kind as there was in the service. By far the larger part of the men were under twenty-one, active and thoroughly posted in the drill, and capable of doing as effective work as it was possible to do. We had been drilling nine months, and there were few men who, if called upon, could not take any position on the piece and do the work perfectly.

The battery consisted of six brass guns called "light twelves," or "Napoleons." They were smooth bore, and our ammunition was of twelve-pound shot and shell, spherical in form, and canister, which consisted of thirty-two quarter-pound iron balls, contained in a tin case.

Now with such guns and ammunition as these we had been told, if we would stick to the guns, no troops could live in front of us as long as our ammunition lasted; and on this very afternoon of which I write we proved the truth of that assertion. We had been in position perhaps a half hour, when we had orders to begin shelling the woods that were in our front. We had seen great clouds of dust in the direction of Manassas Junction pike, and very soon it was said that Longstreet had come up on Jackson's right, and was swinging in on our left with the intent of doubling us up.

Soon they began to show themselves, and we kept up a pretty lively fire on them with solid shot and shell. We must have made it rather warm for them, as the writer noticed they covered as soon as we got the range. They suddenly appeared in our front and formed for a charge, two or three regiments front, and several lines in the rear at close intervals. Soon the gunners called for canister, and we began to send that into them; then we double-shotted it, breaking off the cartridge from one of the cases and ramming it home on top of the other. Our gunners had been taught that in firing canister to prevent wasting it, it was best in close action to ricochet it, having it strike the ground just far enough in front of the enemy to have its rebound reach them breast high. Now imagine the execution of six guns, handled by cool gunners as these were, and can you wonder that they fell back? They soon rallied, however, and came for us again, and this time we staid

195

with them until we used every round of ammunition we had, then limbered and started for the rear, taking off every piece and caisson. The batteries on our right had all been captured or driven off, and when we started for the rear I do not remember seeing any of our troops anywhere near us.

I went into this action as driver of the lead team on the caisson, but early in the fight one of the lead horses of the piece was disabled, and my team was taken to replace it. This left me without anything to do for awhile, but as the limber of the piece was soon emptied, I found plenty of employment in bringing up ammunition from the caisson to the piece. I finished this just about the time that the Johnnies started on the second and last charge, and I had nothing to do but stand around and watch things, which was just the thing I did not care to do. The rebels had planted some artillery on our left, and opened a heavy fire on us with shell and canister, and it seemed to me that the air was full of screeching shells; then canister would come bounding through our battery, so nearly spent that I could watch them, and it did seem to me that if I got out of that place alive it would be a miracle. Just then I heard the order, "Limber to the rear," and I remember calling as loudly as I could, repeating the order, to Corporal George Eldred.

The caisson had left while I was calling to Eldred, and the piece followed closely. Corporal Eldred had passed me on his way to the rear, he being the fastest runner, but we had not gone a hundred yards when I heard a shell coming behind us, and just as it reached a point directly over my head and not a great way above it, it burst, the concussion from it nearly knocking me down. Then I heard the *whirr* of a part of the shell as it flew in front of me, and the thud as it struck poor Eldred square in the back of his neck. I shall never forget the sound that he made as he fell forward, nor the last sight I had of him as I passed a moment later. His head was bent under him a little, showing a great gaping wound in his neck.

A singular thing in connection with his death was the fact that he had always declared he should be killed in the first battle that he should participate in. The boys had tried to laugh him out of the notion. The night before, in our old position, some half dozen of us were lying around the gun, and Eldred had again assured us that if we went into action on the morrow he would be dead at night, and no amount of chaffing could dispel his melancholy.

Soon I caught the piece and jumped on the trail, which I had hardly done when we jumped a wide ditch, and I thought I had been hit with a hundred pound shell, but clung to my place, and rode along until the battery was halted and ordered into position again, for what purpose I never could understand, as we had no ammunition, unless as a piece of unadulterated bluff. Nothing came of it, however, as the Johnnies seemed to have had enough for the present, and did not follow us far. We limbered again, and started towards the stone bridge, which, fortunately, we succeeded in crossing without much trouble, and moved on a mile or so towards Centreville. We then turned into a lot and took a short rest. Later we moved on to Centreville, where we unhitched and fed our horses, made some coffee for ourselves, and I lay down to get a little sleep.

It was rather disturbed, however, as I was continually hearing shot and shell whirling around me, and I frequently awoke trying to dodge them. We remained all day at Centreville replenishing our ammunition, and the next day,—September 1st,—started for Washington. When just about halfway between Centreville and Fairfax Court House, Jackson opened upon our corps at a place called Chantilly, and a very severe battle, but of short duration, took place. The battery did not take part in this, as the lighting was done principally by infantry. How it rained that night; we were wet through, but were so tired that we spread our blankets and lay down on the wet ground, threw the blankets over our heads, and were soon fast asleep.

The next day we moved on, and at night reached the vicinity of our old camp at Munson's Hill, very tired, very hungry, and very much discouraged. A brigade of infantry made camp on the opposite side of the road from us, and I remember hearing some of them say that it was fortunate that the officers had concluded to make camp just as they did, as they could not have gone a step farther for anyone.

Just about dark on this same night—September 2nd,—we heard cheering away off down the road towards Alexandria. Of course we were all very anxious to know its meaning. Soon we could distinguish a large body of horsemen approaching, and the troops on either side would rush out into the road and cheer with all their might. We rushed with the rest, and when the cavalcade got near enough we saw that it was General McClellan and staff, and word was passed that General Pope had been relieved and McClellan had assumed command again. What a transformation took place in those troops! All signs of discouragement had passed away, and I fully believe, if he had asked them, tired as they were, to recommence their march, or go into fight that night, they would willingly have obeyed, such was their confidence in him.

For a week or more we remained around the defences of Washington, doing a little picket duty now and then. Finally, on the 6th of September, we left camp near Dupont about 9 p.m., and marched to Washington , passing through the city about midnight, and on the 7th we camped about twelve miles beyond the city, on the Maryland side of the Potomac River. We remained here until the 10th, and then went to Lisbon. We reached New Market on the 12th, and went to Frederick City the next day. Here we began to skirmish with the rebels, and on the 14th and 15th our troops had a severe fight with them at South Mountain. We did not become engaged, but the fighting was in plain view from our position.

We had a little excitement on the afternoon of the 14th. Our men, together with some from a regiment that lay just across the road from us, participated in a raid upon a sutler who was unfortunate enough to happen along just as they were very much in need of something nice to eat, but had no money to pay for it, and his possessions were speedily reduced to the horse and running-gear of his wagon, without any collateral to show for it. He complained at headquarters, and every effort was made to find his goods, but not a single thing was found.

The battery moved down towards Sharpsburg on the 16th, and took a position soon after dark. The rebels shelled us until about 9.30 p. m., and it made a very pretty display as the shells passed through the air, leaving a track of tire behind, and I think we should have enjoyed it if it had not been so dangerous. I laid down that night on the top of a caisson, about ten o'clock, and went to sleep. Just about daylight I awoke with a start. I think that the *whizz* of a shot must have awoke me; at any rate, just as I raised my head, one passed over me, so close that I thought at the time it could not have been more than an inch above me; but I suppose it really was several feet. I jumped down from that box quickly, and for ten or fifteen minutes the Johnnies threw a stream of shells through our battery.

They had a perfect range on our position, and for a little while made it very warm, but we happened to have in position on that hill about twenty guns, unlimbered and ready for action, and it took but two or three minutes for our cannoneers to get to them, and then in a moment twenty projectiles of various kinds and size were flying towards that rebel battery. That treatment was kept up until we had the pleasure of seeing them limber and run away.

We remained in our position, if I remember rightly, until shortly after noon, firing whenever we could see anything to fire at, and watching the fight on our front. Immediately in front was a thin belt of woods, and just beyond this an extensive cornfield, in which was done as stubborn fighting as I ever saw. First one side, then the other, would hold possession of it, charging back and forth, leaving the dead and wounded on the field until they lay in windrows from one side of the cornfield to the other. Early in the forenoon, if my memory serves me, Captain Monroe was ordered to take his pieces, leaving the caissons, and go down through that cornfield to the farther end, and if possible, silence a rebel battery that was giving our men trouble.

Well, we started, and what an awful journey it was. We no sooner reached the field than we were greeted with the groans of the wounded, and some of them that lay in our way had to be moved to one side. Some were horribly mangled. Such sights as these, and the constant *zip* of the minies (which sound I always disliked very much more than that of the shot and shell) had completely unmanned me, so that when we had unlimbered and I was called upon to cut a fuse, I found that my right hand was trembling so I could not use the cutter, and I called upon the wheel driver to help me. In a moment it had passed away and I was myself again.

Our gun did the most rapid firing here that I ever knew it to do, and in a very short time we had silenced those guns. I learned afterwards that we knocked that battery almost to pieces. We then limbered and went a little way back and halted, while one of our pieces was prolonged off. The sharpshooters had nearly used up both men and horses on that gun, in attempting to limber. I think they shot five men, one after the other, just as fast as they attempted to take hold of the trail, but the men succeeded in attaching the prolong to it and dragging it off by hand.

While we lay in that hollow, a division of nine months troops came out into the field. We knew they were fresh from home by the newness of their uniforms and the fresh look about their colours, and also from their full ranks. They marched out in fine style, stepping over the old line of battle where the men were lying down, and charged towards a stone wall behind which the rebels were. Some of the old fellows chaffed them a little by asking where they were going, and telling them to be sure and not go beyond the stone wall; and they did not, but very near it, and a brave fight they made of it, so brave that the vets gave them a rousing cheer when at last they gave way and fell back.

Soon after this we went back to our old position. It was getting dark by this time, and pretty soon the firing ceased and everything was quiet except a shot now and then from the pickets. Thus ended the Battle of Sharpsburg, or Antietam.

From our standpoint we could not tell whether it had been a victory for us or not. We certainly did not suppose it was over, and expected to commence fighting at daylight; but next morning, everything being quiet, we investigated and found that there had been a cessation of hostilities asked for and granted, for the purpose of attending to the wounded. All that day we remained in position, expecting every moment to be called upon. It began to be rumoured around that Lee was getting away as fast as he could, and some very forcible remarks were made about allowing him to get away without making any attempt to crush his army. Every soldier that I heard express himself was in favour of fighting. General McClellan has said that the troops were not in condition to follow, but that was certainly not the case with any of the troops around us.

On the 19th we started, as we supposed, in pursuit, but only marched a short distance and went into camp. After we had finished our camp duties, some of us went back over the battlefield, and I shall never forget what I saw there. A great many of the dead lay just as they had fallen two days before. Burial parties were engaged in digging trenches fifteen to twenty feet long, about six or eight feet in width, and four to five feet deep, in which they would lay the dead as closely as possible, then cover them up. Most of the bodies were in a terrible state. It had rained the previous night, and the sun coming out very hot the next morning hastened mortification, turning the exposed parts of the bodies black, while they were swollen to two or three times the natural size.

I remember seeing a young boy, who had evidently been mortally wounded and had dragged himself up near a stone wall to die. He had taken a daguerreotype of his mother from his pocket for a last look before he died. A horse sitting up like a dog, with his nose deeply imbedded in a haystack, dead, was among the singular things I remember to have seen on that field.

September 20th we moved near Sharpsburg and made camp, in which we remained until October 20th. During this time we were reviewed by President Lincoln.

October 20th we went to Brownville, where we remained three days, camping with the division of artillery, and we expected to build winter quarters here, but on the 23rd were ordered to pack up, and after marching until 9 p.m., went into camp in a mud-hole. On the 27th moved three or four miles to Crompton's Pass, and on the 28th continued through the pass and camped near Knoxville, Md. On the 30th went to Berlin. November 1st went into Virginia and camped at Berryville, and on the road passed the Seventh Rhode Island. On the 3rd camped at Bloomfield, meeting the Fourth Rhode Island. On the 5th marched to Rectortown, thence to Warrentown. On this day we went into position in a furious snow storm.

On the 10th McClellan's farewell address was read to us on parade, the army was reviewed, and Burnside took command and his address was also read. On the 11th we marched to Waterloo, remained here until the 17th, when we went to Morristown, where it was said we were to quarter for the winter; but on the 22nd we marched to Brook Station on the Fredericksburg and Aquia Creek Railroad, and from there back to Waterloo. From this time until December 4th we remained at Waterloo. The weather was very cold and stormy. On the 4th we were ordered to pack up, but it began snowing very fast, and the order was countermanded. It stormed all day and part of the next, the snow was three to four inches deep.

We did not move until the 7th, when we went four or five miles, and the battery became so mired we were obliged to make camp where we were. Rations were very short at this time, and we could not get a square meal. On the 8th we went to Fredericksburg, and on the 9th made camp opposite the city. On the 11th the battle of Fredericksburg was opened. Some time before daylight on the morning of the 11th, artillery had been posted along the heights opposite the city, reaching from one end to the other of the town. I do not know just how many guns were in that line, but should say from seventy-five to one hundred. About 5 a.m. a signal gun was fired, and then they all opened, and for three hours there was a constant roar from these guns that fairly shook the earth.

There was a brigade of rebel sharpshooters in Fredericksburg at this time, and for a long time they effectually prevented the laying of our pontoon bridge. Our men would be shot down as soon as they showed themselves, and finally orders were given for the artillery to concentrate their fire upon them, and at the same time volunteers were called for to cross in the boats and drive them, which was speedily done, when the bridge was laid and our army began to cross, and heavy skirmishing was carried on all day. The next day a very heavy force was thrown across the river, and our battery went with it.

We were not called upon, however, but lay all that day and until just before dark the next, under cover of the buildings in the streets of Fredericksburg. Just before dark on the 14th we were ordered into position on a hill just beyond the town, and opened fire; but no sooner had we done so than a perfect shower of shells and Minies, we being within rifle range of their works, poured in upon us, which shut us up about as quick as you could a jacknife, and we were very glad to seek the protection of the bank, coming back, however, as soon as it ceased, and opened fire again, with the result of reproducing the shower.

About this time we discovered a new danger. It seems that just before we occupied this position another battery had moved out of it, and they had piled their ammunition up near their pieces to have it handy. It was so dark when we drove in that we did not see it. We had been firing over it, and soon a spark from our guns set fire to a fuse, and we suddenly found ourselves in a hornet's nest. Some of us did not have time to get under the bank, and for fifteen minutes or so we hugged the ground for dear life. After remaining here long enough to become satisfied that the only service we could do would be to act as a target for the Johnnies to draw their fire, we were ordered out of it, and went down into the town, seeking shelter under the lee of the buildings.

We remained here until about 2 a.m. of the 15th, when we re-crossed the river and returned to our old camp. This ended the battle of Fredericksburg, lasting four days, every one of which was filled with hard fighting. The battery was under fire constantly, as the rebels kept up an almost constant fire, and so accurate that we could but re-mark the wonderful improvement their gunners had made.

Later we were able to understand the reason of this remarkable shooting; diagrams of the surrounding country were found, the prom-inent points in which, such as streets in the city, farm-houses and intersecting of roads, etc., had been marked with the degrees of el-evation necessary to reach the spot, the result of an actual survey. A perfect dub could have made a good shot with such help.

We moved on the 17th of December back about a mile and a half, into a grove, and began to build our winter quarters. My chum, Peter Botter, and myself, finished ours in a day or two, and made ourselves quite comfortable. Our house consisted of a cellar about a foot and a half deep, six feet long and four feet wide, boxed around with pine slabs. Then the dirt was tamped hard around the outside of the slabs, a ridge-pole raised in the crotch of two upright poles and covered with our shelter tent; a mud chimney was built on the outside, the tent being tacked tightly around the fireplace. We had a bunk on either side, raised from the ground and filled with boughs. When the house was done and we had built a good rousing fire in the fire-place, we were just as comfortable and happy as it was possible for soldiers to be. From this time until the 6th of February, 1863, we spent our time in performing the ordinary duties of the soldier, such as drill, having inspections, etc., varied between January 10th and 21st by being under marching orders for the purpose of crossing the Rappahannock river on an expedition against the rebels, and a large part of the army did leave their quarters and make the attempt, but the weather was so bad and the roads so muddy the idea was abandoned, and the troops returned to their old camps, completing what is known in history as the celebrated mud march. Our battery was fortunate enough not to have left their camp.

On the 6th of February we received orders to pack up and be ready to march in an hour, and at 8 a m. we pulled out of our winter camp and started for Belle Plain, on the Potomac River, about twelve miles distant. It rained very fast and the roads were exceedingly muddy, so that the very best we could do in all day was between five and six miles. The pieces and caissons would become fast in the mud, and we would have to double our teams to pull them out. You may imagine our condition: tired out, wet through, and no way of protecting ourselves from the cold storm, which continued through the night. We succeeded after great difficulty in pulling the guns and caissons through to the landing on the next day, but the battery wagons and forge not having arrived, six teams of horses were sent back after them, and they were found about five miles back, the forge being bottom side up in a creek, having run off the bridge the night before. After four or five hours of hard work, we got it out, and after great trials and tribulations we finally landed the battery at our destination, having been just three days going twelve miles.

At two o'clock a.m., on the 9th, we commenced to load the battery on canal boats; by 9 a. m. were loaded, and at 4 p.m. started down the river in tow of a steamer, but went only a little way because of the rough condition of the river. On the 11th we again started, but as we reached the bay the captain decided that it would not be wise to attempt to cross in the canal boats, so we made harbour at St. Mary's, where we lay until the 13th. The oysters were so plenty here that the boys would take a boat and row over to the rocks, returning in a very short time with several bushels. We did just have a feast while here; we ate them in every style, raw, fried and stewed. I can remember even after this lapse of time how good they tasted.

At daylight on the 13th we started once more, but after running down opposite Point Lookout were obliged to lay to again on account of the weather, until three o'clock, the wind having gone down, we pushed on and reached Hampton Roads at daylight on the morning of the 14th, and immediately disembarked, and the next day went into camp near Hampton, which must have been a beautiful place in its day, before the rebel General Magruder burned it. When we arrived it was largely occupied by negroes, and here it was that I first attended a genuine negro meeting. The boys used to go frequently, more as a place of amusement, I am afraid, than for a better purpose.

From the 15th of February until the 4th of March, we remained in camp at Hampton, with very little to vary the monotony.

On the 14th of March we moved over to Newport News, where we remained until the 19th, and at six o'clock on that day we started for Fortress Munroe, when a furious snow storm came on and we made camp at Hampton. How it did snow that day! At night it was eight to ten inches deep, but next day we pushed on to the Fort. From the wharf at this point we embarked on a schooner, and early on the 22nd sailed for Baltimore, arriving there at sunrise on the morning of the 23rd, and commenced immediately to load the battery on cars. At three p.m. we left Baltimore over the Baltimore and Ohio railroad. It was my duty to look after the pieces and caissons on the first two flat cars until midnight, at which time I was relieved. We had just changed engines for the middle section run and I had made friends with the engineer, who invited me to take a seat in the cab. It was a camel-back engine, and the cab was on the top of the boiler. How warm and nice it did seem to me.

When we arrived at the middle of his run, which was on the very tip-top of the Cumberland Mountains, he invited me to go to lunch with him, which I gladly accepted. I remember that I thought it a great lay-out, and just filled myself. As we were leaving to return to the train he handed me a dozen sandwiches, and I tried to convince him that I thought he had the biggest heart of any man I ever met. Whether I succeeded or not I do not know. We ran all the night of the 24th and all day the 25th, arriving at Parkersburg on the 26th, when we loaded our battery on a steamboat, and on the 27th started down the Ohio river. We had a delightful sail down the river, and ran our nose on the bank some six or eight miles above Cincinnati about eight o'clock p.m. on the 28th. The next day we ran down to Covington and transferred the battery from the boat to cars. Unfortunately for the physical condition of many of the men in our company, there lay around that depot several hundred barrels of whiskey, brand-new stuff just from the distillery, almost white in colour, and containing enough fusel oil in a wine-glass to kill a man, unless he was of the toughest kind.

Well, there were about twenty-five men in the company, who the moment they discovered that whiskey were determined to possess as much of it as possible; so at about ten p.m., when we rolled out of that depot, we had a barrel of the whiskey aboard, and just as soon as we were fairly under way, the head was knocked in, and very soon every canteen, water-bucket, in fact everything that would hold whiskey was full of the stuff. The sequel of this bounteous supply, rivers of whiskey as it were, was, that on our arrival at Lexington next morning, about eight o'clock, nearly fifty *per cent*, of our men were incapacitated for duty, and it consequently fell upon the temperance element of the company to do all the work.

The battery was finally unloaded, and we moved about a half mile from the city and went into camp. Two of our sergeants, Taft and Sullivan, were reduced to the ranks for misdemeanour on the trip. We remained in this camp from March 30th to April 8th, doing general duties, visiting the city, and among other places the plantation formerly belonging to Henry Clay. Late in the evening of the 8th we were ordered to pack up, and marched eight or ten miles, bivouacked for the night, and starting early next morning, made twenty miles, reaching Camp Dick Robinson, where we remained until the 26th.

My recollections of this camp are very pleasant. Just below and across the pike from our camp stood the Hoskins mansion, a spacious house built very much after the style of the houses on the large and wealthy plantations of the South; very large on the ground, and having a wide *piazza* on all sides. At the time of our visit the house was occupied by Mrs. Hoskins and some half-dozen slaves, all that remained, as she told me, of seventy-five that she owned at the beginning of the war. I made an informal call on the lady very soon after our arrival. She received me pleasantly, and as dinner was ready she invited me to sit up.

Our conversation during this meal developed the fact that madam had about everything that was good to eat on her plantation, but no money. We had money, but nothing good to eat, and it was arranged that some dozen or more of us should part with a dollar each day and receive two good meals in exchange. Mrs. Hoskins fulfilled her contract to the letter, and rounded it off by spreading for us on the last day of our stay a perfect banquet.

We left Camp Dick Robinson on the 26th of April, and from then until May 7th spent our time in marching around the country, visiting Stamford, Columbia and Carpenter Creek, for the most part over fine roads and through a beautiful country.

We reached Somerset on the evening of the 7th, and remained there until June 3rd, leaving there at sunrise, and marched towards Lexington, stopping over one day at Stamford to receive pay, and reached Lexington about ten a.m. on the 8th. Began immediately to load the battery on the cars to commence our journey to Vicksburg, but after having nearly loaded the battery the order was countermanded, and we went about three miles from Lexington and camped. That night Louis La Fount, a member of our company, was brought to camp, dead, having fallen or been thrown down stairs in the guardhouse at Lexington, and his neck broken. On the 10th we marched to Nicholsville, and the next day went about five miles to Camp Nelson and remained there until July 12th, a most delightful camp in a very beautiful country.

On the 4th we celebrated by firing a salute, and in order to make as much noise as we could we cut grass, and putting as much as we dared in the guns, rammed it home, and instead of being satisfied with the noise of one gun at a time, we fired by battery: that is, the six guns in unison, and as you may imagine the report was a loud one. In the afternoon we went to the village and celebrated. On the 5th rumors of Morgan's approach began to fly about, and soon the citizens began to drive in their horses and cattle. For our protection we placed four pieces in position, and the infantry threw up earth works; but Morgan was not the fellow to come when he knew we were prepared to receive him. He gave us a wide berth, and by the 11th we knew that he had crossed the Ohio River into Ohio.

On the 12th we started at 9 a.m. for Lexington, and loaded the battery with all possible haste, starting as soon as loaded for Cincinnati, arriving at Covington at 8 a.m., on the 13th, and immediately crossed the river into Cincinnati. The city was very much excited, as Morgan was reported to be within ten or twelve miles, and the citizens expected to see him ride into their streets at any moment.

Our battery was the only veteran organization in the town at this time, and from the moment we landed on that levee we began to receive an ovation. The citizens met us with open arms, as it were, and seemed to feel as though there was some chance of taking care of Morgan now that we had come. The demonstration grew as we got farther into the city, and when we crossed the Rhine, a canal that run through the town, it reached a climax. This part of the city was largely occupied by Germans. There was a lager beer saloon on every corner, and sometimes one or two between. As soon as we reached their neighbourhood the saloon-keepers came out to us with both hands filled with glasses of beer.

Most of us indulged once, some two or three times, and others so frequently that when we arrived in camp on the outskirts of the city, we found that history had repeated itself, and the temperance men had to do the duty The next morning the battery was divided into sections and sent out on the three prominent roads entering the city from the north. My section went about two or three miles, and came into position on a pike. We were supported by the Washington Rifles, good fellows—some of them. Their relatives and friends in the city sent them a large load of nice things, which they shared with us. We had rare fun the next morning, before light, stopping the market wagons as they came along on their way to market. They were considerably frightened at seeing two cannon in position in the road, and when they were halted by the sentry, the sergeant of the guard called, and the demand made that their wagons should be searched for contraband goods, they were too amazed to resist, and we would go through the wagons, taking a few bunches of grapes for our trouble.

On the 17th we moved back into the city. On the 19th we hitched up and marched through the city, visiting the various market-places as a sort of intimidating act, there being some indication of a riot. The next day, thanks to General Burnside, we were ordered to Ninth Street, and made a novel camp. The pieces and caissons were placed in a wagon-yard, the horses in a stable, and the men quartered in a hall, and from this time until the 10th of August we enjoyed ourselves very much. We had little to do, Sunday morning inspection on the levee being about the only real duty that was required of us.

The citizens on Ninth Street invited us out to tea, detachment at a time, and entertained us in fine style. All this was immensely enjoyed by us, but we knew that it was not soldiering, in the full acceptance of the term, and that it must end, which it did on the 10th of August.

We crossed the river to Covington, boarded the cars and were taken to Lexington, from which place we were to commence our march of 250 miles over the Cumberland mountains into East Tennessee, where we passed through a winter's campaign of suffering and privations that was not experienced by any other army during the war.

Campaign of Battery D, First Rhode Island Light Artillery, in Kentucky and East Tennessee

Ezra K. Parker

Campaign of Battery D, First Rhode Island Light Artillery, in Kentucky and East Tennessee

In March, 1863, Gen. A. E. Burnside, having been relieved at his own request of the command of the Army of the Potomac, was soon afterwards assigned to the Department of the Ohio. Upon his special request, the Ninth Army Corps was also detailed for service in this department, and at once preparations were made for the transportation of the corps from Virginia to Kentucky. Battery D, First Rhode Island Light Artillery, Capt. William W. Buckley, was at that time attached to the Ninth Corps and was sent with its corps to the west. This battery had been at the beginning of its service attached to the first division of the Army of the Potomac, and when the army was divided into army corps, this battery was included in the first corps commanded by General McDowell. Its first active service was in the short and successful campaign to Fredericksburg, in April and May, 1862. Then it went through the campaign of the Army of Virginia, under Gen. John Pope, losing heavily at the battle of the second Manassas, then again under General McClellan, in his successful campaign of South Mountain and Antietam.

Meantime, General McDowell had been succeeded by General Hooker in the command of the First Army Corps. It was in the Fredericksburg campaign under Burnside, and was by his order transferred from the First to the Ninth Army Corps. After a not unpleasant march, both by rail and steamboat, the battery reached Lexington, Ky., on

First Lieut. Ezra K. Parker
(Picture taken June, 1908)

March 30th, 1863, and went into camp on the Fair grounds. Here it remained but a week, and then the line of march was taken up for camp Dick Robinson. On the 26th, the battery began its march from camp Dick Robinson to Somerset, near the Cumberland river, completing it on the 7th of May, 1863, and there it remained until the 7th of June. It was now expected that within a few days the march for East Tennessee would commence. Although we, members of the battery, well knew that the campaign would be arduous and full of dangers, still we were all anxious to advance.

In consequence of orders to General Burnside to send a part of his command to Vicksburg to assist General Grant, and in consequence of the raid of Gen. John Morgan, it was not until the 21st of August, 1863, that the expedition started. The Twenty-Third Army Corps was the only corps that commenced at that date the march over the Cumberland River and mountains. General Hartzuff commanded the corps, consisting of three divisions commanded by Generals White, Hascall and Carter, respectively. We were attached to Gen. Hascall's division, and marched with our division by way of Stanford, Crab Orchard and Cub Creek to the Cumberland River. The Ninth Corps was reported to be at Cincinnati and to follow close upon the tracks of the Twenty-Third Corps. The strength of the Twenty-Third Corps was, perhaps, 15,000 or 20,000 men of all arms.

The march over the Cumberland mountains was full of adventures and labours. It would require a much longer paper than this to describe the many incidents that befell us on that famous march. We had no snow nor ice to encounter, but otherwise I doubt whether or not Napoleon's crossing of the Alps was more fraught with dangers and hardships than was this crossing of the Cumberland mountains by the Army of the Ohio. On the 4th of September, 1863, we arrived upon the bluffs of the Tennessee River, opposite Loudon. Here we remained, recuperating, until the 15th of September.

The enemy had hurriedly retreated upon our arrival at Loudon, leaving horses, mules and beef cattle, which we duly appropriated to our own use. A large amount of wheat and corn was found in the possession of the farmers, which was seized by the quartermasters. A steam flour-mill was found in good condition and was employed in grinding up the wheat and corn. We supplemented our rations with chicken and fresh pork while we were encamped at Loudon.

We were on the main line of railway from Virginia to the Southwestern states. In their retreat from Loudon, the enemy had burned the bridge across the Tennessee at that point. It was several days before we were able to place across the river a pontoon bridge. From the south, in the direction of Chattanooga, Gen. N. B. Forrest often threatened us. From the north, a General Jones was daily reported to be advancing down the valley of the Holston upon Knoxville.

About the time that our battery arrived at Loudon, Gen. Burnside made a public entry into Knoxville. General Burnside was not a little disappointed in not having with him the Ninth Army Corps as early as he expected. The corps had been transported from Vicksburg (after having done excellent service before that city and also at Jackson) to Cincinnati, Ohio. In consequence of the great heat at Vicksburg and of the arduous service required of the corps, nearly 50 *per cent* of the men were sick with dysentery and ague. They were sent into Kentucky as soon as possible to find a healthy camp for a few weeks. Crab Orchard was the place selected for the camp on account of its medicinal springs and salubrious surroundings.

On Sept. 25th, 1863, the first division of the Ninth Army Corps arrived at Knoxville, after being subjected to long, fatiguing marches over bad roads by way of Cumberland Gap and Morristown. Our repose at Loudon was broken by orders to place knapsacks and the ammunition chests of the caissons upon flat cars in order to expedite a contemplated forced march. The railroad from Loudon was in operation to a point up the Holston valley beyond Knoxville. The order to move was received upon the 15th inst. We made camp on the night of the 15th near Knoxville, about thirty miles from Loudon. On the 16th we advanced to Strawberry Plains, and on the 17th to New Market.

We remained in New Market two days, and then received orders to counter-march to Loudon. We had been absent about a week, and had covered in all about 200 miles. The cause of this rapid movement from Loudon to New Market was a rumoured attack by the enemy upon our forces in southwestern Virginia. The cause of our return was a dispatch from General Halleck to General Burnside, notifying him that two divisions of General Lee's Army of Northern Virginia had been sent to reinforce General Bragg, and he desired him, General Burnside, to go to General Rosecrans' aid as soon as possible.

On the 23rd of September our battery crossed the Tennessee at Loudon by the aid of a single flat boat large enough to take over only one team and carriage at a time. It took all day and most of the night to effect the crossing. Soon after crossing, we took up the march for Sweetwater, a station sixteen miles south from Loudon, on the east

Tennessee and Georgia railroad. We had no sooner arrived at Sweet-water than we were ordered to countermarch, and away we went back to Loudon. On our arrival there, we were ordered into a rebel fort to the right of the village facing south. This hill was in a bend of the river. A pontoon bridge had been laid across the river and troops of all arms were continually crossing to the south bank. There strong lines of battle were formed, and in expectation of a severe conflict, we awaited the approach of General Forrest, who was steadily driving back our cavalry and mounted infantry upon Loudon. We were all anxious for a brush with the famous General Forrest, and had he assailed our position he would have met with a hot reception. This was the 28th of September, 1863.

Forrest was reported to be advancing with a large mounted force, estimated by citizens and negroes from 3,000 to 15,000 men. We supposed that on the morning of the 29th we would have a royal battle on the banks of the Tennessee. But day dawned and no attack was delivered, and soon word came from our mounted force that Forrest had commenced his retreat down the valley during the night, while we were watering and feeding our horses and mules and inspecting ammunition. From October 1st to the 5th, we were busy collecting forage. In our wagons, and carefully covered by the forage, were carcasses of hogs and sheep. Our company cooks served up rations which could only be fully appreciated by eating. Men, horses and mules were growing fat, sleek and handsome.

On the 6th of October, we received orders to report to our first division of the Ninth Army Corps at Blue Springs, in the valley of the Holston, distant about ninety-eight miles from Loudon. The enemy were reported to be threatening our communications with Cumberland Gap, and the Ninth Corps had been ordered to prevent all interference with this line.

The infantry were transported by rail, but the battery was sent forward on foot. In order that the battery should arrive as soon as possible after the infantry it was forced along at the rate of about thirty miles per day. We found the roads in very fair condition. At dark, on the 9th, we arrived at Bull Gap, a gorge in one of those spur ranges of mountains that extend out from the main chain, and which, at a distance, resembles somewhat a large windrow of hay. On the next day we passed through the gap and soon came up with our division, posted in lines of battle along Lick Creek.

Our arrival was duly reported and we were ordered to hold ourselves ready to take position and open upon the enemy. Here we found General Burnside, and he gave us a hearty greeting, calling us his Rhode Island boys. We responded sincerely and vociferously. Soon after this the general gave the order for our line to advance, as the enemy made no diversion against us. Someone facetiously said that probably the general had waited for our battery before he ordered the attack. We replied to such remarks by retorting that this showed the general's good judgment. A Colonel Foster was in command of a brigade of cavalry, and General Burnside sent him around by the enemy's right flank to seize and hold his lines of retreat. As soon as it was probable that Colonel Foster had reached the desired position, a charge was made upon the enemy's position.

A sharp and hotly contested fight ensued. We drove the enemy from his position about dark. We here formed a new line and lay upon our arms for a renewal of the fight at dawn. The advance was duly made, but the enemy had fled, and Colonel Foster, as it usually happens in such cases, had not got into position to intercept them. Our battery had been in position all day, but was not called upon at all until about dark to fire a few shots at a battery of the enemy that soon withdrew. We pursued the enemy twenty miles up the valley. At noon, we passed through the village of Greenville, and read the sign over a building, with the simple legend, "A. Johnson, Tailor." A mile beyond Rhea Town we went into camp. On the 12th, the cavalry reported the enemy to be so scattered that further pursuit was useless. On the next day, we started back for Knoxville, and arrived there on the 16th of October, 1863. From Loudon to Rhea Town, and from Rhea Town to Knoxville, made a distance of 226 miles, a daily average of a little more than 22 miles. For two days we lay at Knoxville.

On the 20th, we marched again for Loudon. We camped that night at Campbell's Station, seventeen miles from Knoxville. We next encamped at Lenoir's Station. This was a very large plantation owned by a Dr. Lenoir. Its lands were very extensive and beautifully situated. The village consisted of a railroad station, the owner's mansion, large farm buildings, yarn factory, houses for overseers and a hundred or more cabins for his slaves. He, the doctor, was a large slave owner, and a violent rebel. He had extensive fields of maize; one of which was estimated to be four miles in length. The width was considerably less. Most of the corn was as high as a man could reach on horseback.

On October 22nd, we marched to Loudon and crossed the river. The village of Loudon is on the left bank of the Tennessee. Soon after the retreat of General Forrest, referred to above, the writer was detailed to open a recruiting office in the village of Loudon, as our several batteries were all short of men. I duly opened the office in a small building contiguous to a hotel owned by a Mr. Hoss, called by our men "The old hoss." I had two men with me, one a corporal, I appointed clerk; the other man acted as guard and orderly. Handbills were printed and distributed in the vicinity, and on the morning of the second day, as I looked out of the office, I had an idea that a large squadron of cavalry was drawn up before the hotel. The men were thin and lanky, also their horses were the same. All carried guns, some double barrel shotguns; some ancient rifles, and a few modern carbines. I remained in my office, and soon two of the riders dismounted and presented themselves before the guard, who, with drawn sabre and revolver in belt, upheld the dignity of the United States Government in the eyes of these horsemen.

The United States flag was duly floating in the morning air, and all around were nailed the handbills asking for recruits for the U. S. Volunteer Military service. The men who dismounted represented the whole squad. They inquired of the guard if they could "jine" the Union army, and the guard referred them to me for an answer. They came inside and said "Howdy." I responded by a dignified nod of the head. I at once entered upon business, and told them the conditions upon which they could become Uncle Samuel's volunteer soldiers. I stated that I would call a surgeon in order to ascertain if they were physically qualified to enlist. I asked them what they proposed to do with their horses, suggesting that if they were serviceable, they would be bought for our service. They then said that they came from the mountains that lay partly in North Carolina and partly in Tennessee; that they wanted to keep their horses and go home upon them once a week.

I explained that if they enlisted in our service they could go home only at times when furloughs might be granted them, and that meantime they would be expected to be in camp or with their commands at all times, day and night. This they said they could not agree to. They would be ready at any time to a fight, if their services were required, and this they thought was all that should be required of them. Under such conditions, it is evident that the fifty or more mountaineers did not enlist. This ceremony took place on each of the two or three following days, and I tired of this service.

I did not secure a single recruit, and when our battery was ordered to Blue Springs, I was only too pleased to turn over the office to a captain of infantry, who was as successful recruiting as I had been. Another little episode happened to me just before I entered upon the recruiting service. It became necessary for Captain Buckley to send to Knoxville a commissioned officer to report to General Burnside. Our pickets extended about two miles out from Loudon towards Knoxville, and from Knoxville toward Loudon about the same distance. The railroad was not in use at that time, so it was necessary to make the twenty-six miles outside of our lines.

It was about four p.m., when I learned from the captain that I was the favoured officer to report at Knoxville. It was suggested that I need not start until dawn next morning, still I was at liberty to leave at once. I considered the matter a moment and decided to leave that day at dark. There was no moon, but it had all the indications of a bright starlight night. I had my best horse, a thoroughbred Kentuckian, fed at once. I took my sabre and revolver, with a light lunch, and at dark I quietly left camp for my ride to Knoxville. The road to Knoxville was direct and plain. Nearly half the distance it passed through woodland, with but little underbrush. I decided, as the country outside of our lines was infested with rebel scouts and guerillas, to ride rapidly through the open country, but to walk through the wooded part, as it was so dark there that I could not see.

If I walked, I could use the sense of hearing, and so be warned of the approach of either friend or foe. Should I hear advancing steps, I could easily ride out of the road into the woods out of sight, as there were no fences that bordered the road. I met with little adventure. Once, just as I was passing a farmhouse, a voice in the rear, near the house, called out in a loud tone, "halt." I did not obey the order, but touched lightly the flank of my thoroughbred with my spur and he left the house behind like the wind. Two or three times I thought I heard approaching footsteps in the woodland, and I rode a few rods out of the road and waited for a few minutes in expectation, but it proved to be all imagination, and I returned to the road, scratching my face more or less in the branches of the trees.

I had calculated that I could make the ride of thirty miles in about four hours, but in consequence of the slow progress through the woods, it took me much longer, and it was some time after midnight that I discovered several hundred yards ahead of me a fire just outside of the road, partly screened by bushes. I knew that it ought to be a Union picket thrown out by our troops in Knoxville, but I deemed it best to make sure. Most of the way on this road there were few stones, large or small. It was generally a dry loam, and hence a horse though shod, upon the walk would make but little noise. I walked along slowly upon one side of the road towards the fire, ready to turn and race down the road if it should be necessary for my safety. Some additional fuel was cast upon the fire, and it lighted up so that I could distinguish a soldier in our uniform, and I at once went boldly forward. I soon was observed by our picket and duly challenged. After I had given the countersign and shown my pass to the officer in command, I was taken to the picket station and well entertained. Early in the day I reported to General Burnside. When I was about to leave, he questioned me about my journey from Loudon, and instructed me to return with a column that would leave for Loudon that afternoon. I returned to our camp the next day about 2 p.m., in fair condition.

On October 29th, our battery was parked near Lenoir's Station, on the edge of a fine grove of pine trees. Here we were informed that our winter quarters would be. Our men at once entered upon the construction of log cabins for the command, as well as stables for our animals. This work went rapidly forward, as the pine woods furnished ready and ample material. We also utilised a large barn built of weather beaten boards which stood near our camp. The boards furnished floors for the cabins and roofs for our stables. The roofs of the cabins were covered with paulines. By the 13th of November, the camp was completed and we all looked forward for a pleasant time during the approaching winter.

The scientists of the battery had captured a still on one of their foraging expeditions, and in a week or so more the intention was to furnish a liberal supply of pure whiskey at moderate prices. But "man proposes and God disposes," and on the morning of the 14th, our short, sweet dream of cosy winter quarters was broken. Soon after *reveillé*, before the men had fallen into line for roll call, there was the sound of heavy artillery firing at Loudon. We proceeded with the regular camp duties and at the usual time ate our breakfast. Soon we learned the news. General Longstreet, of the Army of Northern Virginia, with his famous corps which had done good service for the rebel arms at Chickamauga, had been sent by General Bragg from Chattanooga to capture Burnside and to clean out the Tennessee and Holston valleys from Southern Tennessee to the southern boundary of Virginia. The veterans of Longstreet had been told that some 15,000 raw troops were scattered from Loudon to Knoxville, who would retreat in confusion at the first appearance of General Longstreet.

It seems that it was not generally known that the Ninth Corps had arrived in the valley. The rebels attempted to lay down a pontoon bridge at Hough's Ferry, a short distance below Loudon. The troops sent to oppose the crossing were from both the Ninth and Twenty-Third Corps. The enemy was not a little surprised at the successful resistance which our troops made to his advance. He was held all day from advancing from the river, and the opinion was that Longstreet would be defeated on the morrow. General Grant had requested General Burnside to maintain himself for a short time, until he, Grant, could fight the Battle of Missionary Ridge; then he would promptly send him assistance. General Burnside, it seems, was so confident that he could hold his own with Longstreet, that he proposed to allow Longstreet to cross the Tennessee so that it would not be possible for him to return to General Bragg in time to aid him in the coming fight.

So, on the night of the 14th, it was decided to fall back, and on the 15th General Burnside gave orders to retreat slowly as far as Lenoir's. Our battery remained in camp all this time, ready to move. It was not until 5 p.m., on the 15th, that we began to move on the main road to Campbell's station. This night march was the most horrid of all my nearly four years' experience in the United States Army. Language will fail to do it justice. I was chief of the left section and brought up the rear, or was supposed to. It had rained for twenty-four hours and the frost was about all out of the ground. The soil was a rich clay, two or three feet in depth. Our horses were not very strong, and after they had dragged the guns and caissons about a mile, their strength was gone.

I was instructed to retreat slowly and in case our rear guard, composed of infantry and cavalry, should find it necessary to make a stand, I was to go into battery. The right and centre sections had gone far ahead of me, as the road was not cut up so bad for them, and it literally seemed, in the language of the poet Horace, that the "*Devil would take the hindmost.*" After the first mile we came to a long, deep bed of sticky mud. I rode in advance, and found that about a half mile ahead there was a little knoll of cleared land, comparatively dry, and skirted by a high, worm fence of good oak rails. So I went back and ordered an advance. By pushing hard, we were able to move our tired teams. Before we had made 200 yards, we were stalled. Then we all, non-commissioned officers, privates and myself, put our shoulders to the wheels and made another 200 yards.

We were all wet inside by sweat and outside by mud and water. Never have I seen men do better. At last, somehow, near morning, we reached the knoll, a mile and a half from camp, physically used up. The caissons in front with guns to the rear, we drew up by the roadside and replenished the smouldering fires with rails. Our horses, poor things, were reeling, scarcely able to stand under the weight of their harness.

One of the buglers had been detailed to accompany me, and I sent him forward to report to the captain our condition and to ask for orders. Meantime, the colonel in command of the rear guard sent word that the rebel skirmishers were pressing him hard, and that he could not hold them back much longer. I roused the weary men and sent a sergeant to select an easier way through the fields. Before he reported, the bugler returned with orders from the captain to destroy and throw away my ammunition. I had never disobeyed an order, but in this case I knew that we had a short supply of ammunition for our 12-pound Napoleons in all the Tennessee Valley; that guns without ammunition were useless, and so I hesitated.

One round was thrown into the mud by a corporal, who heard the report of the bugler to me. I immediately stopped further destruction and proceeded to place my pieces in battery for opening upon the advancing rebel lines, and I had asked our infantry to unmask our front so that we could have a clear field. I gave the order to "load with solid shot," and immediately my men were as active as ever under the excitement of a fight. Before the order was executed I heard my name called, and an officer reported to me with four fresh, 6-mule teams.

General Burnside had burned a large quartermaster's train in order to save his artillery and its ammunition. The arrival of the mules prevented the destruction of our ammunition and the skirmish which I had arranged. I was informed that I should make all haste, as General McLaw had been sent by the Kingston road to cut off our retreat. The two roads, one from Kingston and one from Loudon, intersected a mile south from Campbell's Station. The drivers unhitched their horses and were sent on ahead in order to be out of our way. As soon as the mules were attached to our guns and caissons, they were started, and away they went, through the deep mud, up hill and down, until they passed safely the Kingston road about 10 a.m., and we parked in the open field with the rest of our battery.

A sharp fight took place at the junction of these roads, in which our people more than held their own. We made some coffee, ate a little corn bread, and all of us felt young again. My men and myself were still covered with mud. While our battery and its division were halted, columns of troops were rapidly moving forward and deploying north of the village of Campbell's Station. The position was this: Here was an opening in the woods about three miles long from north to south, and from a mile to a mile and a half in width. The south end was higher than the middle. From the middle to the north was quite a rise of from fifty to 100 feet, where was spread out a broad plateau, which commanded the whole open tract of land. The village was in the lowest part of the tract. Upon the plateau at the north, General Burnside was placing a portion of his troops, including three or four light batteries.

Our battery soon had orders to move, and on we went, followed closely by our rear guard, which itself was closely pursued by the rebels. Our front line of battle was partially in the village of Campbell's Station, protected very well by the buildings. Our battery did not halt until we arrived upon the plateau. Soon we were assigned a position to protect our extreme right and right flank. After getting into position, we had nothing to do but to observe the movement of the enemy. We soon beheld a splendid exhibition of war. The rebel skirmishers first appeared in the open, carefully examining the ground to find if we had a concealed line of battle near. They soon advanced a half mile or less and found no opposition. There they rested, and we soon saw the rebel columns debouch from both the Loudon and the Kingston roads. At last there came a battery of 20-pounder rifled guns, with several white horses, and went into position on the right of the road.

This battery we had often met in the East. It was one of the batteries of the Washington corps of artillery of New Orleans. This was an excellent battery. The enemy soon formed two strong lines of battle clear across the open country, about 200 yards apart. Light batteries came forward, halting in front, and took positions between the brigades. On the flanks the cavalry was seen in the open woodland. This scene was all spread out before us. In all our great battles, such as Manassas and Antietam, we rarely saw more than a fourth of a mile of our enemy's line.

About 12 m., the signal was given, and the rebel lines, with flags flying and batteries firing, advanced against us. The fighting for the last forty-eight hours had evidently convinced Longstreet's veterans that they had worthy foes to meet. Four rifled batteries planted upon the brow of the hill, under General Burnside's personal directions, opened rapidly upon the enemy's lines of infantry, paying no attention apparently to the enemy's artillery fire. The very first discharge sent havoc into their first line and killed a colour bearer. In five minutes their heavy lines were fearfully torn, but still closing up and keeping up a wonderful alignment they moved right on. To us spectators, it seemed that they would overwhelm our own lines of battle. The enemy had not stopped to fire a rifle, neither had our infantry discharged a piece. Suddenly a change came over the wonderful scene. The Twenty-Third Corps opened with terrific volleys, followed closely by the Ninth. The lines of the rebels halted, opened fire and sought such cover as the surface of the ground afforded them.

Soon the smoke of battle shut in the grand scene and we looked to our own commands. The Washington artillery began throwing over our way its twenty-pounder compliments. As the flank of our battery was nearly in line with the fire from the rebel battery, it seemed sometimes as if they would rake our whole front. Fortunately for us, they did little damage. Lieutenant Benjamin, chief of artillery, paid his special attention to the Washingtonians, and the result was that they were satisfied to keep quiet, one of their guns burst in full view, and this seemed to take their attention away from us.

Soon a regiment or two of the enemy were seen to pass to our extreme right under cover of the skirting woodland and into the wood. At once we were ordered to open fire upon this piece of woodland with shell and shrapnel. We sent twenty-five or thirty shells in rapid succession into the wood, and soon we saw the rebels going to their rear upon the run. It seems that a portion of the Ninth Corps was in position to enfilade the rebel line, and after they had received a few volleys and our shells they beat a hasty retreat. During the remainder of the battle there was no further trouble on our right flank. This affair on our right flank convinced us that however strong mules were for drawing over heavy roads our artillery, they were not at all well behaved in battle.

Of course, as soon as we opened upon the flanking rebels, several batteries of the enemy gave us special attention. The shells burst fast and furious all around us, but it did not interfere with our shelling the woods. I heard deep and loud profanity, and turning around saw my two mule teams start towards each other, and when they met they began to climb up each other.

We had extra men detailed from the infantry to help us manage the mules, and it was from our infantry friends that the loud talk came.

After getting up in the air a good distance, the leading pairs of each team fell over. Underneath each was thrown a man. When the rebels retreated from the wood, we ceased firing and our cannoneers went to the assistance of the mule guards. One man was severely bruised, though no bones were broken. We had the mules taken out of the line of the enemy's fire and they soon quieted down. General Longstreet was present in command of his forces, reported to be 20,000 strong. Various assaults were made by him against our lines that November afternoon, but we repulsed them all with heavy loss to him. It was now nearly dark. The plan of General Burnside was to withdraw to Knoxville as soon as he could leave his lines in safety, under cover of night.

All the batteries went to the rear, except Benjamin's, and one section of Buckley's under my command. I was instructed to take orders from Lieutenant Benjamin and not withdraw until he so ordered. His battery was slowly and accurately firing and much annoying the rebel batteries. When it was so dark that one could not see twenty-five yards, he ordered me to withdraw and proceed as fast as possible to Knoxville, not waiting for him. I directed that my right or fifth piece should be first limbered up. The men in charge of the mules that hauled this piece attempted to drive them round to the trail, but they made only a few steps and then planted their forward feet in the soft ground and stood firm as Gibraltar. The guns were about 100 yards front of them, and I soon decided that it would be easier to run our pieces back by hand than to attempt to move the mules. Men from our division came to our assistance, and we soon had the guns ready for marching.

My caissons, after having supplied from them the expended rounds of ammunition from my gun limbers, had been sent back with the rest of the battery, so that I had only my two guns to care for on my night retreat. My cannoneers were so tired that I allowed them to take turns in riding upon the limbers. This was our second night out and we were all thoroughly exhausted. For thirty hours the men had not slept and had partaken of but little food, mostly a small ration of corn bread. We were preceded by the rest of our battery in Knoxville. I reached Knoxville about 5 o'clock in the morning, and was directed to camp on the right of our two sections just in the rear of Fort Saunders.

There was an Ohio battery attached to the Twenty-Third Army Corps. We made the march with them from Kentucky, and we were not a little chagrined at the way these sons of Ohio overlapped us in foraging. We had no serious difficulty with this command, still we all felt that it was composed principally of the porcine element. When we went to the Ninth Corps we parted company with this battery with regrets, for we felt that we had not been able thus far to even up our accounts with them. This Ohio institution had seen no service except marching and camping. At Campbell's Station, it was in the front line of artillery, first on the left of the Knoxville road in a very prominent position. For a while it was rare fun for these men to rake the rebel lines, but when the rebel artillery opened upon this first line of our batteries, there was a most sudden change in the situation. The Ohioans had a man or two wounded and a caisson blown up. When the explosion occurred, the zeal of the men vanished, from officers and all.

The captain limbered his battery to the rear, hauled out into the road and advanced toward Knoxville upon the trot. Whether he had orders to do so or not, we never knew. As they passed along the road by our battery in position, our men joked them to their hearts' content. It was loudly said that they were after hogs, poultry and sheep. We all felt that Ohio had been settled with, and just as we wanted it to be done. Had this battery seen as much service as the Ninth Army Corps, they never would have done as they did.

We placed our guns in position, as before stated, in the rear and to the right of Fort Saunders. The drivers took care of the mules, and the cannoneers at once dropped upon the ground and slept until aroused to assist in fortifying our position. We were on a commanding ridge looking to the southwest. A section of our battery was to occupy embrasures in the fort. The other two sections were outside and to the right of the fort. This fort was an unfinished rebel earthwork, which commanded the Loudon road, and was named by them Fort Loudon. Col. Orlando Poe was the engineer in charge, and we soon had staked out for us works to be raised to protect our guns.

As our men were so wearied out, it was difficult for them to accomplish much in the digging on this 17th of November, 1863, the day of our arrival. Late in the day details of citizens came upon the ground, and before light the next morning we had excellent protection for our guns. It was reported that General Burnside had taken all males, irrespective of colour or politics, and set them to work upon the fortifications around the city.

Knoxville then rested entirely upon an elevated plateau, skirting along the right bank of the Holston River, which is the main branch of the Tennessee. This plateau was divided into three portions by two creeks, named first and second creeks, respectively, from the north. Third creek was just south of our position at Fort Saunders. This name was given the fort about the 20th of November, in honour of Colonel Saunders, who was killed at Armstrong's House. This division of the plateau gave one the impression that the city was built upon three hills. On all prominent points strong works were erected, some of them enclosed. These forts were joined by strong rifle pits. Also there was an inner line of enclosed works. On the left or south bank were several knobs 200 or 300 feet in height. The river was crossed by a pontoon bridge. We had possession of the most commanding knob, had a good road to its summit and it was well fortified.

We had a large mounted force which operated principally on the left bank of the river. Forage and other supplies were sent down the French Broad and Holston Rivers. In fact, during the whole siege, we were never very much interfered with on the south side of the river opposite and above Knoxville. Our force was about 15,000, and that of General Longstreet's 20,000 men. On the 18th we, from Fort Saunders, witnessed a gallant fight for the possession of the Armstrong House, on the Loudon road, about a mile and a half from Saunders. This position was held by 2,000 or 3,000 of our mounted men, and it required the whole force of McLaw to capture the house.

As soon as our forces retreated down the road under cover of our works, the rebels immediately took possession of the house. Lieutenant Benjamin then made a beautiful shot, sending at the first trial a 20-pound shell into the house, setting it on fire. Had the rebels not extinguished the fire the house would have been burned down. On the 20th we erected a flagstaff and sent up a flag in the fort. This created much enthusiasm all along our line. Our fortifications were greatly strengthened by bales of cotton, covered with green cattle hides. We felt by this time that we could easily hold our own against the enemy.

A house on the north side of the Loudon road, from which its owners had fled, was taken possession of by the enemy's sharpshooters. It was outside of our lines, but was near enough to our fort to cause us much annoyance. General Ferrero, who commanded this portion of the line, decided to capture the house in a night attack. This was made in the evening at 8 o'clock, so quietly and quickly that the enemy were surprised, and some surrendered and some ran away. The house was destroyed.

A little incident occurred in the fort at this time that I have never forgotten. I had held the view, with most others, that it is a matter of instinct for a person to jump or dodge if anything unexpected comes upon him through any one of the senses. Lieutenant S. N. Benjamin, the chief of artillery of the army, often reprimanded his men for dodging, and so did General Ferrero, and General Ferrero told a story how a soldier was hit when he dodged; had he gone right along the bullet would have missed him. I had noticed Lieutenant Benjamin on several occasions under a warm fire, and he paid no attention to the whistling balls. On the night in question General Ferrero and staff and about every commissioned officer in the fort were standing inside Fort Saunders awaiting the advance of our Seventeenth Michigan regiment upon the house. We had waited several minutes after 8 o'clock, and began to wonder why the attack had not been made. Suddenly there came right at us a heavy volley from the house. This was so unexpected that down went General Ferrero, and Lieutenant Benjamin was almost prone upon the ground. My opinion is that all present dodged more or less, but none so low as the officers named.

On the 21st, Saturday, the work upon the fortifications still went steadily on. The garrison of Fort Saunders consisted principally of the Seventy-ninth New York Highlanders and Benjamin's and Buckley's batteries. Other infantry was close at hand, which could be called upon in an emergency. From the 21st to the 28th nothing unusual occurred. The enemy seemed to be busy on the south side of the Holston occupying a high knob with artillery, but so far off that we gave it but little attention. With 24-pound howitzers they could nearly reach our own main line. Had he been able to capture the knob which our people had strongly fortified, it would have been very disastrous to us.

Nov. 28, 1863, opened cold and rainy. The outside of the parapet of Fort Saunders was coated with ice. From indications that all observed, it seemed that the assault upon our line was near at hand. The enemy seemed to be pushing troops toward the right of Fort Saunders, and were constantly attempting to force back our pickets in that locality. The location of the several guns of Battery D at 10 p.m., on the 28th, was as follows: the second and sixth pieces were in Battery Galpin, on second creek, enfilading the creek and railroad; the third, fourth and fifth in Fort Saunders, and the first in Battery Noble, on the left of the Loudon road. At 11 p.m., the rebels made a determined attack upon our lines from Battery Galpin to the river, and our battery did considerable firing. This movement of the enemy was to drive in our pickets and to get as near our main line as possible.

We all knew that by daylight we should be attacked with all the fury which General Longstreet could command. Ammunition was brought up in extra rounds, ready for use. Nobody slept. General Burnside was visiting his troops, especially those in Fort Saunders. Two companies of the Twenty-ninth Massachusetts had been added to the infantry. His staff were all busy directing and encouraging the men. It was not until half past six o'clock on Sunday morning, Nov. 29, 1863, that a signal gun was fired from the enemy's battery on Armstrong's Hill. There was then a lively artillery fire opened from all the enemy's guns in position on both sides of the river. Our artillery made no reply. When the rebel artillery stopped firing we all knew that the assault would promptly follow. We were peering through the fog and smoke and darkness to see the advancing gray lines of the rebel infantry. We well knew that in a minute they might be upon us, as they had crowded up to within 200 yards of Fort Saunders.

In front of the fort telegraph wires had been wound round the stumps of trees lately cut down, and this wire, not being known to the enemy, threw them into much confusion. Lieutenant Benjamin's 20-pounders were not well adapted to the short range required to repel the assault, although they were as well served as any men could serve them, so that it devolved upon the three brass Napoleons of Battery D to do the effective work. As soon as the charging "columns by division closed *en masse*" of the enemy appeared, Battery D sent in to the columns double rounds of canister at fifty yards. The veterans of Fredericksburg, Chancellorsville, and Chickamauga began to quail. It was not possible for them to stand such an onslaught from big guns and rifles. Many fell from the deadly fire and others on account of contact with the entangling wire, but then in the fog and smoke, it was not possible to tell why it was that nearly every man in the first rank fell.

To those brave men it seemed death to advance or retreat, and by force of numbers they pushed on, and some got into the ditch in front of the fort, it being some eight feet deep and twelve feet wide; to the top of the parapet was at least twenty feet, and the outside of the parapet was covered with smooth ice. When they gained the ditch they were sheltered from our fire. It was not an agreeable duty for our infantry to peer over the top of the parapet to shoot the rebels below, so Lieutenant Benjamin took a number of his shells, lighted the fuses and rolled them over the parapet into the ditch among the enemy. A half dozen explosions of these shells brought them to terms, and soon something as white as anything they had, was raised upon a ramrod. They were told to enter by a certain embrasure, leaving their arms in the ditch. They came along rapidly, about 300 of them, and were marched into Knoxville. The rest of the charging columns fell back, and the battle was at an end. Four brigades, consisting of nineteen regiments, from 4,000 to 6,000 men, were sent forward against Fort Saunders.

News soon came that General Grant had won a decisive victory at Chattanooga, and that General Sherman was rapidly coming to our relief. Joy reigned in Knoxville, and in all the hearts of the thousands of loyal people in East Tennessee.

APPENDIX.

INCIDENTS (PERSONAL)

At Campbell's Station Sergeant Gideon Spencer, of the fourth piece, had a close call. He was taking his piece from its position and passing along the Knoxville road. A high worm fence was standing by the side of the road and one of the slanting stakes in it hung out over the road so that the sergeant on horseback had to turn his head over to the right in order to avoid a collision. Just as he turned the head, a 20-pound shell came from the Washington artillery and cut off the stake, opposite the sergeant's head. In this case, dodging paid.

During the siege of Knoxville Private William Oakes was down in a ravine near the teams. A bullet fired from the rebel lines came over and passed through his head just above the tongue, carrying away two or three of his teeth. He was in a hospital a short distance away, and the next day after he was wounded I went to see him. I found him with his cheeks swollen to an enormous size. I shook his hand and expressed my regret at his misfortune, and hoped that he would soon be out of the hospital, etc. I did not think that he could articulate. I saw that he was about to speak, or to attempt it, and so I leaned over to catch his words. He managed to say in a distressed voice that he was unable to eat popcorn. I thought that he would get back to Rhode Island, and told him so.

While lying with my section on the right of Fort Saunders, on a cold, wet day, the colonel commanding the brigade to which I was attached directed his quartermaster to furnish me with a tent. There was sent round an old sibley tent and my men pitched it a short distance in rear of the line, on a slightly elevated dry patch of ground. I went inside, but found that as the top of the tent was above our parapet, the rebels were shooting bullets through the top in a lively manner. I went outside and estimated about how low the shots could come through the tent. I made a mark on the inside, and those who happened to be in the tent kept heads below the line. The colonel referred to this line as the dead line. A soldier brought to me a beautiful copy of the works of the Latin poet, Virgil, and I spent the time in reading his poetic account of the siege of *Lofty Ilium*.

On the morning of the great assault upon our lines, Sergeant Charles C. Gray was in charge of the fourth piece of our battery. He often loaded his piece with double canister and fired with terrible effect, for the range was only from fifteen yards to fifty yards. He moved his piece from its first position *en barbette* on the right of the fort, to an embrasure that more effectually commanded the rebel advance. Here he fired with great rapidity, until the enemy appeared to recoil. He had his gun loaded with double canister and ceased firing. At this time a rebel officer climbed out of the ditch, and standing at the muzzle of the cannon placed his sword upon it and said: "Surrender this gun." The man who held the lanyard was ready to fire, and asked for the order. Sergeant Gray replied: "Don't waste double canister on one man."

At this juncture, three other rebels came into the embrasure at the muzzle of the gun, and then the order was given to "fire." Of these four men, nothing was left but atoms. The brave sergeant was publicly thanked and congratulated by General Burnside a few hours later. The Governor of Rhode Island, at the general's request, sent him a commission as second lieutenant. This case is unique. Nothing but the stout heart of Sergeant Gray made him a commissioned officer. He owed his promotion to no political or personal influence with the Governor of Rhode Island.

Sergeant Frank Tucker, of Battery D, was a cool, brave man, and the best shot in the whole battery. Some 600 or 700 yards from our lines, just in the edge of a piece of woodland, a rebel sharpshooter, with a big target rifle that sent explosive bullets, had secreted himself in a pine tree. A number of men had been killed by him. General Ferrero had barely escaped a bullet through his head. The general sent for me, as my section was in position nearly opposite the sharpshooter, and requested me to open fire upon him. I stated that nothing would please me better, but as Lieutenant Benjamin had ordered me to waste no ammunition, I did not feel that he would permit me to open fire on one man. He gave me a written order to proceed, and so I went back to my section to carry out the order. We placed a cap upon a ramrod and slowly raised it above our parapet. I looked through a field glass while the men looked with naked eyes.

The cap had no sooner come above the parapet than a ball was put through it. We all saw the smoke about ten or fifteen feet from the ground. I directed Sergeant Tucker to load with solid shot, to take his time about computing distance, elevation of piece, and aiming it. When he had the gun ready, we once more raised the cap, and promptly the bullet came. The sergeant had his piece ready aimed and he quickly said "fire." The next I saw the pine tree break off and topple over, and down fell a man with his gun in his hand. Our men sent up a great shout. General Ferrero was delighted with such an exhibition of marksmanship. I noticed that as soon as the reb. struck the ground he jumped up and ran into the thicket to the rear of his tree. I said nothing about this, and it was understood that Tucker had dropped his man at the first fire.

CONFEDERATE LOSS IN ASSAULT UPON FORT LOUDON, *ALIAS* SAUNDERS ON NOVEMBER 29, 1863.

Killed, 129   Wounded, 458
Missing, 226   Aggregate, 813
War of the Rebellion, Official Records, Vol. 31, Part 1.

General Burnside makes Confederate total loss about 500.
Ibid.

Union entire loss about 20,
Ibid

In the assault *upon* Fort Saunders, November 29, 1863, I do not find that Battery "D" suffered any loss.

E. K. Parker.